Peripheral Centralities

NICHOLAS A. PHELPS / ROGER KEIL / PAUL J. MAGINN (EDS.)

PERIPHERAL CENTRALITIES

INSTANCES OF
ANTICIPATORY URBANISM

jovis

Table of Contents

Agency

Technologies

Acknowledgements

This volume is based on contributions to the third of four seminars on the theme of peripheral centralities, which were held in person at York University, Toronto, in October and online in December 2022. Not all presenters were able to contribute to this volume, and we would like to express our appreciation to all those who participated in these discussions. We thank the Urban Studies Foundation for funding these events with a Seminar Series Award grant and Joe Shaw for his encouragement throughout. We could not have hosted the in-person seminar without the logistical and organisational assistance we had from the Faculty of Environmental and Urban Change and the City Institute at York University. We are grateful for the generous support we received from the Faculty of Architecture Building and Planning and the Yencken Trust at the University of Melbourne, which helped us to realise this publication. Finally, we appreciated the professionalism and flexibility of the editors at jovis at all stages of the publication, especially the guidance of Franziska Schüffler and Felix Torkar.

Nicholas A. Phelps, Roger Keil, and Paul J. Maginn
Melbourne, Toronto, Perth, March 2025

The Periphery at the Centre

Nicholas A. Phelps, Roger Keil, and Paul J. Maginn

The peripheries of cities are where the architectural, design and planning, and citizen imagination has the greatest license. The margins and in-between spaces of metropolitan regions are, as Tom Sieverts has pointed out, the contemporary living space of the majority and a working landscape; the product of countless rational decisions in everyday urban life, and the projection space for the centrality of the state and corporations.[1] Yet we understand very little about the *centrality* of urban peripheries as the sites and spaces for some of the most imaginative, anticipatory, and purposeful instances of urbanism. The imagination of a variety of urban professions remains fixated on what the architect Lars Lerup has called 'the stone city: all of the built-up centres of thousands of cities detached from the biology of their surroundings—all of those ever-present downtowns—[...] that still [dominate] our readings of the urban'.[2]

Certainly, there is a seductiveness to the urban core. Its powerful architecture and morphology, the concentration of economic activity, the sensory overload, opportunities for social interaction, and the sense of risk—not to mention the fact that all roads and rail lines lead, both literally and metaphorically, to the urban core—make it an alluring object of scholarly inquiry as well as a potent force in our imaginations. In contrast, the periphery tends to sit out of sight and mind. Despite many observations to the contrary,[3] what exists 'out there' in the periphery continues to be perceived as aesthetically and morphologically homogenous, socially conformist, and monoculturalist. Such is the expansiveness of the periphery, comprised by an archipelago of residential sub-divisions and road networks. For some, it constitutes a *brutalscape*.

Forming part of the extended urban, the suburbs have often been misunderstood. There is a long-standing academic and popular preconception that suburbia is nothing more than a patchwork quilt of *blandscapes*.[4] To put it bluntly (and perhaps unfairly), suburbia has been stereotyped as the place where culture goes to die. This chapter, and this book more broadly, aims to challenge these negative preconceptions and stereotypes. It does so by advancing the argument, illustrated by numerous case studies from across the globe, that the periphery is just as central to 'the city' in defining contemporary metropolitan regions.[5]

The seemingly oxymoronic term 'peripheral centralities' describes how new *activity centres*—to use Australian planning terminology—are imagined and built in the periphery. It also highlights how these concrete instances of urban development prompt us to understand and theorise the growth and decline of cities from a peripheral vantage point. Furthermore, the term helps us to understand the deeply symbiotic relationship between 'the urban' and 'the suburban'. This volume foregrounds the centrality of (sub)urban peripheries in all their diversity with a view to reworking conceptions of the urban and suburban found across architectural, landscape and urban design, planning, sociological and geographical disciplines. Moreover, it strives to rethink urban theory from the outside in. The book examines the relationships of those new peripheral centralities to the metabolisms, assemblages, and urban political ecologies beyond the built and imagined 'stones' of their immediate presence.

Urbanisation: Peripheral and Central

Running parallel to conventional and long-standing connotations of the suburb as somehow 'less than' the urban—as the locus of people and spatial functions that are unwanted within the city—there is an equally long history of suburban peripheries holding the physical and imaginative space for counterparts and/or major extensions to cities. Here, the urban periphery emerges as a focal point for the desire of ordinary citizens to approach the city and its amenities, as with the informally developed edges of southern European and Latin American cities.[6] Frequently, these desires consolidated into deliberate re-imaginings of the suburbs: designs for new and improved urban futures were envisaged by numerous powerful actors in society, underpinned by innovative ways of 'seeing' the potential centrality of urban peripheries. For example, the organised expansion of the City of London in the 1600s and 1700s was, at times, a stately affair led by royal courts and landed estates.[7] Elsewhere, the Garden City movement in the early twentieth century, in particular the development of Letchworth and Welwyn, is an early example of how residential–commuter peripheral centralities preserved functional proximity to London. And, in the 1940s and 1950s, London's extension was infused with social ambitions for better housing conditions and a better society.[8] All three modalities of suburban governance—capital accumulation, the state, and private authoritarianism—are apparent in patterns and processes of peripheral urbanisation throughout those periods.[9]

The centrality of urban peripheries to contemporary processes of urbanisation in the Global North has been recognised since the 1960s, in writings by urban geographers and urban historians, as well as the self-styled 'Los Angeles School' with its notions of the city turned inside out.[10] The LA School's postmodern take on the city region represented a direct challenge to the Chicago School of Ecology's privileging of the urban core. Fundamentally, the evolution and dominance of the human ecologists' take on 'the city' in the early twentieth century is a result of migration stemming from a constellation of peripheries in various southern states across the U.S. as well as Europe. As Chicago grew in terms of population, economic power, and physical scale, this gave rise to two peripheral zones—residential and commuter—as seen in Burgess's classic concentric zone model. These residential peripheries generated much of the city's lifeblood, as suburbanites made the daily commute to their jobs in the central business district.

More recently, in cities of the Global South, the noticeable swell of urbanisation has contributed to new approaches focusing on 'southern' and 'massive' forms of urbanisation at the periphery.[11] Within this context, a mix of formal and informal planned settlements have emerged, offering a complex array of living conditions ranging from private gated communities in mansions and/or luxury apartments (i.e. *brutopianscapes*) through to state or UN-controlled refugee camps or tent cities (i.e. *brutalscapes*) for those fleeing war, civil unrest, and persecution.

Peripheral centralities continue to be visible in the imagined homes for major corporate, university, and science city campuses, in addition to edge cities or suburban employment nodes, airports, and new planning models (such as 'aerotropolis') and staples of suburbia, such as regional shopping malls and entertainment complexes.[12] Moreover, they appear on an altogether grander scale as part of planned economies past and present: in the massive formations of suburban housing in the UK, France, and the former Central and Eastern European nations, as well as planned new towns, economic and technical development, and smart city zones across East Asia and India.[13]

In architectural design and planning practice, the future possibilities for greater density, walkability and, ultimately, urbanity of the suburbs have been heralded in normative agendas focusing on the retrofitting of suburbia, and by planners/geographers with research interests in suburban regeneration.[14] Centrality and density as antidotes to traditional, single-family residential suburbanisation have been subject to much planning debate. This is intensified in view of the challenges to cities posed by climate change and the emergence of planning idea(l)s such as the fifteen-minute city, transit-oriented development (TOD), and the return of edge cities. The latter is underpinned to a large extent by the recent COVID-19 pandemic, with academic speculation and analysis as well as media coverage alighting on the demise of urban centres and the rise of the outer suburbs.[15]

As such, apart from their physical manifestation, peripheral centralities crystallise extant and shifting distributions of power in society. They draw attention to social conflicts over the best use of land, alongside the alternative private, public and public–private modes of development and financing that lie at the heart of analytical and normative questions typically addressed in the field of urban studies. The challenge of the present century will be the task of re-imagining, retrofitting and regenerating middle- and outer-ring suburbs, especially since so much of present-day suburban build-out takes place with little thought for the need to generate meaningful centralities across the urban periphery.

Figure 1. Toronto Aerotropolis. Source: Photo by Roger Keil, 2022

Peripheral Centralities: Instances of Anticipatory Urbanism

This edited volume of visual essays brings together a multidisciplinary mix of scholars and practitioners—from urban history, sociology, geography, environmental studies, planning, architecture, landscape architecture, urban design and property development—to further define, theorise and empirically analyse instances of peripheral centrality, unpacking how they help inform an understanding of the significance and nature of suburbanisation processes. Where urban theory has sought to engage processes of extended urbanisation and move research and writing beyond 'methodological cityism', it has rarely done so from an explicitly and empirically rich (sub)urban peripheral vantage point. This volume seeks to further define the value of examining urbanisation processes from a peripheral vantage point—rethinking urban theory from the outside in.[16] It contributes to our own ongoing work to better define and develop the field of research centring on processes of suburbanisation.[17]

Further, this book emphasises peripheral centralities as some of the best instances of *anticipatory urbanism*—manifest here as pre-figurative public sector planning or real-estate-dominated visions of new urban frontiers.[18] These anticipations tend to arrive in the form of numerous, seemingly unconnected 'projects'—centres to themselves—that spread across urban peripheries. Too often, these projects are treated as 'out of sight out of mind', or unfinished sites of storage and speculation.[19] They are thus perceived as having limited implications for the shaping of metropolitan and wider societal futures. Yet, urban peripheries are also subject to grander plans with both internal (subjective) and external (objectivised, mass) representational power.[20] In short, peripheral centralities are key vectors through which we can examine the continual remaking and reimagining of cities and their metropolitan regions. However, the urban peripheral vantage point on this remaking process is one that reveals the fragmentation, rather than the presumed unity, of cities and their metropolitan regions.

The structure of this book uses the thematic repertoire we have developed as part of our academic praxis to try and make sense of the historical, empirical and theoretical dimensions of peripheral centralities through 'centring the periphery' in terms of (sub)urban theory.[21] It selectively develops this thematic framework, reusing the themes of the 'pervasiveness', 'agency' and 'social relations' apparent in the imagining, planning and making of peripheral centralities. This thematic repertoire is also extended by considering the 'technologies' implicated in the centring of urban peripheries alongside the variety of 'ways of seeing' centrality within urban peripheries. The latter theme represents a novel contribution to the literature on suburbanisation.

Pervasiveness

Periphery is everywhere and, unsurprisingly, the execution of designs in urban peripheries—by states, citizens and corporations—is pervasive. Urban peripheries may appear economically marginal within urban systems, as displayed in the classical bid rent and central place theories that have informed models of urban spatial economic structure. They may additionally seem aesthetically undesirable and 'ugly' from an urban planning, design or landscape perspective, as we describe below. However, some of the most unsuitable or potentially 'costly' urban peripheral sites continue to attract the attention of citizens and developers as places to implement dreams, whether big or small.

The fact that land is empty and remains either empty or underutilised may also bear no reflection on the intensity of speculative interest in that same land. The term 'planning blight' tends to imply an inert scenario in which 'active' interest in particular sites is curtailed or cut short. However, what planning blight often really conceals is the opposite—namely, an incredibly intense and focused interest among a variety of parties. Developers may wait patiently on the sidelines, like a cat stalking a bird. Indeed, they rarely wait passively or act disinterestedly—instead, they lobby continuously and intervene in blighted sites through stealth. Civil society groups may also wage continual campaigns regarding those same spaces, however unattractive they may appear when afflicted with planning blight. Some of the most spectacular master-planned city failures have sought to tap into the potential of vast unoccupied stretches of land peripheral to extant urbanisation—as with the failed development of California City, once intended to be the third largest urban agglomeration in the state.

Social Relations

The urban periphery is relational in a fundamentally physical sense since it is home to both intensive and extensive development of infrastructure. The development of infrastructure and the interstices it produces are intrinsically relational. Not only do they physically connect one place to another but, as a result, they are socially relational—connecting people and designs through those same spaces.

However, urban peripheries may be relationally central in metropolitan areas in a variety of social senses. Not least in this respect are the diverse (im)migrants for whom urban peripheries are central as reception and assimilation zones. For these populations, the urban periphery is an adjunct to the city which harbours the prospect of the 'right to the city'. Here, homes are established and identities forged in a distinctive fashion, across distances and cultures. In relational terms, this involves acculturating to new norms of civic participation, translating between old notions of home and its construction and those that prevail in the new host context. While such spaces may appear less than ideal when it comes to normative planning, urban design and landscape standards, they nonetheless hold great affection for residents and users.

Agency

The urban periphery is a powerful source of agency for various types of actors. While states may have designs on urban peripheries, these spaces exist to varying degrees within government and policy blind spots. This lack of visibility, combined with the relative absence of the state, provides ample space and opportunity for the exertion of citizen agency through the informal appropriation of urban peripheral spaces.

One consequence of this is that urban peripheries—or peri-urban and rural fringe areas—appear messy in terms of urban planning and design as well as landscape architecture. They have been described as 'drosscapes'.[22] This messiness can be hard to read analytically and difficult to deal with practically for planning authorities; those elements of 'centrality' within it can be difficult for states and analysts to 'see'. Yet, this messiness may nevertheless be a resource or opportunity for some citizens and corporations. This apparent disorder is also the definition of urban life for the urban majority. The massive 'messiness' of the periphery, to quote AbdouMaliq Simone, 'means both the voluminous expansion of speculative accumulation, extraction of land value, replication of vast inequities and dysfunction, and the continuous emergence of new forms of urban inhabitation, a constant remaking of the social field by what has been called the urban majority.'[23] From an intellectual standpoint then, any desire to better understand urban peripheries in terms of their definition, significance and potential necessitates engaging methods of unveiling centrality within urban peripheries—a challenge that the various contributors to this volume embrace.

Technologies

Urban peripheries are hardly empty. Indeed, they are the locales of many forms of intensive technological and infrastructural development—especially those technologies and infrastructures needed to make the urban core, the compact city or the fifteen-minute city function. They are bisected by major freeways, rail routes, overhead and underground power lines, water and sewerage systems. Additionally, they are the location for major intermodal transfer points and associated logistics as well as warehousing activities designed to underpin the circulation of goods, services and people in urban economies. If the city is a terminus, then the urban periphery is an 'interplace', shot through with major transportation and infrastructure networks and peppered with numerous urban interstices.[24]

Thus, one specific way in which designs on the urban periphery have been repeated in recent history is that they afford space for experimentation with new technologies, including new technologies of mobility. In the last hundred years or so these technologies have arrived in the form of specific proposals for urban-peripheral monorails, personal automated transport systems, and even the use of flying boats in urban peripheries that are adjacent to major bodies of water.[25]

In addition, technological changes in the life of the urban periphery also extend to the social technologies of everyday life, quotidian politics, and governance that make the spatial margin so central to how modern capitalist societies are governed—as attested to by several of our contributions.

Seeing the Urban Periphery

If states 'see' in particular ways, then the sightline of government rarely extends beyond the 'core': often, they do not see the *desakota* or *Zwischenstadt*—the in-between spaces of urban peripheries in East Asia and Germany.[26] As we have briefly described above, this does not mean that the urban periphery is invisible to other important actors, such as corporations and citizens. Indeed, we might speculate that their ways of seeing are alive to the opportunities afforded by urban peripheries. When some authors talk about a transformation of democracy in today's urban world, they explicitly have in mind an extended view of the urban.[27]

However, a second issue follows. Namely, how can we 'see' the urban periphery in academic terms? What analytical and practical skills can be mobilised to see the urban periphery and those elements of centrality that it may embody? Contributors to this volume present a variety of ways of seeing the centrality of urban peripheries—from desk-based big data to the transecting of peripheries on foot and bicycle. As these contributions reveal, urban peripheries are ripe—if a little challenging in their sheer scale and physical impenetrability—for psychogeographical methods of exploration and data collection.[28]

Conclusion

The chapters in this volume provide important glimpses into the centrality of urban peripheries to contemporary processes of urbanisation as well as the anticipatory imagination that is vital to the centring of urban peripheries. They signal not only that the urban theoretical imagination can be helpfully de-centred. But, further, that greater appreciation and investigation of the imagination of built environment practice (as applied to urban peripheries) will be a much-needed part of any theoretical move beyond 'methodological cityism'. The term peripheral centralities is far from oxymoronic. Rather, it signifies that in an era of massive planetary (sub)urbanisation centrality is no longer premised on a fixed Euclidian concept of the centre. Instead, it proposes that centrality is always multi-dimensional and relational.

Figure 2. Vaughan Metropolitan Centre. Source: Photo by Roger Keil, 2022

Endnotes:

1 Sieverts, T. The In-Between City as an Image of Society: From the Impossible Order Towards a Possible Disorder in the Urban Landscape, in: D. Young, P. B. Wood, and R. Keil (eds.) *In-Between Infrastructure: Urban Connectivity in an Age of Vulnerability.* Praxis (e) Press, 2011.

2 Lerup, L. *The Continuous City.* Park Books, 2017, p. 109.

3 Keil, R. Towers in the park, bungalows in the garden: Peripheral densities, metropolitan scales and the political cultures of post-suburbia, *Built Environment, 41* (4), 2015, pp. 579–596.

4 Maginn, P. J. and Phelps, N. A. Making Sense of Twenty-First Century (Sub)Urban Landscapes: Blandscapes, Blendscapes, Brutalscapes and Brutopianscapes, *Built Environment, 49* (1), Spring 2023, pp. 5–22.

5 Phelps, N. A., Maginn, P. J., and Keil, R. Centring the periphery in urban studies: Notes towards a research agenda on peripheral centralities, *Urban Studies, 60* (6), 2023, pp. 1158–1176.

6 Leontidou, L., Afouxenidis, E., Kourliourios, E., and Marmaras, E. Infrastructure related urban sprawl: mega-events and hybrid peri-urban landscapes in southern Europe, in: C. Couch, L. Leontidou, and G. Petschel-Held (eds.) *Urban Sprawl in Europe: Landscapes, land-use change and Policy.* Blackwell, 2007, pp. 71–101; Reis, N. and Lukas, M. (eds.) *Beyond the Megacity: New Dimensions of Peripheral Urbanization in Latin America.* University of Toronto Press, 2022. Roitman, S. and Phelps, N. Do gates negate the city? Gated communities' contribution to the urbanisation of suburbia in Pilar, Argentina, *Urban Studies, 48* (16), 2011, pp. 3487–3509.

7 Barratt, N. *Greater London: the story of the Suburbs.* Random House, 2012.

8 Phelps, N. A., Mace, A., and Jodieri, R. City of villages: stasis and change in London's suburbs, in: N. A. Phelps (ed.) *Old Europe, New Suburbanization.* University of Toronto Press, 2017, pp. 183–206.

9 Ekers, M., Hamel, P., and Keil, R. Governing suburbia: Modalities and mechanisms of suburban governance, *Regional Studies, 46* (3), 2012, pp. 405–422.

10 Muller, P. O., The suburban transformation of the globalizing American city, *The Annals of the American Academy of Political and Social Science, 551* (1), 1997, pp. 44–58; Fishman, R. *Bourgeois utopias: The rise and fall of suburbia.* Basic Books, 1987; Harris, R. and Larkham, P. Suburban foundation, form and function, in: R. Harris and P. Larkham (eds.) *Changing Suburbs: Foundation, Form and Function.* Routledge, 1999, pp. 1–31; Kruse, K. M. and Sugrue, T. J. Introduction, in: K. M. Kruse and T. J. Sugrue (eds.) *The New Suburban History.* Chicago University Press, 2006, pp. 1–10; Dear, M. and Dahmann, N. Urban politics and the Los Angeles school of urbanism, *Urban Affairs Review, 44* (2), 2008, pp. 266–279; Soja, E. *Postmetropolis.* Blackwell, 2000; Keil, R. *Los Angeles: Globalization, Urbanization, and Social Struggles.* John Wiley & Sons Ltd., 1998.

11 Bloch, R., Mabin, A., and Todes, A. Africa's Suburban Constellations, in: R. Keil and F. Wu (eds.) *After Suburbia: Urbanization in the 21st Century.* University of Toronto Press, 2022; Güney, K., Keil, R., and Üçoğlu, M. (eds.) *Massive Suburbanization: (Re)Building the Global Periphery.* University of Toronto Press, 2019; Wu, F. and Keil, R. (eds.) *Changing Asian Urban Geographies: Urbanism and Peripheral Areas.* Routledge, 2023.

12 Mozingo, L. A. *Pastoral capitalism: A history of suburban corporate landscapes.* MIT Press, 2016; Day, J., Phelps, N. A. et al. From edge city to city? Planning intentions for edge cities, *Journal of the American Planning Association, 88* (4), 2022, pp. 565–577; Kasarda, J. D. and Lindsay, G. *Aerotropolis: the way we'll live next.* Farrar, Straus and Giroux, 2011; Stevens, N., Baker, D., and Freestone, R. Airports in their urban settings: towards a conceptual model of interfaces in the Australian context, *Journal of Transport Geography, 18* (2), 2010, pp. 276–284.

13 Phelps, N. A. *Interplaces: An economic geography of the inter-urban and international economies.* Oxford University Press, 2017; Güney, Keil, and Ucoglu (2019) *op cit.*; Peiser, R. and Forsyth, A. (eds.) *New Towns for the Twenty-First Century: A Guide to Planned Communities Worldwide.* University of Pennsylvania Press, 2021.

14 Dunham-Jones, E. and Williamson, J. *Retrofitting Suburbia.* Wiley, 2009; Phelps, N. A. *Sequel to suburbia: Glimpses of America's post-suburban future.* MIT Press, 2015; Ruming, K. *Urban Regeneration in Australia.* Routledge, 2018; Talen, E. *Retrofitting sprawl: Addressing seventy years of failed urban form.* University of Georgia Press, 2015.

15 Keil, R. and Hertel, S. Fixing Post-suburbia: Recalibrating the Way we Think, Speak, and Act Upon Toronto's Periphery, in: P. J. Maginn and K. Anacker (eds.) *Suburbia in the 21st Century: From Dreamscape to Nightmare?* Routledge, 2022.

16 Brenner, N. and Schmid, C. The 'urban age' in question, *International journal of urban and regional research, 38* (3), 2014, pp. 731–755; Keil, R. Constructing Global Suburbia, One Critical Theory at a Time, in: J. Harrison and M. Hoyler (eds.) *Doing Global Urban Research.* Sage, 2014, pp. 169–181; Keil, R. *Suburban Planet.* Polity, 2017; Phelps, N. A., Which city? Grounding contemporary urban theory, *Journal of Planning Literature, 36* (3), 2021, pp. 345–357.

17 Keil, 2017 *op. cit.*; Maginn and Anacker, 2022, *op. cit.*; Phelps, N. A., Wood, A. M., and Valler, D. C. A postsuburban world? An outline of a research agenda, *Environment and Planning A, 42* (2), 2010, pp. 366–383.

18 Anderson, B. Preemption, precaution, preparedness: Anticipatory action and future geographies, *Progress in human geography, 34* (6), 2010, pp. 777–798; Davoudi, S. Prefigurative planning: performing concrete utopias in the here and now, *European Planning Studies*, 2023, pp. 1–14; Garreau, J. *Edge City: Life on the New Frontier.* Doubleday, 1991; Phelps, N. A., *The Urban Planning Imagination: A Critical International Introduction.* Polity Press, 2021.

19 Hopkins, L. D. & Zapata, M. Engaging the future: Forecasts, scenarios, plans, and projects. Lincoln Institute of Land Policy, 2007; Simone, A. The Surrounds: Urban Life Within and Beyond Capture. Duke University Press, 2022.

20 Neuman, M. How we use planning: Planning cultures and images of futures, in: Hopkins and Zapata, 2007, *op. cit.*, pp. 155–174.

21 Phelps, Maginn, and Keil, 2023, *op. cit.*

22 Berger, A. *Drosscape: Wasting land in urban America.* Princeton, 2006.

23 Simone, M. Imagining collectives: A missive on the massive, *Discover Society*, 2020; https://archive.discoversociety.org/2020/06/03/imagining-collectives-a-missive-on-the-massive/.

24 On infrastructure: see Cidell, J. Distribution centers among the rooftops: the global logistics network meets the suburban spatial imaginary, *International Journal of Urban and Regional Research, 35* (4), 2011, pp. 832–851; Keil, 2017, *op cit.*, Hesse, M. *The city as a terminal: The urban context of logistics and freight transport.* Ashgate Publishing Ltd., 2008. On interstices: see Brighenti, A. M. *Urban interstices: The aesthetics and the politics of the in-between.* Routledge, 2016; Phelps, N. A. and Silva, C. Mind the gaps! A research agenda for urban interstices, *Urban Studies, 55* (6), 2018, pp. 1203–1222.

25 Phelps, N. A., Keil, R., and Maginn, P. J. (eds.) *Peripheral Centralities: The Lost and Past Urbanity of the Suburbs.* Routledge, 2025.

26 Scott, J. C. *Seeing Like a State: How Certain Schemes to Improve the Human Condition Have Failed.* Yale University Press, 2000; Ginsburg, N. Extended metropolitan regions in Asia: a new spatial paradigm, in: N. Ginsburg, B. Koppel, and T. McGee (eds.) *The Extended Metropolis.* University of Hawaii Press, 1991, pp. 27–46; Sieverts, T. *Cities without cities: an interpretation of the Zwischenstadt.* Routledge, 2023.

27 Beveridge, R. and Koch, P. *How Cities Transform Democracy.* Polity, 2023; Hern, M. *Outside the Outside: The New Politics of Sub-urbs.* Verso, 2024.

28 Coverley, M. *Psychogeography.* Oldcastle Books, 2018.

P
erva
siveness

Pervasiveness

Incremental Metropolitanism: An Assessment of Retrofitting Suburbia's Endgame

June Williamson

Introduction

In an epilogue to *Retrofitting Suburbia: Urban Design Solutions for Redesigning Suburbs*, Ellen Dunham-Jones and I hypothesised that by 2050 a future landscape of *incremental metropolitanism* would emerge in major northern American metropolitan areas[1], resulting from an accumulation of suburban retrofitting projects. These retrofits would improve 'the sustainability of the system as a whole by incrementally redirecting growth from the periphery inward', restructuring towards a diversified, polycentric geography and logic, envisioned as more sustainable, interconnected, and cooperative.[2]

Our 2008 narrative included predictions about new drivers of suburban retrofit. We proposed that the U.S. Surgeon General would warn that unwalkable superblocks are dangerous to public health; the 'Step it Up!' call to action was issued in 2015.[3] We speculated that gasoline would top $10 a gallon; in summer 2022, a spike in gas prices assisted the (overdue) passage in the U.S. of a historic climate bill to accelerate decarbonisation.[4] We anticipated severe water shortages in the continental south and west; this is coming to pass, along with unprecedentedly destructive wildfires and severe storms.

With a degree of optimism, we imagined the transformations that could be achieved through the methods of urban design, producing an accumulation of ever-more innovative retrofits on redundant *greyfields* (paved parking areas), along suburban arterial corridors, and in selected edge-city-type nodes. Our focus then, as now, was on large and small opportunity sites—primarily commercially zoned, populated by dead and dying malls, abandoned office parks, vacant strip centres and gas stations, decommissioned airports, and the like. Many of these sites, particularly when located near mass transit (or with potential for its addition), would be densified through combination strategies of infill and selective *redevelopment* or *reinhabitation* (reuse). Other sites would be de-densified by *regreening*.

The endgame, if there is such a thing in an ever changing urban world, would be the radical redistribution of built density and uses into many discrete centres, efficiently interconnected, with more resilient landscapes and places in between, a process we defined as *incremental metropolitanism*.[5] Through suburban retrofitting—supported by good governance, progressive planning and environmental policies, and responsible real estate development tools and financing—existing metropolitan areas could sustainably accommodate projected population growth, demographic changes, and the introduction of new and diversified uses over time without increasing the overall footprint of urbanised land area. Cumulatively, a range of retrofits, focused primarily on sites built with obsolete, underperforming, redundant, and sometimes actively harmful twentieth-century suburban forms, would serve to geographically redistribute built density across metropolitan regions.

It is now more than a decade and a half later. What is the current state of this vision of a suburban retrofitting agenda? What progress, if any, has been made in increasing sustainable and resilient polycentrism in the major metropolitan areas of northern America? To assist with assessing the extent of progress, I share some examples from a recent book-length study, *Case Studies in Retrofitting Suburbia*. These case studies are presented in the wider context of the urgent challenges facing the current generation of suburban retrofits, including the need to leverage social capital for equity and add water and energy resilience.[6] After two decades of collaborative study of the deep and rich history of suburbanisation—the ideals and design visions, the contested policies and politics, the economic and social forces—as well as the collection of many, many case study examples, Dunham-Jones and I continue to advance a framework exploring how processes of retrofitting individual suburban form sites—pieces of actual property—may add up over time. The goal is to reverse the most harmful twentieth-century patterns of sprawl over the next generation. Some of this involves the emergence of new peripheral centralities wherein suburban life is recast.

Challenge: Leverage Social Capital for Equity

Social justice activist Angela Glover Blackwell succinctly clarifies what is at stake:

> America's history of racial exclusion repeats and deepens itself as low-income people of color are displaced from newly chic neighborhoods, shut out of all but the lowest-wage jobs, and isolated in aging, disinvested communities—these days, in the suburbs.[7]

While it has taken a long time, recognition is finally gaining that the suburbs of northern America are not physically homogenous, nor are suburbanites all the same. However, they remain highly fragmented and segregated by income, race, and ethnicity; it has been systemically structured that way over many growth cycles, and the barriers to decreasing segregation and inequality stubbornly persist.[8] Ongoing research demonstrates the increasing concentration of U.S. income and wealth in the top 1% of the population since the 1980s. The number of suburban U.S. census tracts with high levels of poverty has grown. Yet, while poor places get poorer, many rich places continue to get richer, and the uneven playing field gets more inequitable.[9]

Within the context of suburban retrofitting, social capital is the introduction or enhancement of social infrastructure within a project. Simply put: a strengthened social infrastructure increases urban resilience—that is, the capacity of a place, with its inhabitants, to survive, adapt, and even grow in the face of both chronic and acute stresses and shocks, be they economic, climatic, political, or all three. How do retrofits address the challenge of leveraging social capital in ways that increase resilience and measures of equity? Urban scholars make cases for the role of weak ties in fostering community and trust both at metropolitan-wide and neighbourhood scales, and outline roles for design in enabling and sustaining social diversity.[10]

The three primary suburban retrofitting strategies can be mixed and matched (see Figure 1). *Reinhabitation* of commercial spaces can support the flourishing of locally owned businesses, particularly in working-class suburbs and 'ethnoburbs', places where recent waves of immigrant populations have concentrated. *Redevelopment* can add and preserve jobs, housing affordability and choice.

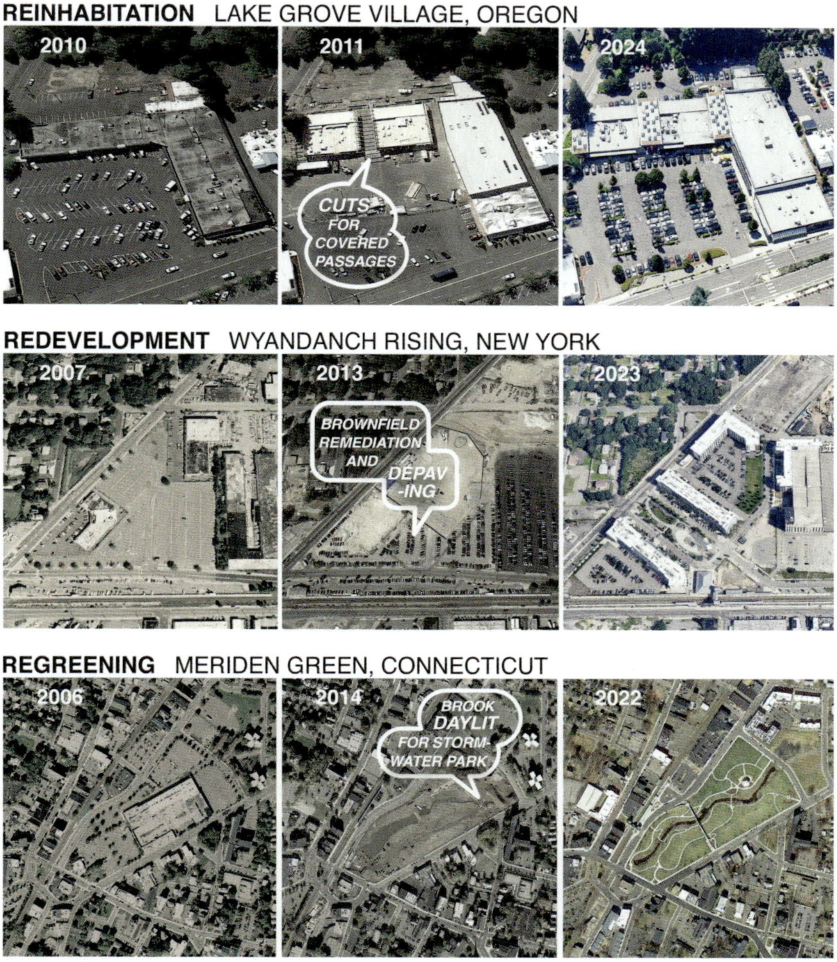

Figure 1: These sequences of aerial photographs document suburban retrofits of three sites discussed in this chapter. (top) Lake Grove Village, the reinhabitation of a strip mall near Portland, Oregon, illustrates the urban design tactic of subtracting narrow passages to break up the building mass, add access to the rear, and provide shared areas for 'third place' sociability. (centre) Wyandanch Rising, in the Town of Babylon on Long Island, New York, is gradually infilling depaved commuter parking lots and industrial brownfield sites adjacent to a newly rebuilt train station, offering deeply affordable new housing and community amenity spaces. (bottom) Before regreening, the urban renewal-era Meriden Hub mall sat squat in a parking lot. The mall was demolished, the brook daylit, and the land regraded into a stormwater park. A sophisticated piece of green infrastructure, Meriden Green is surrounded with new and relocated subsidised housing. Source: Diagram by June Williamson, 2024

And *regreening* can provide equitable access to an enhanced civic realm of public and shared green spaces, helping assert a 'right to the suburb'.[11] These strategies can and should be employed both in suburbanised communities with high rates of poverty, where needs are greatest, and in more prosperous places with existing access to a greater range of opportunities.

Third Place Redux

Several retrofits have been successfully designed to invoke the sociological concept of the 'third place'.[12] A third place is not home, nor a site of work; instead, it is an informal gathering place where people regularly go to socialise in convivial company, including in public squares, gardens, playgrounds, and outdoor art installations. Countless small strip shopping centres (often oriented around a grocery store) have the potential to be consciously reshaped into third place neighbourhood anchors, with the addition of covered seating, breezeways, decent coffee, and management policies that tolerate some degree of purposeful 'loitering'. Big box stores can also accommodate public third place uses, such as branch libraries, recreation gyms, and wellness centres.

The owners of Lake Grove Village, near Portland, Oregon, removed and recycled part of the original grocery-anchored strip mall to create two covered passages with ample seating and open pedestrian access to the rear. This *subtractive* act of remodelling increased potential hangout places, while additionally strengthening pedestrian connections to the surrounding neighbourhood.

Ethnic shopping centres are central to the lives of immigrant suburbanites, both in terms of shopping for specialised items and services, and forging bonds with others.[13] Many of these are reinhabitations of older malls. In Fort Worth, Texas, a shopping mall—originally built as the Seminary South Shopping Center in 1962, on the site of a drained lake by the development arm of Sears—has become La Gran Plaza de Fort Worth, a highly successful Hispanic-themed mall (see Figure 2). The centre is anchored by a department store that has been converted into a 12,000-square-metre, three-level *mercado* featuring many small, individually operated stalls—basically a small business incubator. La Gran Plaza regularly hosts events such as Mexican wrestling in the atrium and coordinates live music festivals in its parking

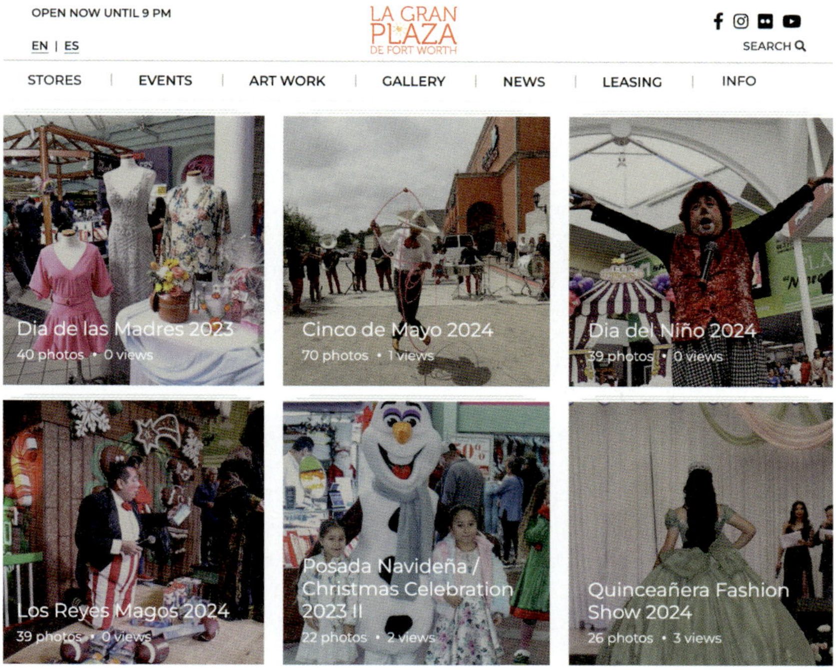

Figure 2: La Gran Plaza, a Hispanic-themed shopping mall in Fort Worth, Texas, frequently hosts community-serving activities and events. Photos and videos on the website document *lucha libre* wrestling matches, *quinceañera* fashion shows, and Cinco de Mayo celebrations. Source: La Gran Plaza de Fort Worth website

lots. In response to demographic shifts, mall reinhabitations have in several instances become locales for political assembly and protest.[14]

Expanding Housing Types, Tenure and Choices

Past recessions exposed the risk of over reliance on a singular suburban housing 'product'—generally typified by detached houses organised into subdivisions, varying only in dwelling size and price point. Residential development monocultures are obsolete precisely because they are not resilient in the face of economic shocks. Permitting and infilling with *missing middle* housing types—including duplexes, fourplexes, cottage courts, and so on—can incrementally introduce more choices to housing monocultures, at a greater range of prices and rents.[15]

The population of the unincorporated hamlet of Wyandanch, a persistently distressed area of Long Island, is predominantly Black and Latinx. Generations of residents have endured a shameful history of racial segregation and public neglect.[16] Two decades in the making, Wyandanch Rising is an ambitious, overdue retrofit (see Figure 3). Located on cleaned-up brownfields and greyfields, next to a formerly underused commuter rail station, the plan calls for several new buildings with hundreds of apartments (including a variety of types) arranged around a civic green. Extensive community-organising groundwork went into creating a network of trust with dozens of civic and religious groups. The master development agreement for the retrofit included a labour requirement for all sub-contractors to hire first from a local resident pool, trained through a community centre on-site. One of these residents was a mother of three living in a shelter when she applied for training. She excelled, becoming a working member of the local carpenters union.[17]

A Right to the Suburb? The Public Realm

A third approach redresses the public or civil realm, often an impoverished aspect of conventional suburban form. French theorist Henri Lefebvre's concept of the 'right to the city', birthed in the social upheavals of 1968, has been reframed by some scholars as the 'right to the suburb', in recognition of a need to theorise areas in the urban

Figure 3: Delano Stewart Plaza is framed by new affordable apartment buildings in Wyandanch Rising. Designed by Olin Studio, the plaza is named after a long-time African American community activist. On its opening day in 2018, dozens of local kids learned to ice skate on the seasonal rink, a focal point of the plaza. Source: Photo by Phillip Jones, 2018; courtesy of RetrofittingSuburbia.com

periphery where most now live and work.[18] This is as true in France as it is in northern America and, increasingly, across the globe. In the northern American context that is our focus here, a suburban public realm may be co-created through retrofits that insist that spaces that *look* public in form—spaces that have sidewalks, street trees, and such—should afford real rights to all people.

New York City is perhaps the U.S. city least associated with suburban form, though this typology exists in relative abundance in the outer boroughs. For instance, a failed auto-oriented strip shopping centre located on the outskirts of Queens is now being replaced with 1,700 sorely needed units of affordable rental housing and supporting spaces, spread across several ten to fifteen-storey buildings. The design of Far Rockaway Village includes a walkable spine of civic spaces reconnecting the southern terminus of a subway line (the A train) to the Long Island Rail Road terminus in neighbouring Nassau County (see Figure 4).

Challenge: Add Water and Energy Resilience

Twentieth-century suburban form was based on an industrial model of segregation and optimised engineering of separated systems, rather than interdependency.[19] For example, countless wetlands were filled in and creeks channelled into concrete culverts to prepare large land parcels for commercial development. There is now far greater recognition of the collateral damage such systems have wrought on our environment and of how climate change is increasing risks of extreme weather, flooding, droughts, wildfires, and urban heat island impacts. However, upgrading the performance of already existing suburban water and energy systems is difficult. And this is precisely where retrofits can come in.

Negative impacts can be mitigated by *redevelopment* of suburban form using walkable, transit-served, compact urban form. And, where suitable, by *reinhabitation* of existing buildings to retain embodied energy. Further, we can engage in *regreening* by introducing soft, natural systems infrastructure in place of grey, hard infrastructure for managing stormwater, reducing overall energy use, and integrating renewable energy sources.

Figure 4: Far Rockaway Village replaced the derelict 1960s-era Far Rockaway Shopping Center in outer Queens, New York. A new walkable central spine reconnects two regional rail termini. Developed by venerable non-profit Phipps Houses, the ambitious strip mall retrofit is designed by Marvel Architects. Source: Photo collage by June Williamson, 2024

Retrofitting Water for Resilience

Suburban form tends to exacerbate problems of water quality and water quantity. Stormwater run-off becomes excessive and degraded with oils, salts, and fertilisers. About a tenth of all occupied U.S. housing units are sited in floodplains, half of them built since 1980.[20] This is a particularly acute problem across metropolitan Houston, Texas. At Exploration Green, volunteers are leading the conversion of a defunct, 180-acre golf course, which is now being reimagined as a linear nature park featuring stormwater detention ponds with capacity to protect thousands of nearby households.

In the downtown of working-class Meriden, in central Connecticut, a creek was erased from the visible landscape decades ago, diverted into an underground concrete culvert, and the Hub Mall built over it. The site flooded, frequently and catastrophically. In a comprehensive regreening process, the mall was demolished, the creek 'daylit' and the area landscaped into a stormwater park, called Meriden Green. Traversable by a spanning bridge, the Green is designed to completely fill with water in the event of a severe storm—as it did in summer 2021 after Hurricane Elsa caused torrential rainfall.

Retrofits in arid areas with too little water, increasingly susceptible to very high heat and drought, can increase shade and evaporative cooling for people with tree canopies, bioswales, high-albedo coatings, and fountains and misters in paved areas. These types of site-specific, localised regreening features can really add up, particularly when paired with depaving measures, to decrease the amount of exposed impermeable surface area and reduce the damaging heat island effect.[21]

Conclusion: Retrofitting Suburbia for Energy Resilience

Solar panels, wind turbines, and geothermal wells are all highly viable in suburbanised settings, far more so than in city centres. For Guthrie Green Urban Park in Tulsa, Oklahoma, a block-sized cultural and wellness park replaced a truck loading facility parking lot. The project features an array of solar panels and extensive geothermal wells installed beneath the turf. After this depaving retrofit, the park has become an anchor and magnet for a larger, emergent cultural district. Not only has the form changed significantly, but also the uses of the surrounding area, as various buildings are beginning to be restored and reinhabited.

These case study snippets briefly survey the current state of the vision for incremental metropolitanism. The second generation of suburban retrofitting projects—located in peripheral areas across northern America—provide vital evidence that some scattered progress has been made in implementing the vision through the gradual accumulation of innovative projects on already urbanised sites in the metropolitan periphery. Fewer of the projects surveyed here exhibit the kind of hybridity or the compromises found in the first generation of retrofits; indeed, many of them are seeking (and achieving) layered goals. By leveraging social capital to increase equity, enhancing water and energy resilience, and disrupting car dependency, they redefine the baseline conditions for any credible suburban retrofitting project.

Endnotes:

1 With the term 'northern America', I mean to refer principally to the continental United States and Canada, excluding Mexico, countries and territories of the Caribbean, and other places or nations that—by the basic geographic definition—are considered part of North America.

2 Dunham-Jones, E. and Williamson, J. *Retrofitting Suburbia: Urban Design Solutions for Redesigning Suburbs.* Wiley, 2008, p. 233.

3 Dr. Vivek Murthy was U.S. Surgeon General from 2014–2017, when the 'Step it Up!' call to action was issued. He was appointed again in 2021.

4 The Inflation Reduction Act of 2022 was signed into U.S. law on August 16, 2022.

5 Dunham-Jones and Williamson, 2008, pp. 9–12, pp. 230–233.

6 Williamson, J. and Dunham-Jones, E. *Case Studies in Retrofitting Suburbia: Urban Design Strategies for Urgent Challenges.* Wiley, 2021.

7 Glover Blackwell, A. The Case for All-In Cities, in: T. Griffin, A. Cohen, and D. Maddox (eds.) *The Just City Essays.* Next City, 2015, pp. 57–58.

8 Rothstein, R. *The Color of Law: A Forgotten History of How Our Government Segregated America.* Liveright Publishing Corporation, 2017; Mitchell, B. and Franco, J. *HOLC 'Redlining' Maps: The Persistent Structure of Segregation and Economic Inequality.* National Community Reinvestment Coalition report, 2018.

9 Kneebone, E. and Berube, A. *Confronting Suburban Poverty in America.* Brookings Institution Press, 2013; Allard, S. *Places in Need: The Changing Geography of Poverty.* Russell Sage Foundation, 2017; Piketty, T., Saez, E., and Zucman, G. Twenty Years and Counting: Thoughts about Measuring the Upper Tail, *The Journal of Economic Inequality, 20* (2022), pp. 255–264.

10 Pastor, M. and Benner, C. *Equity, Growth, and Community: What the Nation Can Learn from America's Metro Areas.* University of California Press, 2015; Talen, E. and Lee, S. *Design for Social Diversity.* Routledge, 2018; Talen, E. *Neighborhood.* Oxford University Press, 2018.

11 Dunham-Jones, E. and Williamson, J. Dead and Dying Shopping Malls, Re-inhabited, *Architectural Design, 249* (2017), pp. 84–91; Li, W. *Ethnoburb: The New Ethnic Community in Urban America.* University of Hawai'i Press, 2009.

12 Oldenburg, R. *The Great Good Place: Cafés, Coffee Shops, Community Centers, Beauty Parlors, General Stores, Bars, Hangouts, and How They Get You Through the Day.* Paragon House, 1989.

13 Lung-Amam, W. *Trespassers: Asian Americans and the Battle for Suburbia.* University of California Press, 2017.

14 Williamson, J. Protest on the Astroturf at Downtown Silver Spring: July 4, 2007, in: C. Niedt (ed.) *Social Justice in Diverse Suburbs: History, Politics, and Prospects.* Temple University Press, 2013. pp. 54–69.

15 Parolek, D. *Missing Middle Housing: Thinking Big and Building Small to Respond to Today's Housing Crisis.* Island Press, 2020.

16 Wiese, A. Racial Cleansing in the Suburbs: Suburban Government, Urban Renewal, and Segregation on Long Island, New York, 1945–60, in: M. Silver and M. Melkonian (eds.) *Contested Terrain: Power, Politics, and Participation in Suburbia.* Hofstra University, 1995.

17 Reported in the Long Island paper *Newsday* in July 2014.

18 Lefebvre, H. The Right to the City, in: E. Kofman and E. Lebas (eds.) *Writings on Cities.* Blackwell Publishers, 1996, pp. 147–159; Carpio, G., Irazabal, C., and Pulido, L. Right to the Suburb? Rethinking Lefebvre and Immigrant Activism, *Journal of Urban Affairs, 33* (2011), pp. 185–208; Harris, D. The Rights to the Suburb. *The Aggregate blog*, 2015; http://www.we-aggregate.org/piece/the-rights-to-the-suburb.

19 Brown, H. *Next Generation Infrastructure: Principles for Post-Industrial Public Works.* Island Press, 2014.

20 Rosoff, S. and Yager, J. *Housing in the U.S. Floodplains.* Data Brief. NYU Furman Center, 2017.

21 Jiang, Y., Yuan, Y., and Piza, H. A review of applicability and effectiveness of low impact development/green infrastructure practices in arid/semi-arid United States, *Environments, 2* (2015), pp. 221–249.

From Swamp to Satellite: The Case of Cassia Township, Penang

Sharifah R. S. Dawood

Introduction

Dynamic socio-spatial processes make today's cities more complex systems than ever, presenting numerous challenges for urban governance. Presently, smart growth is one of the most sought-after governance models, evident in its acceleration at a global scale. In Malaysia it has been applied within the normative planning framework, especially in the case of urban peripheries. Many new satellite townships and smart developments have been conceptualised based on the notion of smart growth. These include the newly emerging township of Cassia, Penang, which is the subject of this chapter. The narrative of urbanisation currently playing out in this periphery aims to synergise advanced economic and cultural operations with the core region, enabling it to modernise and develop sustainably. Planners and architects are now implementing the idea of a smart eco-city in Cassia, through designing, master planning, and executing individual projects. Notable in this regard is the heavy reliance on global and local investors in property development.

These urban expansion projects are manifest as what K. Murat Güney, Roger Keil, and Murat Üçoğlu have termed 'massive suburbia'.[1] These urban economic enclaves[2] form part of a mega property investment frontier of exclusive utopias targeted at the rising urban upper middle class. Reflecting on the *'global suburbanisms'* major international research programme, they assert that we live 'in the age of the urban periphery'.[3] Keil claims that urban peripheries exhibit greater diversity 'than perhaps anywhere else in the modern history of city-building and re-building'. It is clear that today's urban peripheries are marked by a mixture of dynamism and stagnation; they also mirror affluent lifestyles and socioeconomic inequalities[4]. These satellite towns have become very prominent and influential in planning and development models, illustrating how the urban periphery is a potent source of planning and policy elements that are globally mobile.[5] In Malaysia, the satellite town model has been seen as a highly effective way of attracting new and additional sources of investment and human capital. Satellite cities concretely reflect the current politics of urban development in this country, with its aspirations to network individuals, communities, and regions into the global economy. They rely on branding as a strategy to draw in international investors, using terms such as eco-city, smart city, and techno city to represent a new frontier in real estate investment—one in which prosperity thrives as a direct outcome of these swiftly emerging urban utopias. Nevertheless, while the idea and mission of making a township such as Cassia smart, green, connected, and resilient might appear easy to plan on paper, its realisation in practice is altogether a different matter.

The History and Idea behind the Eco- and Smart City Models

The formation of Bandar Cassia (BC), or Cassia Township, was based on earlier initiatives instigated by the Penang state government. It was given the name Cassia in honour of the genus of trees that bear vivid yellow blossoms, namely the *Cassia siamea* species which is a species native to the area. Due to its proximity to the Second Penang Bridge on the Penang Mainland, the township has grown quickly. Located in *Seberang Prai* (formerly known as Province Wellesley), it was the most undeveloped district in Penang in the 1980s. However, the state government has always felt a responsibility to develop this area, paralleling the rapid development on Penang Island. In 1989, Tun Dr. Lim Chong Eu—Chief Minister of Penang at the time—instructed the Penang Development Corporation (PDC) to designate a location in South Seberang Prai for the development of an economic hub. Through this scouting process, Batu Kawan—originally a swampy area with a few dispersed sugarcane, coconut, rubber (and later oil palm) plantations, as well as a few scattered villages or *kampungs*—was identified as a suitable location. The state government acquired Batu Kawan in 1990 and, due to its strategic location and size (spanning about 6,781 acres), it was chosen as a new growth centre. Eventually, PDC purchased about 6,326 acres of land from this area, which it later named Bandar Cassia.

To build and accelerate the new township's growth in accordance with the contemporary conventions (and rate) of development, the government proposed that it should represent a globally desirable and attractive model of city development. The concepts of the eco-city, low carbon city, and 3Rs (reduce, reuse, and recycle) were collectively adopted alongside other green initiatives at the 2014 UNEP-IETC & Global Environment Centre (GEC) meeting, drawing on the example of Kawasaki Eco-Town in Japan.[6] These learning experiences eventually led to the adoption of the eco-city concept. Borrowing from ideas and concepts implemented successfully in Japan, Penang planners and architects integrated the Kawasaki experience in their development planning process to create the province's eco-town.

Subsequently, PDC spearheaded the development effort as the Penang state government designated the greenfield regions for new industrial sites and urban development on the mainland. Thus, the creation of the eco-city—which PDC, the area's self-described architect, had imagined as the first smart, eco-city with a futuristic vision—came to pass. Once a quiet little 'island' surrounded by mangrove swamps, Batu Kawan is now set to be transformed into a township that will encapsulate the future of Penang and, perhaps most importantly, compensate for the dearth of space on Penang Island. After years of meticulous planning, deal-making and construction, Batu Kawan has been gradually transformed through the arrival of major establishments, including the Swedish home furnishing retailer, IKEA, and the commercial centres of Vervea, as well as the educational and residential properties in Utropolis and Eco Horizon. At the time, there was a lot of expectation that the completion of the second Penang Bridge in 2014 would serve as a further catalyst for the acceleration of Cassia Township's development, owing to the increased accessibility and connectivity to Penang Island's mainland. This was claimed as the primary attraction for island-based homebuyers flocking to the newly developed Cassia Township.

Known as the third satellite city of Penang [the first being Bayan Baru and the second being Seberang Jaya] and dubbed as the '*Damansara* of Penang' (a reference to the similarly named luxurious, affluent, upscale suburb in Kuala Lumpur), the eco-city of Cassia aspires to be a sustainable city where its citizens can enjoy the best possible social, economic, and environmental quality of life. Bandar Cassia, which was a swampy marshland only a decade ago, is fast transitioning into a dynamic satellite city that boosts new housing, industry, commercial precincts, and malls. The eco-friendly development of BC is expected to be completed by 2030, and the finished city will cater for some 230,000 residents. Nine key elements of the eco-city concept have been implemented to make BC a growth centre and to realise the state's intention to prioritise eco-friendly development, grounded in green technology and low carbon emissions. In this case, the Municipal Council of Seberang Prai (MPSP) has developed a thorough set of guidelines for BC eco-city in collaboration with technical organisations and stakeholders (city planners, government, and tech specialists) as summarised in Figure 1.

The Transformation of a Swampy Periphery into a Modern Utopia: How far can Urban Governance take Control?

The state government of Penang aimed to establish a township with the purpose of transforming BC into a satellite township and an eco-smart metropolis capable of generating sustainable growth. The following nine essential components form the foundation of the eco-smart city development concept: affordable housing, solid waste management, ecology preservation, accessibility, safe city, zero renovation, green building, and green neighbourhood.

Although construction was already underway, Cassia Township's property development did not really get underway until 2010. Development mostly consisted of residential buildings, ranging from luxury condominiums, serviced apartments, and landed houses to affordable housing projects. Among these were the Vertu Resort, Viluxe, and Ashton @ Eco Horizon. The Design Village, IKEA Batu Kawan, Vervea @ Aspen Vision City, Sensasi @ Utropolis, and Borealis @ Eco Horizon were among the completed commercial developments. Meanwhile, education centres include the UOW Malaysia KDU campus (University of Wollongong Australia global network) and Peninsula Ship Campus (in partnership with University of Plymouth) (see Figure 2). The aim was to create the Utropolis, making Batu Kawan the first university metropolis in Penang (Figure 3).

Figure 1. Eco-city initiatives in BC. Source: MBSP [City Council of Seberang Prai], 2018

Figure 2. The Peninsula Ship Campus, one of the iconic buildings in BC.
Source: The Ship Campus Sdn Bhd

Figure 3. Utropolis Batu Kawan. Source: Paramount Property

Furthermore, Penang's Batu Kawan industrial region was identified in Malaysia's 2021 budget as a promising site for high-tech industry investment. Larger industrial corporations and well-known global brands, such as Western Digital, Boston Scientific, Lam Research, and Hewlett-Packard, were further drawn to this area. As for the top three real estate developers, they are: Paramount Property with Utropolis Batu Kawan; Aspen with Aspen Vision City; and Eco World Development Group with Eco Horizon. They have all constructed various types of property, ranging from high-rise residential and office buildings through to terraces, semi-detached houses, and bungalow units. An aerial view of the development can be seen in Figure 4.

A strong anchor for the integrated mixed-use development township is the Swedish furnishing company, IKEA, which now serves as a new centre for residential, commercial, and industrial activity. Other notable anchors include Design Village Outlet Mall, Aspen Vision City, Eco Horizon, and the Utropolis Education centre. The creation of a new 'art city', utilising container art pieces in several locations, adds a creative aspect to the township's development and planning (see Figure 5). This is part of a strategic action to promote BC, generating a unique sense of local identity in the face of modernisation and peripheral urbanisation. Additionally, it encapsulates and narrates the identity of Penang's local communities by enhancing the creative ecosystem of Province Wellesley—which was formerly a sluggish, backwater space. The aim here was to inject a sense of creativity and work–life balance into the city, enhancing BC's desirability as a commercial and leisure destination, and thus bridging the gap between the island and the mainland of Penang (especially in terms of tourism).

From Vision to Implementation: Tough Challenges Ahead

Despite intellectual reservations, 'smart' digital innovations have become widely accepted among policymakers as key to improving the economic, social, and environmental quality of life, including in urban peripheries.[7] Thus, using digital solutions to help address important issues like public safety, utility management, and traffic congestion is also one of the ideas driving BC's development. Another is to encourage more effective urban planning by state agencies, real

Figure 4. Property development in BC. Source: ASPEN

Figure 5. Container artwork in BC, showing the local fisherman.
Source: Photo by Sharifah R. S. Dawood, 2023

estate developers, municipalities, and local councils. The pace of digitalisation among local authorities can potentially boost the efficiency of public services and allow the public sector to flourish, but urban governance will nevertheless encounter numerous challenges.

To provide its residents with new technology capabilities, the positioning of a smart city in BC depends not only on local authorities and their infrastructure but also on the continuous transformation of industry and business. However, due to the COVID-19 pandemic and various funding issues, numerous obstacles have hindered the progress of several planned projects—among them the construction of a private hospital and a theme park which have been delayed and the latter cancelled. Successive lockdowns have slowed real estate development. Other issues have also recently arisen around traffic congestion, waste management, road construction issues, river pollution, and water supply. In addition to this, there is poor coordination between the public and the private sector in the development process. Despite the state government initiating numerous collaborative arrangements with businesses in the private sector, it seems to lack transparency in planning and implementation. For instance, the state government initially engaged an external consultancy firm from Singapore to develop projects involving some 11,800 apartments on an 80.9 hectare area, making this the state's largest affordable housing project. However, it was cancelled due to internal issues and local criticism. Moreover, the affordable housing project seems to be mismatched with the needs of the local community since even 'affordable' housing ends up being housing for the wealthy. Although low-cost housing may seem an outdated concept in a cosmopolitan region like Penang, the reality is that low-cost housing is still very much in demand by the working classes. Relying on external developers also generates volatility in the market and the corollary issues that arise with it. As peripheral centralities like Cassia Township become increasingly networked into global neoliberal capitalism, the profit imperative drives imbalances in supply and demand in the highly speculative processes of property development.

Perhaps the largest obstacle to BC's implementation plan is the lack of financing. To incorporate digital technologies in cities, sophisticated infrastructure must be deployed. The government must meet all standards, hire a sufficient number of computer specialists and urban planners, and the installed hardware requires regular audits for maintenance. Moreover, there are resource-related issues pertaining to the shortage of human capital, most notably qualified experts who can develop plans to ensure the success of eco- and smart city initiatives, identifying areas for technology deployment and operating systems.

Besides this, the high-speed internet connectivity needed to fulfil the requirement of 4G and 5G mobile systems still lags in the region. Without the improvement of human resources and systems, there is the prospect of Cassia Township becoming a smart city anti-model of cybersecurity risk—where data from parking lots, CCTV cameras, EV charging stations, and GPS systems (containing citizens' private information) is at potential risk of leaking.

More broadly, the limitations of this model suggest that Cassia Township may yet be a 'white elephant' project unless all stakeholders collaborate proactively. Will this satellite township offer architects and real estate developers a chance to create a distinct centrality in the urban periphery of Penang—a new metropolis, a middle-class paradise? The case of Cassia raises the question of how sustainable the privatised peripheral centralities found across Southeast Asia[8] truly are, and casts challenges on the ability of national and local governments to co-fund their development.

Conclusion

Emerging from a swampy marshland, Cassia Township has the potential to become a sustainable new centrality on the periphery of urban Penang. The satellite township makes use of a development strategy in which the system of governance transforms and creates a new phase of peripheral urbanisation with an emphasis on smart and eco growth. The development of bridge and road infrastructure, industrial parks, malls, business districts, condominiums, and luxury homes has rapidly altered the partially swampy and sparsely settled plantation estate. Nonetheless, BC's prospects remain mixed.

Certain elements of this contemporary eco-city development ignore the needs of local populations, even displacing them as local government struggles to finance affordable 'smart eco-cities'. Understanding of urban peripheries and the changes occurring in Cassia Township can be strengthened by approaching them from an international, comparative viewpoint. It is necessary to re-evaluate the risks that privatisation presents to public values and to consider the various roles played by investors as well as the extent to which technology generates development and added value. As this chapter has made clear, there is still much to be re-evaluated in the credentials of this emerging model of smart eco-cities—not least what its spread across peripheral centralities in Malaysia (and elsewhere in South-east Asia) signifies in terms of social balance, governance, and supply of sufficient services.

Endnotes:

1 Güney, K. M., Keil, R., and Üçoğlu, M. *Massive Suburbanization: (Re)Building the Global Periphery.* University of Toronto Press, 2019.

2 Phelps, N. A., Miao, J. T., and Zhang, X. *Polycentric urbanization as enclave urbanization: a research agenda with illustrations from the Yangtze River Delta Region (YRDR), China.* Territory, Politics, Governance, 2020.

3 Keil, R. *Suburban Planet: Making the World Urban from the Outside In.* Polity Press, 2018.

4 Padgham, J., Jabbour, J., and Dietrich, K. *Managing change and building resilience: a multi-stressor analysis of urban and peri-urban agriculture in Africa and Asia.* Urban Climate, 2015.

5 Phelps, N. A., Maginn, P. J., and Keil, R. Centring the periphery in urban studies: Notes towards a research agenda on peripheral centralities, *Urban Studies, 60* (6), 2023, pp. 1158–1176.

6 Planning of Eco-city and Green Technologies in Province Wellesley, Penang, Malaysia; https://eri-kawasaki.jp/wp-content/uploads/2018/02/43535ff2c35363d-f56776bd4 aa40167d.pdf

7 Meth, P., Goodfellow, T., Todes, A., and Charlton, S. Conceptualizing African Urban Peripheries, *International Journal of Urban and Regional Research, 45* (6), 2021, pp. 985–1007.

8 Dick, H. W. and Rimmer, P. J. Beyond the Third World City: The New Urban Geography of South-east Asia, *Urban Studies, 35* (12), 1998, pp. 2303–2321.

Golf Courses as New Suburban Centralities: The Case of Johannesburg

Federica Duca

Introduction

Golf courses in Johannesburg, South Africa, represent new forms of peripheral centrality, conferring centrality upon initially peripheral areas. They have been a constitutive part of the city since its inception and have maintained their relevance through to the present day. Indeed, golf has taken on a new centrality by virtue of the type of space it creates and represents, space which is related to the sport only in a tangential sense. The presence of golf infrastructure throughout the city (taking the form of ordinary golf courses and newly built golf estates) means that such spaces are pivotal for understanding spatial transformation—or lack thereof—in a city deeply scarred by apartheid planning. Golf courses serve numerous different purposes for the city and its residents, going beyond the practice of the sport itself.

The creation of new peripheral centralities through golf and golf courses reveals the role of the sport in creating a layered space that is peripheral and central at the same time. The generation of these spaces through establishing golf clubs contributes to the creation of new centralities that cement Johannesburg as a 'city of clubs'. Although golf courses have historically been spaces of exclusivity, the general decline of the sport has made it imperative to devise new spatial functions as a source of revenue creation. While their need to renew their relevance means that the use of golf courses has diversified in the last ten years, they have only apparently become less exclusive. Indeed, this 'diversification' has nevertheless contributed to defining a city that is characterised by new centralities implemented through enclosure and different forms of exclusion. What does this mean for the broader structure of the city and for the perpetuation of spatial and social inequality?

Working with the concept of peripheral centralities proves to be a generative entry point for thinking about the multifaceted functions a space has in constituting both centrality and periphery at the same time.[1] Thinking of peripheral centralities allows one to locate the different functions of a space; in this case, taking the golf course as vantage point affords us the opportunity to reflect on the different facets of enclosure. In this chapter, I demonstrate that the periphery and centre can co-exist and that the golf course as a space exemplifies this. In Johannesburg, this means formalising a new centrality in a process that involves the gradual abandonment of the original 'inner city' and its expansion through the creation of clubs.

Golf Courses in Johannesburg

In Johannesburg alone there are at least forty golf courses, including old golf clubs and new golf estates. Golf courses in Johannesburg are both hidden and visible. It is almost impossible for residents or visitors to the city not to notice the pervasive presence of manicured greens, especially when driving through the city's older suburbs. These are not always open to everyone and access is not straightforward unless one is a member. Despite being gated, however, they remain highly visible and even those unable to enter these spaces are able to observe them from the outside.

On the contrary, those courses located *inside* golf estates—which, in the 1980s and early 1990s, were situated in the new suburban peripheries but now exist as new centralities—are hidden to the eyes of the visitors, though they remain central to the imaginaries of existing residents and those that aspire to live in them.

Golf courses began appearing in Johannesburg in the early 1900s, when the city first developed. At the time, golf courses represented the apex of the 'gentlemen's game': a white, male-dominated sport which was characterised in the South African context by racial discrimination and dispossession of land. While playing in what was then 'the outskirts' of the South African city, golfers still felt they were connected to the heart of the Empire and its lifestyle. During apartheid, the city was formally segregated and the subsequent development and sprawl towards the north—starting in the 1970s—brought with it the reconfiguration of the city centre, through the creation of a new central business district, Sandton.[2]

Later, in tandem with the end of the apartheid regime, a new urban residential model made its appearance, namely that of the golf estate. During the transition to democracy, it was seen as a simple reproduction of the apartheid city. Over time, it has contributed to forming a new configuration of the post-apartheid city, wherein what were once deemed the peripheries have now become centralities, transforming the role of the old city centre, which is now seen as derelict, inaccessible, and dysfunctional.

Golf courses in Johannesburg are a pivotal space through which to analyse this change in that they contribute to social polarisation and environmental injustice alongside promoting selective inclusion.[3] However, being that they are both highly ambitious and lucrative, they also constitute new centres of gravity and emerge as important networks in the city. When built on gated estates they contribute to the outward expansion of the city and are justified by the rhetoric of inclusivity, even though golf courses largely remain sites of exclusion. Such rhetoric is based on the need for golf courses and clubs to maintain their lush appearance at a moment in time where this has become a financial challenge.

The Different Uses of the Golf Course

Golf courses are central to the imaginary of Johannesburg as a city; residents aspire to live in close proximity to golf courses because they add value to properties and provide a tranquil, secluded, and prestigious environment. They thus offer both material and symbolic value. Though this happens in different ways, it always involves some degree of exclusion through creating a 'city of clubs'. In what follows, I explore three different ways in which golf courses have become the new suburban centralities in Johannesburg. This happens through a blended use of the golf course which provides a space for selective belonging.

In the first instance, gated golf estates are used for residential and sporting entertainment purposes. Blair Atholl Golf and Equestrian Estate was built on a farm existing since the 1940s, on land that was at that time designated 'countryside'[4]. It was later established as an estate when the South African golfer, Gary Player, the farm's subsequent owner, decided to sell it and design a state-of-the-art golf course. The golf estate is now established but not yet fully occupied. The estate prides itself on being exclusive and class homogeneous. The signature golf course gives centrality to a space that is geographically removed from the traditional urban centres. Early on, potential buyers saw this as an appealing space precisely because it was both central and peripheral at the same time. It is near a newly built airport and will be at the heart of the new Lanseria Smart City plan—recently announced as the first 'post-apartheid city'.

The golf course is central to the estate, making it highly aspirational. The golf course's grandeur was confirmed with its selection as the host of the prestigious SA Open tournament in November 2022. This meant that the golf course and estate assumed a centrality that extended beyond golfers, encompassing the array of visitors who were allowed to enter the estate upon purchase of a ticket over the tournament period. During the event, the golf estate also became a commercial site, with food stands and sporting gear on sale. Visitors came from all over the country, and the estate acquired a new appearance of centrality by virtue of the golf course.

Adding a more symbolic layer, a second example of the different uses and meanings ascribed to golf courses is provided by newly built golf estates which now constitute new centralities and that advertise themselves as sites which instantiate a new post-apartheid country, despite being located in initially peripheral spaces and displaying features of exclusivity. Steyn City offers one such example. The South African developer, Douw Gerbrand Steyn, made a point of choosing South Africa as his home. Moreover, he has highlighted that the promotion of his new gated development, endorsed by Nelson Mandela, is the ultimate expression of his involvement in the transition process and his commitment to building a democratic South Africa[5]. He envisages the new gated estate not only as a new city, but as an expression of the new country. Developments like these are now being marketed as the new face of democratic dispensation. Yet, their management is based on the existence of a highly selective club.

As with many other golf estates built in the last twenty years, the golf course at Steyn City is aspirational. The estate is composed of different internal centralities (in the form of amenities, various types of housing and internal suburbs) all of which take the golf course as their reference point, being a large open space within the estate. In this case the golf course is invisible from the outside and is accessible only upon entrance to the facility, gained through a selective process.

While marketed as the ideal of a new South Africa championing selective diversity, many are drawn to the estate because the presence of the golf course and other amenities make for a good investment, adding value to any property purchased.

Finally, golf courses are also explicitly a site of commercial value, accessible but not visible. Located in proximity to Sandton, the financial CBD of the city—the new centre outside of the 'traditional' inner city—a nine-hole golf course is attached to a restaurant, designed as an easy course for non-professionals to enjoy a casual game. This golf course is hidden but accessible to those who frequent the restaurant.

The owner of the restaurant confirms that the little golf course adds value to the restaurant. Patrons enjoy having a meal and then going for a recreational game. But, perhaps most importantly, given that this is not solely a space for golfers, the nine-hole course is appealing to those who enjoy a walk after their meal. In this instance, the presence of the golf course becomes an incentive for visiting the restaurant, thus creating an appearance of centrality. The golf course is also presented as accessible to non-members of the club.

The examples given so far offer a view of the golf course's centrality in spaces which were initially spatially peripheral. The next example provides a vignette of a golf course that has lost its centrality due to its proximity to the original, now-defunct city centre.

Conclusion: New Peripheral Centralities

The original city centre in Johannesburg has been abandoned in the imaginaries of the middle and upper classes. New imaginaries and actual planning have largely departed from the inner city, which has become the new periphery of the metropolitan area of Johannesburg.

Golf courses, usually located in areas that were once peripheral, are spaces of aspiration, which exert a pull that produces new centres of gravity and networks in the city. Even golf courses in private gated estates are embedded in the process of massive urbanisation and citywide expansion, led by the false rhetoric of inclusivity. Built in line with a politics of urban sprawl dating to the 1980s, golf

Figure 1. SA Open tournament. Source: Photo by Federica Duca, November 2022

courses are seldom contested by citizens despite being socially and environmentally detrimental.

Owing to the changing nature of the sport, which is beset by structural and financial challenges, golf courses in Johannesburg have assumed additional functions in relation to commerce, sport, and identity. Today, they appeal to a wide variety of actors. Indeed, those who argue in favour of constructing courses are not just golfers; rather they are people who can extract value from these sites. In Johannesburg, the transformation of such spaces is not necessarily linked to opposition.[6] Golf courses change, perhaps in unexpected ways, and are not always representative of the 'gentlemen's game' in the same way they were a century ago. Golf courses within estates, even when they are located on the outskirts, have now become essential to imagining what constitutes the 'good city'.[7]

Golf courses become central because they create added value in numerous ways, both symbolic and commercial. Yet, as in many processes of value creation, their value is unevenly distributed, and they aggravate various forms of dispossession. Indeed, the cases I have illustrated here show how they foster division while at once presenting themselves as spaces that can bridge social and spatial inequalities. While, for instance, the SA Open gave temporary centrality to the golf estate through greater access during the tournament, entrance was subject to purchase of a ticket and under normal circumstances it remains ringfenced and unreachable. Likewise Steyn City may be an aspirational space, but it is also an exclusive estate that is inaccessible to the vast majority. Historically, centrality has been linked to imperial networks.

The current predominance of golf clubs in Johannesburg entails a similar process of partitioning the city, creating an isolationist world of members clubs. This city of clubs is only capable of looking inwards at its own spaces. The fairways of golf courses delimit the possibilities of accessing quiet green space in the urban metropolis, with devastating implications for those who are unable to access it. Here, the inner city emerges as a negative alternative. The challenge of this new centrality is that, although it promises to, it does not welcome everybody. This false promise makes it deceptive: while it might seem more inclusive or accessible, it nonetheless remains a club, one which excludes and selects.

In Johannesburg, where the golf course has become part of the new urban core, its vantage point is thus crucial for developing an urban theory that complicates the traditional city centre as the main point of reference. Further, these sites push us to think through new peripheral centralities in the city and their implications for the ways in which the city itself is conceived and inequalities are reproduced.

Figure 2. A view of the golf course by the restaurant. Photo by Federica Duca, November 2022

Endnotes:

1 Phelps, N. A., Maginn, P. J., and Keil, R. Centring the periphery in urban studies: Notes towards a research agenda on peripheral centralities, *Urban Studies, 60* (6), 2022; https://doi.org/10.1177/00420980221135418.

2 For a comprehensive study of the spatial changes of Johannesburg, please refer to Harrison, P., Gotz, G., Todes, A., and Wray, C. (eds.) *Changing Space, Changing City: Johannesburg after Apartheid.* Wits University Press, 2014.

3 Cock, J. Caddies and 'Cronies': Golf and changing patterns of exclusion and inclusion in post-apartheid South Africa, *South African Review of Sociology, 39* (2), 2008, pp. 183–200, https://doi.org/10.1080/21528586.2008.10425085.

4 For the history of the Blair Atholl Golf & Equestrian Estate, see: https://www.blairatholl.co.za/history/ (accessed October 24, 2024).

5 Domisse, E. *Fortunes: The Rise And Rise Of Afrikaner Tycoons.* Jonathan Ball Publishers, 2021.

6 This is not the same as other parts of the country. In Johannesburg, for instance, golf courses are highly contested. This calls for interesting comparative studies of how centralities are built in different cities.

7 Duca, F. Golf, gates and the good life: Johannesburg's private estates offer home comforts, good service – and selective solidarity, *The Sociological Review Magazine*, November 8, 2022; https://doi.org/10.51428/tsr.urxj9865.

R
ela
tions

EXIT 9
Lowry Campus
Colo Nat'l Guard
Buckley AF Base
NEXT RIGHT
Freedom Memorial

R ela tions

Back on the Map?
De/centring the 'Community Benefit' in Weston, Toronto

Sophia Ilyniak

Introduction

Socio-spatial polarisation has been exacerbated by place-based municipal policy, i.e. targeted (versus universal) socioeconomic development. Its tendency to prioritise the inner city contributes to the suburbanisation of poverty and, in turn, to depictions of the periphery as a 'threat' to the urban core[1] and its competitiveness. Attempts to manage this threat have made the urban periphery a key site of neoliberal, deregulatory experimentation underpinned by sophisticated public–private partnership arrangements and non-democratic forms of governance.[2] In their attempts to create new centralities in the periphery, revitalisation strategies and redevelopment projects often have the effect of dispersing working-class concentrations and exerting racist forms of social control, thus playing into the broader political reorganisation of core–periphery relations.[3]

In Toronto, Canada, core–periphery relations have shifted through significant and ongoing re-mappings of city boundaries and districts. Over the past seventy years, the city has seen austerity-led amalgamations resulting in new peripheralisations and subsequent attempts to address disparities through place-based policy. The now *inner* suburbs of Toronto are perhaps less *spatially* peripheral but nonetheless remain *socially* peripheral.[4] They are driven into new competitive relationships and rendered vulnerable to private exploitation of the state-made rent gap. The sharp retrenchment of the state as a redistributive actor can be most prominently seen here. In its place, the third sector—comprising an uneven patchwork of charitable, material, or therapeutic interventions—increasingly defines the *modus operandi* of social change.[5]

This chapter homes in on the case of Weston, an inner suburb of Toronto that is being 'revitalised' to recapture its historic town centre for private investment and middle-class resettlement. The focal point of this revitalisation is a large residential-commercial redevelopment, governed by a public-private-non-profit partnership (PPNP). The non-profit partner is positioned as the public face of the redevelopment. It also plays the double role of providing 'community benefit' while building local consensus for the redevelopment. The revitalisation plans specifically target the living space of the demographic majority, namely racialised, poorer residents. Meanwhile, its proponents—who are eager to place Weston 'back on the map' as a desirable place to live—are largely the middle-class, white minority.

This chapter has three aims: first, to follow state attempts at managing the peripheral 'threat to the core' by recreating Weston's centre; second, to examine PPNP or non-profit-led development as an emerging form of non-democratic governance; and, third, to question the 'community benefit' of redevelopment by highlighting the decentring effects and bringing attention to the surrounding discourse, experiences, and political actions of Weston residents. These accounts were gathered through fieldwork in the lead up to the construction of the redevelopment in 2015–16 and are supplemented by subsequent informal observation of the neighbourhood through my experience as a health outreach worker and supporter of locally-organised tenant actions. The chapter concludes with considerations for the future of inner-suburban communities in the Global North, evaluating the consequences of philanthropic-private investment in place of public reinvestment.

Re-mapping: Toronto's Inner Suburbs

Following the 1998 amalgamation of Metro Toronto and its constituents—including the post-war suburban boroughs of Etobicoke, York, North York, East York, and Scarborough—the new City of Toronto embraced an entrepreneurial stance towards governance that emphasised public–private partnership as a means of repositioning a competitive city on the global stage.[6] Re-urbanisation, or municipally managed gentrification, became an essential component of Toronto's strategy for economic success.[7] A parallel strategy was established in 2006 to address concerns of poverty and related gun violence in the city's new periphery—which posed a threat to downtown's competitive image. So-called 'Priority Neighbourhoods', all within the inner-suburban ring, were identified. The result was not economic reprioritisation (as the name suggests) but rather territorial stigmatisation, incremental surveillance, policing and criminalisation, as well as the increased presence of friendlier, cheaper alternatives offered by non-profit social programmes.

The map was re-drawn in 2014 after acknowledging that the demarcation of Priority Neighbourhoods contained poverty instead of eliminating it. The municipal government chose the bottom thirty-one of its 140 neighbourhoods ranked by 'liveability' as Neighbourhood Improvement Areas (NIAs). Most existing Priority Neighbourhoods remained on this list, though some were curiously excluded despite high service needs. Two inner-city neighbourhoods undergoing extreme redevelopment and gentrification processes—namely Regent Park and South Parkdale—were added. The NIA policy emphasised civic boosterism and competitive place promotion to attract private investment, while the public investment remained marginal. This was the case for Weston, a former Priority Neighbourhood in northwest Toronto which has come under significant redevelopment pressure since becoming an NIA.

Weston

Weston was first established as a British colonial settlement in 1796 along the trading route of several First Nations on *Gabekanaang-ziibi* (the Humber River). The construction of railways in the 1850s and 1860s led to industrial expansion and a local identity was formed around a prosperous manufacturing town. Weston was incorporated into the Borough of York in the 1950s; deindustrialisation followed in the 1960s–70s. With the devaluation of rents throughout the 1980s and 1990s, Weston steadily became home to a poorer population, including recent immigrants from the Caribbean, the Americas, and East Africa. In 1998, Weston (as a part of York) was amalgamated into the new City of Toronto and austerity measures related to this restructuring pushed it into further decline.

At the time of conducting my fieldwork, almost a third of Weston residents fell below numerous state poverty threshold markers and had the highest risk of homelessness in the city.[8] Approximately 50% were immigrants, 60% of them racialised, and 70% were living in multi-storey apartment buildings.[9] However, a minority of white, middle-class residents remained segregated in the northeast quadrant—in heritage single-family homes separated from the rest of the community by railroad tracks.

Many factors led to the pressure for redevelopment in Weston: its NIA status; a high concentration of residential high-rises, which made it an appropriate candidate for a related Tower Renewal programme; and, the construction of a station for the new Union Pearson (UP) Express train, connecting Toronto's downtown train terminal to its international airport. With the help of the Toronto chapter of the Urban Land Institute (ULI), an international non-profit real estate lobbyist group, the *Weston 2021 Revitalization Strategy* was conceived under the premise that Weston had experienced almost no private investment during Toronto's building boom.[10] Underpinning the *Strategy* was the notion that there is 'nothing' in Weston's so-called town centre—a notion shared among the minority white, middle-class enclave and amplified by local politicians.[11] This claim was made despite the area's high residential density and little-to-no commercial vacancy.

Another officially-stated impetus for the *Revitalization Strategy* was a feasibility study for a 'community cultural hub' conducted by a non-profit organisation called Artscape, which concluded that by taking advantage of the 'abundance of affordable space [...] such developments can put challenged neighbourhoods *on the map*'.[12] For over thirty years, Artscape has played a catalytic role in the transformation of the most gentrifying/gentrified downtown Toronto neighbourhoods (among them: Queen West, Regent Park, Distillery District) through the development of subsidised artist housing and commercial-recreational spaces. It enjoys partnerships with some of the biggest developers in Canada, who also see a competitive advantage in practicing 'corporate social consciousness'. Setting its philanthropic gaze on Toronto's inner suburbs, Artscape re-packaged the 'creative city' script as a therapeutic solution to so-called inner-suburban 'blight'. The organisation's first *Creative Spaces Outside of the Core* project in Weston would serve as a model for other inner-suburban neighbourhoods, shifting the focus 'from challenges to opportunities'.[13]

Artscape's proposed community cultural hub was only one component in a much larger residential-commercial redevelopment in Weston. The Artscape Weston Common (AWC) was positioned as the signature initiative of the *Revitalization Strategy*, expected to jump-start a chain of new private investments. The site combined a publicly owned parking lot deemed surplus, an adjacent expropriated vacant lot, and the podium—a multi-level parking garage and largely vacant commercial space—of an existing thirty-one-storey residential building, 33 King Street (henceforth 33 King). The building is predominantly home to low-income seniors and immigrant families and had been previously stigmatised as a site of murderous crime. The publicly owned parking lot served as an important space for community events and a long-standing farmers' market.

A complex PPNP was formed consisting of Woodbourne (owner of 33 King), the Rockport Group (developer), Artscape (non-profit), and the City of Toronto (various departments). AWC's design, conceived by elite architectural and planning firms, included a new-build thirty-storey market-rate residential rental tower. The zoning by-law limit of eight storeys was amended for the tower in exchange for the 'community benefits' it offered. These included Artscape's twenty-six 'affordable artist live/work units' and 'community cultural hub' inside 33 King's podium, as well as adjacent 'publicly accessible open space' to host an 'enhanced' farmers' market.[14] Metrolinx, the provincial transit agency responsible for the new UP Express train line, and an unofficial partner in the project, built a pedestrian bridge over the railway tracks to the foot of the AWC, allowing for movement from the neighbourhood's affluent northeast to the town centre.

Despite the City's facilitator role, the project had no direct impact on the municipal budget. Its contribution consisted of targeted requests for proposals; public land sale to Rockport (of which proceeds were re-directed to the redevelopment); gifted expropriated property; and brokering of density-bonus funds. Additionally, the City waived development charges, permit fees, and property taxes on the basis that this was a *non-profit* redevelopment understood to be operating 'for the benefit of the community'.[15]

Centring: The 'Community Benefit'

Almost none of the AWC redevelopment could have been achieved without Artscape, the non-profit partner in the complex PPNP. It wielded its special non-profit abilities to maintain cost-cutting agendas, re-direct public funds, and legitimise private capital flows. The latter were developed through consensus-building programming, including public consultations. The *Revitalization Strategy* had already formed an alliance between Artscape, Weston's northeast enclave, and its institutions (e.g. business and residents' associations). Included in the process were key local non-profit organisations, many of which had grown out of early austerity in the 1980s and were empowered by the previous Priority Neighbourhood policy. These organisations, which offered charity and recreational programming, were valued by revitalisation proponents as a buffer against visible poverty and anticipated youth criminality. They were positioned as the embodiment of aspiration for Weston's racialised poor residents within the revitalisation area.

Building consensus around the AWC was necessary to displace critiques of it. A faction of middle-class homeowners against densification expressed concern for infrastructural and environmental impacts. Social activists challenged the blatant racism and threat of displacement behind the narrative of 'nothingness' in Weston.[16] Local Caribbean artists clashed with Artscape, calling it the 'Walmart of the arts'.[17] Others calculated that if the revitalisation was truly about the community, the City had the means to develop a community centre independently without resorting to larger private redevelopment.[18]

Critical discourse in Weston was largely drowned out by feel-good, procedural participatory events and visioning activities that tactfully focused on the 'community benefit'—namely the cultural hub—with no mention of the broader AWC redevelopment. The consultations glossed over power relations, failing to discuss, for example, whether Weston residents actually wanted privatisation of publicly owned land. Instead, the PNPP focused on envisioning Weston's cultural regeneration: a medley of community events and artistic interventions embodying vague concepts such as diversity and inclusion. However, the corporate identity and name for the redevelopment, the Weston Common, were non-negotiable for the PPNP. The appropriation of an old concept ('commons') suggests that

Figure 1. Main intersection of Weston (Weston Road and Lawrence Avenue), looking north. Source: Photo by Sophia Ilyniak, 2015

Figure 2. Site to be redeveloped as AWC: public parking lot and 33 King Street. Source: Photo by Sophia Ilyniak, 2015

Figure 3. Ground-breaking ceremony marking the beginning of the AWC redevelopment. Representatives of the PPNP assembled for a photo opportunity, including Toronto's mayor John Tory, who called the redevelopment, 'one of the best examples of a public-private-non-profit partnership' that he had ever seen. Source: Photo by Sophia Ilyniak, 2016

Figure 4. Completed AWC and Weston. Source: Photo by Sophia Ilyniak, 2022

the AWC is neither a public nor private space, but a designated 'third', 'community' space that is separate from the hard sell of the market.

De-centring: The People of Weston

The AWC redevelopment was completed in 2019 with a dramatic colour palette washed over 33 King's exterior. Two years later, it was sold to Dream Unlimited Corp, a real estate investment trust. The cultural hub houses the youth arts non-profit organisation that was most deeply involved in the AWC consensus process. Residents have moved into 'resort-style living' (as advertised) at the new-build thirty-storey tower. The pedestrian bridge allows northeast residents to visit the new farmers' market vendors. The intended spill-over effects of the signature initiative laid out in the *Weston 2021 Revitalization Strategy* appear to be coming to fruition. A number of private residential-commercial redevelopments (currently underway) will continue to radically rearrange and reshape Weston's town centre, while also making use of non-profit partnerships for density bonuses and higher profitability. Property values in the northeast quadrant have increased. Many ethnic-oriented shops, which double as important social spaces, are slowly being replaced by new and corporate chain businesses.

The dialectical-materialist tradition understands that with every advance there is a retreat. Applying this lens to the creation of new centralities in the periphery, it becomes evident how any attempt at centring or re-centring Weston also has the effect of decentring. Racialised, working-class people in Weston's high-rise buildings are experiencing displacement pressures. The residents of 33 King—the heart of the AWC redevelopment—have been harassed, evicted, or had their parking spaces reassigned to new higher-paying tenants. Since revitalisation and AWC planning started, the landlord has applied to raise rents above provincial guidelines (permitted if improvements, often merely cosmetic, are made to common spaces) six times. The local tenants' union stated that Weston had been duped by 'the so-called "affordable housing" development', which not only appropriated public funds and land for private gain but often contradicted its own affordability promise.[19] This contradiction has been exacerbated by the instability caused by Artscape entering receivership in 2023. Meanwhile, in sharp contrast to 'community benefit', residents of 33 King have organised against the repeated and ongoing attempts to push them out of their homes. At the time of writing, hundreds of 33 King residents and new tenants of the AWC redevelopment are entering the fourteenth month of their rent strike.

Conclusion: False-Choice (Sub)Urbanism

The trend of socioeconomic polarisation, in which a number of the inner suburbs remain publicly neglected, continues in Toronto.[20] These peripheral areas suffered the worst impacts of the COVID-19 pandemic[21] and the highest incidence of eviction, which disproportionately affects racialised people.[22] These combined issues made the periphery a key site for tenant organising—under the banner of 'Keep Your Rent'—against mass evictions during the height of the pandemic, which was further complicated by the betrayal of local non-profits partnering with displacing forces.

In attempting to manage the periphery by creating new centralities, place-based policy falsely assumes that locality is the problem, rather than an expression of it. Toronto's NIA strategy of cost-saving revitalisation under the guise of de-stigmatisation—generally taking the form of state-facilitated private exploitation of the rent gap, coupled with the state's continued retreat—only leads to further peripheralisation, as we have seen. As such, the redevelopment of Weston's town centre presented a false choice. To be placed 'back on the map', as promised by Artscape, meant the uncritical acceptance of any/all private investment and its consequences. PPNP or non-profit-led governance, operating in place of public redistributive power, is not only insufficient but is correlated with the decentring of people's homes and lives. Additionally, it has the double-edged effect of sanctioning their political displacement. As PPNP-led revitalisation plans continue to proliferate across the inner suburbs, it is critical to identify residents' challenges to the predominant negotiations of core–periphery relations.

Figure 5. Tenants of 33 King march across the pedestrian bridge connecting the 'two Westons', towards the northeast. AWC is behind them. Source: Photo by York South–Weston Tenants' Union, 2022

Endnotes:

1 Kipfer, S. and Mustafa D. Peripheries against Peripheries? Against Spatial Reification, in: K. M. Guney, R. Keil, and M. Üçoglu (eds.) *Massive Suburbanization: (Re)Building the Global Periphery.* University of Toronto Press, 2019, pp. 35–55.

2 Ekers, M., Hamel, P., and Keil, R. Governing Suburbia: Modalities and Mechanisms of Suburban Governance, in: P. Hamel and R. Keil (eds.) *Suburban Governance: A Global View.* University of Toronto Press, 2015, pp. 19–48.

3 Kipfer, S. (De)Constructing Housing Estates: How Much More than a Housing Question?, in: K. M. Guney, R. Keil, and M. Üçoglu (eds.) *Massive Suburbanization: (Re)Building the Global Periphery.* University of Toronto Press, 2019, pp. 142–161.

4 Young, D. Decline and Renewal in Toronto's High-Rise Suburbs: The Tragedy of Progressive Neoliberalism, in: Guney, Keil, and Üçoglu, 2019, *op cit.*, pp. 111–125.

5 Parlette, V. *On the Margins of Gentrification: The production and governance of suburban 'decline' in Toronto's inner suburbs.* PhD Thesis, University of Toronto, 2012, p. 124.

6 Desfor, G., Keil, R., Kipfer, S., and Wekerle, G. From Surf to Turf: No Limits to Growth in Toronto?, *Studies in Political Economy, 77*, 2006, pp. 131–155.

7 Lehrer, U. and Wieditz, T. Condominium development and gentrification, *Canadian Journal of Urban Research, 18* (1), 2009, pp. 82–103; Slater, T. Municipally managed gentrification in South Parkdale, Toronto, *The Canadian Geographer/Le Geographe Canadien, 48* (3), 2004, pp. 303–325.

8 Paradis, E., Wilson, R. M., and Logan, J. *Nowhere Else to Go: Inadequate Housing & Risk of Homelessness Among Families in Toronto's Aging Rental Buildings.* University of Toronto Cities Centre, 2014.

9 City of Toronto. *Neighbourhood Improvement Area Profiles Share*, 2022; https://www.toronto.ca/city-government/data-research-maps/neighbourhoods-communities/neighbourhood-profiles/nia-profiles/.

10 City of Toronto. *Weston 2021 Revitalization Strategy.* City of Toronto, 2012.

11 For example, as the York South–Weston Ward Councillor, Frances Nunziata, said at the Etobicoke York Council Meeting on November 15, 2015: 'There is going to be a revitalization in Weston. That's what we want. For years and years, I'm hearing from my community, "I don't want to go down to Weston Road. We don't have good restaurants. We don't have coffee shops. We have nothing."'

12 Artscape. *Cultural/Creative Hubs in Priority Neighbourhoods: Feasibility Study for a Cultural/Creative Hub in Weston Mount Dennis.* City of Toronto, 2011, p. 3 [emphasis by the author].

13 As described by Artscape CEO Tim Jones, in a public presentation on 'Culture as Urban Acupuncture' at the 2015 MaRS Global Leadership conference in Toronto.

14 City of Toronto. *22 John Street, 33 King Street and 2 Elsmere Avenue (The Weston Community Cultural Hub) – Official Plan Amendment and Zoning By-law Amendment Application – Final Report.* City of Toronto, 2015.

15 City of Toronto. *Municipal Capital Facilities – Exemption of City Properties from Realty Taxes.* City of Toronto, 2013, p. 2.

16 One local activist, Shadya Yasin, made this point in an interview on June 10, 2016: 'The [Weston Village] Residents' Association, the Councillor, the small group involved—they're complaining that there are too many hair salons. But it's not that it's too many salons, it's just that it's Black people are running the salons. However, the same amount of salons you can count on the Weston Road strip, you go to Yonge and Eglinton [an elite Toronto neighbourhood], you see the same amount of salons and barber shops. That's something I always find fascinating.'

17 Local Caribbean artist, Jacklyn Thomas, in an interview on June 8, 2016: 'I did my research. I looked where the [Artscape] projects were and how they operated ... they were all the same, from one place to the next ... It's like Walmart. As I told [Artscape Vice President] Pru [Robey], "Artscape is the Walmart of the arts. And even when you're not art, you position yourself as art, and when you move in, everything gets sucked out". I told her, I said "you suck the life-blood out"'.

18 In an interview on July 8, 2016, Mike Sullivan, the former Member of Parliament for York South–Weston, insisted that if the community cultural hub cost only CAD $1,500,000 in private 'community benefit' funds, with the remaining public funding not being 'real money' but revenue from the public land sale and 'forgiven money' (exemptions for various development charges), then the City of Toronto could have afforded to build a community centre for Weston independently and avoided the entire AWC redevelopment.

19 York South–Weston Tenants' Union. *Updates*, 2021; https://www.tenantunion.ca.

20 Allen, J. Wealth inequalities and poverty concentration in Toronto: Our first look at 2020 annual income data collected as part of the 2021 Canadian census, School of Cities, 2020; https://schoolofcities.github.io/neighbourhood-income-toronto-2020/.

21 Biglieri, S., De Vidovich, L., and Keil, R. City as the core of contagion? Repositioning COVID-19 at the social and spatial periphery of urban society, *Cities and Health, 5*, 2021, pp. S63–S65.

22 Leon, S and Iveniuk, J. *Forced Out: Evictions, Race, and Poverty in Toronto.* Wellesley Institute, 2020; Lewis, N. *The uneven racialized impacts of financialization: A report for the Office of the Federal Housing Advocate.* The Office of the Federal Housing Advocate, 2022.

Peripheral Centrality as Strategic Process in Urban Redevelopment: The Capitol Theatre and Flint, Michigan

David Wilson and Tilman Schwarze

Introduction

What is now going on in America's Rust Belt cities is perversely deft. These cities, at various stages of struggling to redevelop in punishing global and neoliberal times, ironically turn to a perhaps unexpected element—their Black neighbourhoods—to help reverse their fortunes. Many of these growth coalitions, facing decades of disinvestment and neglect, now strive to 'tourist-up' and 'service-up' their cities through rebuilding and recasting these neighbourhoods to attract global capital and stabilise local tax bases.[1] Poor Black communities—long labour warehouses for subalterns in these cities—have since their inception been peripheral-central spaces within the broader trajectory of their cities' political economy. So situated by growth coalitions, they have always been marginalised, pushed-to-the-border spaces while also being functionally central to the city economy's operation. Now they are becoming peripheral-central in another way: as racialised 'gems' of an emergent service-tourist economy whose appealing symbolic qualities can grace downtowns. To understand current redevelopment in U.S. Rust Belt cities, it is crucial that this new kind of peripheral-centrality—a novel unfolding for these typically unadventurous and staid places[2]—be recognised by contemporary urbanists.

In this context, we study Flint, Michigan, one of America's quintessential Rust Belt cities, with a focus on its much-hyped Capitol Theatre project. We chronicle how the city's current redevelopment governance has begun to use its traditionally peripheralised-centralised, poor Black communities in a new way to advance this and other downtown restructuring projects. Currently, these communities, widely seen by Flintonians as homes to cultural-racial Others, are being framed as 'exotic' tourist attractions that can help shoulder the burden of the city's flagging tourist industry and economy. In this chapter, we show, first, that, with this use of peripheral centrality, the concept denotes more than a morphological description of urban realities and spaces. We identify peripheral centrality as a novel process, a flexible and resilient one, that in Flint is being strategically activated and mobilised by city authorities, entrepreneurs, and developers in their pursuit of entrepreneurial redevelopment. As a process in Flint, cultivation of common imaginings around peripheral centrality does the political and economic bidding of a city's major mover and shaker: its growth coalition.

We show, second, that as exemplified in the case of the Capitol Theatre project, this peripheral-centrality situating depends upon a strategic and vacillating use of the notion Blackness. This term, as a fundamental understanding, is shown to be a complex and elaborately deployed discursive resource, tied to the roll-out of a new 'ghettoised' peripheral-centrality taking place across the city. Blackness—anything but a fixed, monolithic set of meanings—is rather an evolving, 'multi-use' opportunity structure in this context. In the project's narrative frame, constructions of Blackness see-saw erratically, alternating between invoking the 'raw', the 'authentic', and the 'exotic' (what might be considered 'the goodness of Blackness') on the one hand, and the 'scary' or 'transgressive' (what we might term 'the badness of Blackness') on the other. Which way the see-saw dips depends on what is needed at that specific moment to galvanise the redevelopment. The importance of this finding: as shown by the use of this term, this kind of peripheral-centrality redevelopment embodies much instability.

The context in Flint: paralleling decades of economic decline from World War II to the present and scandals around environmental racism and institutionalised discrimination,[3] city developers now strive to economically revive its downtown to welcome new middle-class life (Figure 2). As proclaimed by Mayor Sheldon Neeley in 2022, 'Flint's Central City will prosper'.[4] Yet this process has become deeply racialised, reiterating the city's complicated history of hegemonic dynamics between the centre and the periphery. At one time, the Black poor were blatantly banished from downtown; peripheral neighbourhoods like Carriage Town and Grand Traverse District were considered the 'outside' of a typical inside/outside civic dichotomy.

The sole functionality of these neighbourhoods was straightforward: to store cheap labourers that would help drive the city's industrial base. However, a widely publicised deindustrialisation decimated Flint that was replaced by the rise of a low-wage service economy. As a tourist economy emerged alongside it, poor Black communities assumed a new functional role: to 'spice up' tourist-facing spaces and activities. Suddenly, Blackness became a different kind of resource, one that could be integrated into marketing place.

The Capitol Theatre in Flint, Michigan

Flint's Capitol Theatre, built in 1928, has recently been dramatically renovated to anchor downtown's much-hyped revitalisation. A sum of $1,200,000, invested by the Mott Foundation and funnelled to Uptown Reinvestment to perform the upgrade, has recreated a shiny new Gothic-Roman facility that is now hailed as 'the class of a new burgeoning downtown'.[5] To Flint's previous mayor, Karen Weaver, the Capitol Theatre is 'the gateway to a new downtown'. Designed by noted architect John Eberson and constructed by Henry Vander Horst, it was for decades the centre of Flint's formal theatre scene. But as post-war disinvestment and decline steadily engulfed Flint's downtown, and middle-class departure from the area reduced purchasing power, the theatre closed in 1996 (and remained dormant for twenty years). In 2015, its restoration began, and it was reopened in 2016. Its original design, bolstered by the recent rehabilitation, has recreated an atmospheric theatre designed to look like a Roman garden (see Figure 1).

Today, the Capitol Theatre is the most visible symbol of a drive to redevelop Flint's downtown that has deftly deployed race–i.e. Blackness–in two ways: as a cultural lodestar and as a locus of civic problems. Through this project (and others), the Black poor vacillate in portrayals from mysterious and charismatic to ominous and 'scary.' The politics of fostering 'the Capitol Theatre miracle' and the rebirth of downtown has been strengthened by this. An economic regeneration, underpinned by a racialised imaginary that places clichéd tropes of Blackness at its centre, illustrates how diverse understandings of race are weaponised as powerful political constructions and resources.

Figure 1. Flint's Capitol Theatre. Source: Photo by David Wilson, 2022

Tim Hawkins
Saturday, Nov. 3rd
7:00 PM

As redevelopment efforts prepare downtown to become a site of cultural consumption for the greater Genesee County region, downtown is being remade into a 'live, work, play' destination that will appeal to a racially diverse group of suburban residents, students, and upwardly mobile Flint residents. Led by the Capitol Theatre rehabilitation, Flint's downtown is now forwarded as a site of 'exotic' cultural consumption, ideal for weekend daytrips into the city, an evening out after work, and, for the truly pioneering, a new place to call home. After decades of disinvestment, neglect, and scandals of environmental pollution and racism,[6] it is hoped that the 'new' downtown Flint will revive the city. Crucially, this redevelopment effort privileges a key population, namely a fantasy-infused construct termed 'the new downtowners', envisioned as being made up of middle-class African Americans and middle-class whites. As a planner noted to us in 2020, 'we're a Black and white city, that's our demographic, and renewing the downtown with a responsive, Black middle-class but also with civic whites makes sense'.[7]

Exoticisation—Bring Their Presences In

The first trope: key redevelopment actors—Uptown Investment Corporation, Mott Foundation, Flint City Planning—draw on imaginings of raw Blackness to push the creation of a multi-cultured, middle-class downtown. Their use of Blackness taps into connotations of 'exoticism' to appeal to the new downtowner in their search for 'authentic urban experiences' and 'edgy, interesting engagements'.[8] Thus, Uptown Reinvestment Corporation (2018), downtown Flint's largest developer (having received more than $35,000,000 in endowment funds since 2015), strategically extolls the virtues of the Capitol Theatre project and its nearby street and block transformation—all of which 'blacken-up' their aesthetics.[9] One of its spokespersons, in discussion with us, notes the rationale. 'Our new projects, especially the Capitol Theatre rehab and the downtown redevelopment movement, recognise the magic of our Black people ... it's their fascinating culture, the intrigue of their traditions and tastes, that we need to bring in and portray in the downtown'. Here, the cultural cachet of poverty's aesthetics (its tamed 'edginess') is fruitfully mixed with stable and predictable presences (middle-income people, blocks, homes) downtown to create a vibrant middle-class consumption core.

Figure 2. Housing for Flint's New Gentry.
Source: Photo by David Wilson, 2022

Figure 3. Exoticized Blackness. Source: Photo by David Wilson, 2022

The centre of this 'Black aesthetic' to mix with Capitol Theatre's upgrade is the offer of nearby restaurants, such as Charlie's Smokin' Bar-B-Q (Figure 3). Charlie's is made into an elaborate spectacle of Black goodness, replete with its sea of gritty tables, weathered floorboards, and faux-beaten bathrooms (outhouses). Patrons can further access this 'authenticity' through pictures on walls (decrepit southern shacks, aged Black men), worn tables, and adobe-looking floors. This place, like a number of new downtown restaurants, has been recruited and supported by Flint's growth coalition.

Charlie's emerged out of city planners lobbying for Black-owned eateries downtown. It was coaxed into locating on this particular site—a new, highly visible upscale farmers' market that is seen as going hand-in-hand with the Capitol Theatre development. Since opening, the Genesee County Chamber of Commerce (2019) has aggressively advertised Charlie's, especially through the paper *Flint Side*, as 'the true venue for Black [and Latino] culture that can be shared by tasting the fare and breathing the ambiance'.[10] Residents meanwhile, used to the city's relentless waves of business closures and outflux of capital, widely imagine the benefits of using tamed, exotic Blackness to support a drive to re-entrepreneurialise downtown Flint. Thus, Flint's small upscale dining district on its main drag, Saginaw Street, is widely heralded for both its trendy multicultural motif[11] and clever business practice of inviting racial authenticity.

New downtowners, in this context, are to throw themselves into Flint's new cultural-racial urban core (spectatorship and consumption are to flourish). These footloose cultural dabblers are supposed to move in and out of this new aesthetic improvisationally, employing a kind of playtime-meets-colonising sensibility. The Genesee County Metropolitan Planning Commission, for example, declared at a community development meeting that: 'downtown will be a multicultural collage for our new burgeoning downtown residents, it will be their recreational centrepiece as they will live safe, city-improving lives'. The 'new downtown aesthetic', they note, 'will be a key building block in the drive to provide enriching lives for in-movers and city pioneers'.[12] When the *Detroit Metro Times* speaks of 'Flint's Next Battle: To Become Cool', they reference the city's drive to create a provocative racialised downtown that encourages detailed dalliances for fun-seeking, place-transforming in-movers.[13]

Revulsion and Fear—Keep 'Em Out

The same actors also strategically use Blackness in another way to advance downtown restructuring: they sometimes not-so-subtly impugn the city's Black poor to justify their bodily exclusion from the core area. Amid valorising the Black poor's aesthetics and extolling their cultural products, their actual bodies are presented as not-so-veiled threats to the upgrading core. For instance, the Mott Foundation and Harris Construction routinely describe the Capitol Theatre project and downtown development itself as having to deal with a host of civic inconveniences, among them: 'expanding underclass neighbourhoods', 'growing minority neighbourhoods', and 'ghettos moving into new blocks'.[14] Through the Capitol Theatre and broader ongoing redevelopment, the public is to see and feel racialised poverty/class anxieties and ominous social possibilities around them. Set against this, ameliorative activities are purportedly needed to 'restore social and architectural integrity out of decay', 'deal with minority poverty', and 'reverse the spread of slum blocks'.[15] The affiliation of these concepts with Blackness reiterates colonial, racist logics, further peripheralising Black poor residents as invalid urban citizens.

Of course, impugning the city's Black poor in public forums (and more generally speaking) is hardly new in Flint. Racial fears, particularly anxieties around issues of crime and neighbourhood liveability, have long circulated in the thoughts and actions of Flint's institutions and residents.[16] In the last decade in particular, perceptions have situated Flint as being afflicted by spiralling-up Black poverty—both in intensity and magnitude—making this narrative of decline especially resonant and effective in sowing division.[17] Today, Blackness in Flint—especially in its intersection with poverty—does not merely denote physical attributes, it organises elaborate perceptions about core differences between people and their viability for citizenship.[18] Poor and near-poor Black people (particularly Black youth) are widely imagined as dominating the city's streets, 'scaring' away white residents and investors, while deepening 'ghetto' and downtown decline.[19]

Accordingly, practices of exclusion operating along race-class lines have long been a feature of trying to redevelop downtown. Hence, current zoning, pushed especially by Flint's newest downtown business owners,[20] now aims to tackle what one member of Uptown Reinvestment Corporation termed 'the persistence of ugly ghetto blocks'.[21] This practice, of course, is strategic: it makes downtown unaffordable to the Black poor, unleashing upscale zoning that strategically engulfs new growth blocks, the new restaurant row, the farmers' market, and upscale housing enclaves along Saginaw Street (the main city thoroughfare). Yet this practice—common across U.S. Rust Belt cities in general—has a unique, city-specific rationale in austerity-plagued, crime conscious Flint: it purportedly helps police the Black poor without using police officers, reinforcing this group's peripheralisation from downtown. Revised zoning, suggested one councilperson, 'drives downtown growth as the new unfunded policing mechanism that will help limit crime and enhance Flint's downtown recovery'. To a local government official, 'zoning is beautiful. It does what we need the cops to do—it provides the area with needed growth, safety, and security'.[22]

This does not mean that the police department is totally absent in this latest rendition of peripheral centrality. In fact, the police department's policy of youth policing now blankets downtown. This, in lieu of the standard, brutal cleansing of downtown, takes the form of a nuanced removal done under the auspices of 'therapeutising' the Black poor. They, in stated objective, are to be kept away from downtown for the sake of their own betterment. The idea: Flint's racialised poor supposedly continue to be devastated by toxic communities in the downtown core: 'Poor African-Americans in Flint have already been dinged by living in urban wastelands downtown ... it has hurt them, for their own sake let's encourage their residency elsewhere'.[23] Not surprisingly, then, a youth policing regime—funded by the Mott Foundation—prioritises dispersing downtown congregations, increases on-street engagement with small crimes, operates a network of security cameras across downtown, and establishes a quick-to-indict and remove-from-downtown violations bureau.[24] These activities are concentrated at key street sections of downtown (e.g. the block of the Capitol Theatre, the emergent Saginaw Street 'sushi belt'), as well as evening hotspots (e.g. Cork on Saginaw, Blackstone's Smokehouse) and downtown public spaces and parks.

Conclusion

This chapter reveals the different constructions and uses of Blackness driving the peripheral-centralised redevelopment of Flint's downtown that leads with a prominent project, the Capitol Theatre endeavour. Within this narrative framework, served up by actors in the city's growth coalition, the Black poor are situated as nothing less than ambivalent figures. At the abstract level, they are culturally exotic and desirable; but, at the concrete level, they are bodily toxins to be isolated and ejected from downtown. The abstract symbols of an exotic Blackness are to flourish downtown; but Black bodies are to be nowhere in sight. In Flint, the process of peripheralising-centralising is more than a mere description of material urban realities, infrastructures, and morphologies. Instead, it can be understood as a strategic and political-economic process and resource, forming part of a planning blueprint that is being mobilised to produce re-entrepreneurialised downtown space. This human manufacturing, we have shown, is inexorably tinged by a deeply troubling reliance on shaky and unstable logics of racialisation—which always hover to threaten the downtown's remaking.

Endnotes:

1 Wilson, D. and Heil, M. Decline Machines and Economic Development: Rust Belt Cities and Flint, Michigan, *Urban Geography, 43* (2), 2022, pp. 163–183; Schwarze, T. and Wilson, D. Silencing, Urban Growth Machines, and the Obama Presidential Center on Chicago's South Side, *Frontiers in Sustainable Cities*, 2022; https://doi.org/10.3389/frsc.2022.835674; Schwarze, T. *Space, Urban Politics, and Everyday Life. Henri Lefebvre and the U.S. City.* Palgrave MacMillan, 2023.

2 On peripheral-centrality, see Lefebvre, H. The right to the city, and the new metropolitan mainstream, in: N. Brenner, P. Marcuse, and M. Mayer (eds.) *Cities for People, Not for Profit. Critical Urban Theory and the Right to the City.* Routledge, 2012, pp. 42–62.

3 Pulido, L. Flint, Environmental Racism, and Racial Capitalism, *Capitalism Nature Socialism, 27* (3), 2016, pp. 1–16.
4 Neeley, S. Discussion with Mayor of Flint, August 13, 2022.
5 Edwards, L. Discussion with City Planner, City of Flint, September 2, 2021.
6 *Op. cit.*
7 Keys, L. Discussion with Planner, City of Flint, February 7, 2020.
8 Keys, L. Discussion with Planner, City of Flint, February 24, 2019.
9 Uptown Reinvestment Corporation. Technical document from developer, 2018; https://uptownreinvestment.org/the-rowe-lofts/ (accessed May 14, 2024).
10 Genesee County Chamber of Commerce. Discussion with worker, December 13, 2019.
11 Herman, T. Telling Flint's economic development story is vital. The Davison Index, 2017, pp. 1–3; Sissen, P. 2017. Flint, Michigan, looks to shake off stigmas of the past with a rising downtown. Self-published, 2017, pp. 2–12.
12 Eyck, R. Discussion with worker, Genesee County Metropolitan Planning Commission, August 4, 2019.
13 Atkinson, Scott. Flint's next battle: to become cool, *Detroit Metro Times*, March 15, 2018; https://www.metrotimes.com/detroit-guides/flints-next-battle-to-become-cool-10183028 (accessed October 25, 2024).
14 Harris Construction. Discussion with Officer, June 12, 2019.
15 Mott Foundation. Discussion with Officer, July 23, 2019.
16 Highsmith, A. R. Demolition means progress: urban renewal, local politics, and state-sanctioned ghetto formation in Flint, Michigan, *Journal of Urban History, 35* (3), 2009, pp. 348–368; Highsmith, A. R. *Demolition means progress: Flint, Michigan, and the fate of the American Metropolis.* University of Chicago Press, 2015.
17 Fasenfest, D. and Pride, T. Emergency management in Michigan: Race, class and the limits of liberal democracy, *Critical Sociology, 21* (3), 2016, pp. 331–334.
18 Ranganathan, M. Thinking with Flint: Racial Liberalism and the Roots of an American Water Tragedy', *Capitalism Nature Socialism, 27* (3), 2016, pp. 17–33.
19 Ames, A. Discussion with Housing and Community Activist, Flint, March 9, 2019.
20 Imagine Flint. Technical document, City of Flint, 2019; http://www.imagineflint.com/Plan Implementation/ZoningOrdinance.aspx (accessed June 9, 2024).
21 Uptown Reinvestment Corporation, 2018.
22 Ray, R. Discussion with Councilperson, City of Flint, April 21, 2019.
23 Harris Construction, June 12, 2019.
24 Mott Foundation, July 23, 2019.

Cultivating Suburban Place Affection: Encountering the Pluriverse within Peripheral Centralities

Erica Dorn

Introduction

Aurora, Colorado, a suburb east of Denver, is sometimes referred to as Saudi Aurora. Aurora is a single-family home mecca, making it an excellent habitat for cars. It receives only about fifteen inches of rain and snowfall yearly but is drenched in developer-led sprawl. Oversized and drought-inducing Kentucky bluegrass lawns sprawl across 420 square kilometres of Indigenous prairie, where 400,000 residents now live.[1]

For the urban onlooker, the typical image of American suburbia—one of sprawling tract homes—depicted through aerial views seems an accurate portrayal of Aurora. But this de-contextualised abstraction, which plays off outdated peripheral stereotypes framing the suburbs as homogenous enclaves, drowns out the thriving, diverse communities and interactions that comprise suburbia today.

In fact, many U.S. suburbs have become more demographically diverse than their city counterparts. Owing to various factors, including the COVID-19 pandemic and the surge in remote work, forced migration, and personal preferences, U.S. residents across all demographics are increasingly relocating from city centres to the suburbs.[2] U.S. suburbs have thus become arrival points for diverse immigrant newcomers from across the globe.[3]

Through this global migration, many U.S. suburbs have undergone a form of decay and rebirth that has fundamentally transitioned their *raison d'être*.[4] The suburbs, initially designed around an agenda of homogeneity and exclusion, now face a paradigm shift that is misaligned with their current demographics as well as their modes of civic and community engagement.[5]

To address the outdated image of suburbia and rally more affection for it, this chapter examines the evolving nature of the suburbs as hubs of global migration, rapid diversification, and adapted modes of interaction. I highlight a series of trans-cultural adaptations that are helping to retrofit suburban civic infrastructure for increased engagement and place affection.[6]

In their transformation, many suburbs are becoming diverse cultural hubs wherein futures are being shaped and negotiated.[7] This reformation is evident in various aspects, such as racial and ethnic diversity, economic disparities, and political affiliations. The trend should not be surprising since an estimated one billion people are on the move globally.[8] Over the next twenty years, the United States can anticipate more than 30,000,000 migrant arrivals from Central America alone.[9, 10] As writer Jay Caspian Kang notes:

> The American public still doesn't know all that much about the millions of immigrants that have come into the country since 1965, nor do they fully appreciate how the inroads made by these populations have come in a short period, not just in terms of economic mobility but also in terms of geography.[11]

Caspian Kang argues that suburbs are among the spaces where 'the greater American narrative does not quite make sense'.[12] The geography and culture of some U.S. suburbs are evolving in ways that are not fully acknowledged, especially in terms of their social formation.[13] In Mitra Kalita's book *Suburban Sahibs*, a historian of Edison, New Jersey, describes how quickly New Jersey suburbs transitioned from predominantly white to majority-minority: 'You didn't see it coming. You saw it happen'.[14] Aurora, Colorado, experienced a similar and seemingly sudden transformation. Founded in the late 1800s, Aurora was once a *sundown town*, welcoming only white residents and continuing to be majority white until the early 2000s. Today, the population is 20% foreign-born residents, speaking more than 160 languages, with Spanish, Vietnamese, Korean, and Ethiopian all being widely heard.[15]

No longer spatially and socially subordinate, many ageing and diversifying suburbs like Aurora can be acknowledged as *pluriburbs*,[16] suburbs in which a *pluriverse*[17] is surprisingly taking shape. Sociologist Arturo Escobar uses the term pluriverse to describe what many Indigenous societies already understand: the notion that many worlds can exist within one. However, this belief goes against a predominant neoliberal worldview that seeks universality, a trait for which the suburbs are historically infamous.[18,19]

Given their newfound dynamism, U.S. suburbs like Aurora often lack the robust and inclusive civic infrastructure to facilitate interactions, work across differences, and engage residents in civic life.[20] Indeed, U.S. suburban civic infrastructure was both designed for and hindered by homogeneity, according to Eric Oliver in *Democracy in Suburbia*:

> By determining who can afford to live in a community, how many people it will contain, and what types of public policies it will pursue, local governments set the political conflicts, patterns of social interaction, and salient issues of a municipality. These factors exert a tremendous influence on citizen interest in local affairs and their patterns of political organization and mobilization. If a community is structured in such a way that it generates little internal conflict or seeks nothing more than to maintain a set of policies that most residents agree with, then it provides little motivation for citizens to become civically active.[21]

Current governance and formal modes of civic engagement in the suburbs are often out of step with the reality of programmes, practices, and policies needed to address the conflicts that arise from rapidly changing demographics. Positive place attachment is essential for promoting prosocial and ecological behaviour;[22] fostering at least some affection for these ubiquitous and fast-changing suburban environments is critical to addressing national and global challenges. Since the United States is caught in a web of political polarisation, driven by ever-shifting and reductive ideologies, the suburbs are evolving into politically purple places with varied voting habits and positions that cut across social issues.[23]

Civic activity frequently unfolds in unseen and unplanned ways; thus, engaging in and promoting civic activity where it can be found is essential. Suburban residents, perhaps once hesitant or

Figure 1. Protestors on the interstate in Aurora, Colorado, demanding justice for Elijah McClain. Source: Kevin J. Beaty, *Denverite*, April, 2020

EXIT 9
Lowry Campus
Colo Nat'l Guard
Buckley AF Base
NEXT RIGHT
Freedom Memorial

excluded from expressing political stances, now embrace opportunities to publicly voice their views on social justice, as illustrated in Figure 1. Following the death of a Black teenager named Elijah McClain in Aurora, Colorado, more than a thousand protestors took over the main interstate to demand justice and protest against police involvement in his death. McClain, who played the violin, inspired many protestors to organise around music, leading to a powerful regional call for unity and justice in his name.[24]

Suburbs often face criticism for their perceived lack of public and semi-public areas, which facilitate engagement among diverse residents. However, this critique typically stems from an urban perspective, which may not fully recognise how social interactions unfold in suburban settings.

Mobilising Suburban Gathering Places

Suburbs face intricate challenges related to rezoning, particularly concerning shifts from single-family zoning to multi-family housing and multi-use zoning.[25] Kristen E. Jeffers, known as The Black Urbanist, highlights that the current urbanist agenda, which aims to retrofit suburbs to resemble denser cities, may not necessarily align with the desires of Black, brown, and immigrant communities residing in these suburbs.[26] Jeffers emphasises the need to understand the vision for improved suburbs through the perspectives and experiences of historically marginalised communities living within these areas. Peripheral centralities must be redesigned and retrofitted from the experience of being peripheral. While historically it was more common for white families to reside in the suburbs, many Black, brown, and immigrant residents have been resettled or displaced into suburban areas as historically Black, brown, and immigrant neighbourhoods in downtown areas are increasingly being gentrified.[27] According to Jeffers, initiatives to retrofit suburbia through new urbanist principles can often impose an identity onto a location that does not reflect the diversity of many suburban residents and their perspectives on what constitutes a safe and welcoming environment.

Residents with recent immigration backgrounds often focus on intra-community solidarity rather than engaging in a formal civic process. This is frequently due to a lack of knowledge about how to access or participate and a lack of awareness about the potential impact of their involvement.[28] Residents often report being unaware of how to attend or participate in city council meetings or access other city resources. Joie Ha, a community organiser in Denver, the daughter of immigrant restaurant owners, explained during a civic listening tour in Aurora:

> When it comes to civic engagement in Aurora, many folks are interested in spreading cultural awareness through small businesses, especially food, and are less interested in any political agendas behind this. Something is to be said about how a lot of immigrant communities were barred from engaging specifically in different ways because things weren't written in their language. Another thing to consider about the immigrant and refugee experience is what kind of governments they come from. My mom came from a dictatorial government in Vietnam, where if you said something, you could get disappeared. That affects civic engagement if the older generation doesn't believe their voice would make a difference.[29]

Civic engagement, often seen as a fundamental right, remains a privilege accessible to only certain groups. Assimilation is frequently prioritised over cultural responsiveness, thus missing opportunities to engage excluded voters in cultivating a deeper connection to their place of residence. Many residents are excluded from civic life due to the high cost and burden of attending events like city council meetings, not to mention language barriers and limited public transportation options.[30]

Although suburbs have a history marked by inequity and unsustainability, their development can also be seen as an effort to address these issues.[31] Central to this debate and the various responses is the need to tackle America's massive housing crisis, with an estimated shortage of over 4,000,000 homes.[32] Antiquated and NIMBY (Not In My Backyard) policies that restrict new development often hinder the creation of new homes that could fill in existing blight and underutilised spaces. Given the severity of the housing crisis, leaving zoning decisions solely in the hands of suburban jurisdictions has proven challenging due to the restrictive permitting of multi-family housing. Replacing city-level zoning laws by legislating state-level zoning changes is vital. California has pioneered such legislation, which removes R1 single-family residential zoning to allow for multi-family construction on existing lots and new developments. Enacting state-level zoning changes reduces the ability of metropolitan regions to build enduring bi-partisan strategies that adequately tackle regionalised challenges and opportunities.[33] A significant leverage point for increased civic infrastructure in the suburbs is the expansion of collaborative governance across the metropolitan region.

Shifting policy through participatory and collaborative policy-making requires a better understanding of how diverse suburbanites gather, finding the porous spaces where newcomer and long-standing residents can more easily assemble to mingle, often spontaneously, fostering interaction and community through proximity. Historically, semi-public areas such as porches, front yards, and cul-de-sacs were integral to suburban social interaction. These spaces are crucial for promoting community health, serving as safe, proximate extensions of private life in the public realm, bridging the gap between the two.[34]

While non-commercial and artistic spaces that could unify communities seem sparse within the suburbs, community building and civic engagement opportunities tend to be dispersed throughout the suburban landscape. Where such spaces cannot be found, they can be mobilised through movable public spaces that address the challenges of delivering social services in sprawling areas lacking robust public transit options.

Mobile initiatives such as public libraries, immigration services, and farm stands are effectively bridging geographical gaps within the suburban landscape, providing direct access to crucial services alongside opportunities to build community.[35] Beyond their practical benefits, these services represent a broader movement towards more inclusive suburban communities, where residents of all backgrounds can easily access resources they need daily. Figure 2 demonstrates how social service is mobilised by residents who set up free fridges and pantries for neighbours in need, breaking typical suburban neighbourhood rules around association.

Recognising the importance of fostering a sense of place among diverse newcomers and long-standing suburban residents within a metropolitan area is crucial. Suburban residents often identify with a broader metro region, including their dispersed family connections in other suburban and urban parts of the area. This reality calls for an approach to immigrant integration that promotes anti-racist, global perspectives as integral to national and local identities. Enhancing civic infrastructure requires collaborative and new techniques that weave together proximate and disparate communities, spurring them into collective action.

A collaboration between dozens of community members and organisations within Aurora and the Denver metro area shows intergenerational and multi-cultural Aurora residents attending the Aurora Cultural Celebration & Civic Conversations at a public recreation centre in Aurora. Such intercultural civic engagement offers a glimpse into the value and potential of bridging communities across sprawling landscapes, fostering connection among residents and strengthening connection to place. The celebration, a culmination of a community listening tour conducted in six languages, signals the effectiveness of culturally responsive approaches to civic engagement (see Figure 3).

The project, a partnership between Warm Cookies of the Revolution[36] and Suburb Futures,[37] aimed at creating space for diverse residents, often on the periphery of civic life, to describe and envision possibilities from the periphery for the periphery. Warm Cookies of the Revolution is a Denver-area-based non-profit that engages community members in crucial civic issues by creating innovative, fun arts and cultural programming. Suburb Futures is a social design institute that advances equity and sustainability in U.S. suburbs through network building, education, and storytelling.

Over one hundred Aurora residents attended the Cultural Celebration. The celebration, which facilitated conversations about prescient issues related to public safety, housing, and education, also included henna artists, a mariachi band, and food from many diverse culinary traditions and cultures. Both newcomers and long-standing residents shared a deep affection for Aurora, while others acknowledged that it was simply where they happened to find themselves.[38] Residents all had something in common: a desire to belong where they live.

The power of civic knowledge, and having the resources to engage in it, are essential for creating healthy places and democracies. Given that Aurora and other suburbs have increasing numbers of non-voting residents, adequate democratic representation requires bridge building and civic skill building, together with new policies to better engage the public. The hope is that this engagement will enable suburban communities to build a future where diverse residents can foster a sense of belonging across their differences.

Figure 2. A free fridge in the suburbs. Source: Dorn, E. *Relational Design for Transitions Within U.S. Suburbs*. Pittsburgh: Carnegie Mellon University, 2020, p. 209.

Figure 3. Generations in the suburbs. Source: *From the Hip Photo*, Aurora Cultural Celebration & Civic Conversations, July 2023

Conclusion

The former mayor of New York City, Ed Koch, used to say, 'New York is the city where the future comes to rehearse'[39]; now, the future is auditioning in the suburbs. No longer subordinate socially, spatially, nor geographically, the U.S. suburbs are the distributed arrival points for new immigrants to the U.S. This plurality offers inroads into upgrading civic infrastructure across the dispersed landscape, meeting the needs of residents and the opportunities they now rightly demand for themselves. Pluriburbs like Aurora have tremendous untapped social capital and a strong portfolio of cultural assets; shifting centralised social resources and governance structures towards dispersed, mobile accessibility ensures that services are more responsive to the diverse needs of suburban communities, enhancing residents' sense of belonging and connection to the region.

Recognising that suburbs have become a critical infrastructure—a polycentric cultural, social, and geographic fulcrum for heterogenous socio-cultural networks—can help to build affection for this ubiquitous, distributed urban form. In this sense, some of the stereotypes about the suburban landscapes can be celebrated: 'One of the most famous attempts to describe Los Angeles depicts it as an enclave of communities without a focused core; a collective search for a pulse that does not exist'.[40] This book and, more specifically, this chapter argue that society's pulse has been sought in the wrong place: it is located not in the so-called centre but, rather, on the periphery.[41]

Endnotes:

1 Keaver, W. *City of Aurora Demographics (2017–2021 U.S Census Bureau ACS Data)*, 2023; https://auroraco.maps.arcgis.com/apps/instant/basic/index.html?appid=bbc0287313654a5fa8833ba42f528e12.

2 Frey, W. H. Today's Suburbs Are Symbolic of America's Rising Diversity: A 2020 Census Portrait, *Brookings*, June 15, 2022; https://www.brookings.edu/articles/todays-suburbs-are-symbolic-of-americas-rising-diversity-a-2020-census-portrait/ (accessed September 2023).

3 Lung-Amam, W. *Trespassers?: Asian Americans and the Battle for Suburbia*. First edition. University of California Press, 2017.

4 Keil, R. *Suburban Planet: Making the World Urban from the Outside In*. John Wiley & Sons, 2018.

5 Dorn, E. *Relational Design for Transitions Within U.S. Suburbs*. Thesis. Carnegie Mellon University, 2024; https://doi.org/10.1184/R1/25850455.v1.

6 Maginn, P. J. and Anacker, K. B. *Suburbia in the 21st Century: From Dreamscape to Nightmare?* Routledge, 2017.

7 Keil, 2018, *op. cit.*
8 Nail, T. *Being and Motion.* Oxford University Press, 2018.
9 Jones, R. *Violent Borders: Refugees and the Right to Move.* Verso, 2016.
10 Lustgarten, A. About Our Climate Migration Model, *ProPublica*, July 23, 2020; https://www.propublica.org/article/2020-climate-migration-part-1-methodology?token=WXm9z79e0T7-hUjzwsfdbQxryFu6WxDL (accessed March 28, 2021).
11 Kang, J. C. A Farewell to Readers, *The New York Times*, September 1, 2022; https://www.nytimes.com/2022/09/01/opinion/farewell-to-readers.html (accessed January 2024).
12 Ibid.
13 Bourne, L. S. Reinventing the Suburbs: Old Myths and New Realities, *Progress in Planning, 46* (3), 1996, pp. 163–184.
14 Kalita, S. Mitra. *Suburban Sahibs: Three Immigrant Families and Their Passage From India to America.* Rutgers University Press, 2003.
15 Keaver, W. *City of Aurora Demographics (2017–2021 U.S. Census Bureau ACS Data).* City of Aurora, 2022 (accessed January 2024).
16 Dorn, 2024, *op. cit.*
17 Escobar, A. *Designs for the Pluriverse.* Duke University Press, 2018.
18 Gómez, S. B., Pallanez, M. O., and Dorn, E. Diseño para la Transición: Entretejiendo saberes por medio de la conversación, *Cuadernos del Centro de Estudios de Diseño y Comunicación, 157,* June 1, 2022; https://doi.org/10.18682/cdc.vi157.6845.
19 Walia, H. *Undoing Border Imperialism.* Ak Press, 2013.
20 Oliver, J. E. *Democracy in Suburbia.* Princeton University Press, 2001.
21 Ibid., p. 190.
22 Tuan, Y. *Topophilia: A Study of Environmental Perception, Attitudes, and Values, Morningside.* Columbia University Press, 1990.
23 Dorn, 2024, *op. cit.*
24 Tompkins, L. Here's What You Need to Know About Elijah McClain's Death, *The New York Times*, October 13, 2023; https://www.nytimes.com/article/who-was-elijah-mcclain.html (accessed January 2024).
25 Williamson, J. and Dunham-Jones, E. *Case Studies in Retrofitting Suburbia: Urban Design Strategies for Urgent Challenges.* John Wiley & Sons, 2021.
26 Dorn, 2024, *op. cit.*
27 McGhee, H. *The Sum of Us: What Racism Costs Everyone and How We Can Prosper Together.* One World, 2022.
28 Dorn, E. and De Zeeuw, C. Relational Design for Sustainability in U.S. Suburbs, in: Cumulus Association (ed.) *Design for Adaptation, Cumulus Conference Proceedings Detroit 2022.* Detroit, 2022; https://www.researchgate.net/publication/370716093_Relational_Design_for_Sustainability_in_U.S._Suburbs.
29 Dorn, 2024, *op. cit.*
30 Berger, A. and Kotkin, J. *Infinite Suburbia.* Chronicle Books, 2018.
31 Lacy, K. The New Sociology of Suburbs: A Research Agenda for Analysis of Emerging Trends, *Annual Review of Sociology, 42* (1), July 30, 2016, pp. 369–384, https://doi.org/10.1146/annurev-soc-071312-145657.
32 Schuetz, J. *Fixer-Upper: How to Repair America's Broken Housing Systems.* Brookings Institution Press, 2022.
33 Ibid.
34 Dunham-Jones, E. *Retrofitting Suburbia: Urban Design Solutions for Redesigning Suburbs.* First edition. John Wiley & Sons, 2009.

35 Dorn, E. How Aurora, Colorado Is Using Mobile Public Spaces to Address the Challenges of Suburban Social Service Delivery, *Brookings*, January 13, 2022.
36 Weissman, E. *Warm Cookies of the Revolution*; https://www.warmcookiesoftherevolution.org.
37 Dorn, E. *Suburb Futures*; https://www.suburbfutures.org.
38 Dorn, 2024, *op. cit.*
39 Koch, E. Text of Address Delivered by Mayor Koch at His Third Inauguration, *The New York Times*, January 2, 1986.
40 Carpio, G. and Rutkowski, A. Mapping LA-Tinx Suburbia, *Boom California*, June 27, 2017; https://boomcalifornia.org/2017/06/26/mapping-la-tinx-suburbia/.
41 Keil, 2018, *op. cit.*

Peripheries No Longer? Bringing Greenbelts into Urban Regions

Sara Macdonald, Cara Chellew, and Sean Hertel

Introduction

In response to problems associated with rapid urban and suburban development, cities around the world have enacted land-use policies to manage growth. Among these land-use policies, the implementation of greenbelts has been a key planning approach for the protection of farmland and natural areas. Defined as open lands and natural areas surrounding cities and regions, greenbelts often contain a mix of private and public lands on which there are development restrictions.[1] The main objectives of greenbelt policies include farmland protection, urban growth containment, and nature conservation.[2] While often located in peripheries, the land uses and functions planned and/or developed within greenbelts have profound implications for city-building processes. Thus, what goes on in and regarding greenbelts highlights the centrality of urban peripheries and their role in shaping cities and regions.

Through a lens of peripheral centralities, this chapter examines significant trends influencing greenbelts around the world and discusses the findings of a comparative study spanning eight greenbelts, published in the report 'Greenbelts Around the World Responding to Local and Global Challenges'.[3] Through an analysis of the cases at hand, it is evident that the protection and enhancement of greenbelts is more important than ever for the future of cities and suburban centres.

Foundational, Evolving Elements of Urban and Regional Planning for over a Century

Greenbelts date back to the late nineteenth and early twentieth century, with origins in British town planning and Ebenezer Howard's Garden City concept.[4] Responding to industrialisation, these early greenbelts (e.g. London) were created to contain development, separate urban and rural areas, and provide recreational spaces for residents.[5] Greenbelts grew in popularity in the years immediately after World War II until the 1970s, spreading to cities such as Melbourne, Australia and Copenhagen, Denmark.[6] Since the 1990s, a new generation of greenbelts with diverse policy goals and more complex governance arrangements have been created in places such as Frankfurt, Germany and Ontario, Canada.[7]

Since the post-war era, the greenbelt concept has evolved to reflect changing conditions found within cities and regions. While early greenbelt policies mostly dealt with guiding urban growth, recent policies often have multi-functional objectives. In addition to controlling growth and protecting farmland, greenbelt policies have been expanded to include objectives such as economic development, climate change mitigation and adaptation, and ecosystem service provision.[8] Furthermore, greenbelt governance has become more complex, with private and civil society stakeholders involved in their management. This reflects trends in regional governance, with public services increasingly delegated to the private and voluntary sectors.[9] Greenbelts have become increasingly central to policy discourses related to the future of settlement areas because their multi-functional peripheral landscapes can help to address current challenges such as climate change, food insecurity, ecosystem destruction, and extended urbanisation.

Greenbelts are often located within heterogeneous, spatially fragmented landscapes due to the growth of regions. These peripheral landscapes include a diversity of residential, commercial, and industrial spaces and infrastructures which are central to a city or suburb's functioning.[10] Given the complexity and potential contradictions of these peripheral spaces, policymakers are tasked with determining how to effectively protect and enhance greenbelts, which play a central role in supporting residents' wellbeing.

Eight Global Greenbelts Studied and Contrasted to Reveal Threats and Opportunities

This chapter features the results of a comparative study examining how greenbelts are evolving to respond to current and emerging conditions found within cities and regions, including the following cases:[11]

- British Columbia's Agricultural Land Reserve, Canada;
- Copenhagen's Green Wedges, Denmark;
- European Green Belt;
- Green Heart, the Netherlands;
- London Metropolitan Green Belt, England;
- Melbourne's Green Wedges, Australia;
- San Francisco Bay Area Greenbelt, U.S.; and
- São Paulo City Green Belt Biosphere Reserve, Brazil.

Four themes were examined: 1) nature-based solutions; 2) food and agricultural systems; 3) outdoor tourism and recreation; and, 4) growth management.[12] This comparative study was based on a review of academic literature, media articles, and government policies, along with twenty interviews conducted in 2021 with greenbelt experts.

One of the original functions of greenbelts is to preserve agricultural land in the periphery of urban centres. Agricultural production within greenbelts near cities and suburbs provides residents with local food and supports regional economies by creating agritourism opportunities (Figure 1). For example, the San Francisco Bay Area is located in a highly productive agricultural region which produces a wide variety of fruits, vegetables, meat, and dairy products. The region's agricultural production generates almost CAN $2,700,000,000 billion per year. While nearly 40% of land in the Bay Area is devoted to farming and livestock grazing, since 1984 more than 200,000 acres of farmland across nine counties have been lost to development.[13] To support growing regions, more housing and infrastructure services are required but this often results in the loss of farmland and natural areas. Thus, the pressure to develop protected lands—paired with increased demand for housing—illustrates the challenges in balancing the often-competing interests involved in greenbelt planning.

Figure 1. Farm, Brant County, Ontario. Source: Photo by Sara Macdonald, 2014

Figure 2. View from Toronto north to the surrounding region.
Source: Photo by Michael Collens, 2020

Figure 3. Housing construction, Oshawa, Ontario. Source: Photo by Sara Macdonald, 2014

Figure 4. Silver Creek Conservation Area, Ontario. Source: Photo by Michael Collens, 2022

Many of the greenbelts examined in these cases are forecasted to experience rapid population growth in the coming decades (Figure 2). Strong growth pressures create surging demand for new housing and associated infrastructure, resulting in increased pressure on politicians to release protected lands for development. For example, Melbourne's Urban Growth Boundary (UGB) was expanded numerous times between 2003 and 2012.[14] These expansions have fuelled land speculation in peri-urban areas, with developers lobbying the government to extend the UGB. Although population and housing density has increased in the greater Melbourne metropolitan area over the past twenty years, approximately half of residential growth has taken place in outer urban areas. Thus, the UGB has not been overly effective in encouraging compact development.[15]

Pressure to open greenbelt lands for development is a threat faced by the majority of cases (Figure 3). Development proponents often cite the high cost of urban land, exacerbated by growth boundaries and development controls, as barriers to creating affordable housing. Yet, our research reveals that altering greenbelt boundaries and developing in protected areas is not a solution for addressing housing affordability. Since 2016, there has been a 127% increase of Green Belt land proposed for development in the London metropolitan area. In 2022, local councils in the London metropolitan area were planning to allow development on more than 48,000 acres of the London Green Belt.[16] While there has been an increase of residential development proposed for London's Green Belt, there is little evidence that affordable housing is being built.[17]

With increased housing demands, there is also an urgent need for infrastructure to support these growing communities. Greenbelts are often locations for peripherally central infrastructures, including highways, water and wastewater systems, public transit stations, and airports. As seen in many of our cases, the creation and expansion of infrastructure is needed to support growth in expanding cities and regions, and to facilitate the movement of goods, services, and commuters. However, these infrastructure projects can fragment and destroy farmland and natural areas, influencing future development patterns by enabling urban and suburban centres to grow beyond their boundaries.[18] For example, Highway 413 is a proposed fifty-two-kilometre highway in the western part of the Greater Toronto Area of Ontario, Canada. The proposed route would cut through 400 acres of greenbelt lands and 2,000 acres of farmland.[19]

Environmental organisations argue that the highway would increase air pollution, endanger species at risk by destroying natural habitat, and facilitate low-density development.[20] As an alternative to a new highway, stakeholders have advocated for public transit improvements that will better address mobility needs. The tensions between the costs and benefits of these peripherally central infrastructures (located within greenbelts) highlight the importance of these landscapes, which have a significant impact on the future development of urban regions.

As cities and suburban centres face challenges in terms of agricultural sustainability and housing, our research reveals greenbelts are an important planning approach through which to manage development more effectively. Greenbelts can be effective growth management tools if supported by other policies and integrated into growth management plans. Comprehensive regional plans can effectively manage growth in peripheral areas, while protecting farmland and natural areas.

Greenbelt Roles: Benefits Require Sustained Political and Policy Support

There is growing awareness among policymakers and the public about the important role that greenbelts can play in mitigating the effects of climate change, biodiversity loss, and ecosystem destruction (Figure 4). Greenbelts can provide environmental benefits including water filtration, carbon capture and storage, flood control, urban heat mitigation, waste treatment, and protect habitat for plant and animal species. Greenbelts are increasingly instrumentalised as 'green infrastructure' and integrated into environmental and land-use planning policies. For example, London's Metropolitan Green Belt is described as the 'green lungs' of the city because it assists with meeting some objectives of the country's twenty-five-year national environmental plan—reducing the urban heat island effect, protecting woodlands, and storing carbon.[21]

While the environmental benefits of greenbelts are becoming more important in environmental policy, many people who live in or close to greenbelts are unaware of the valuable services they provide. Thus, there is a need to enhance education for the public, stakeholders, and policymakers regarding the environmental

Figure 5. View from the Oak Ridges Moraine south to Toronto.
Source: Photo by Roger Keil, 2007

benefits of greenbelts. In the San Francisco Bay Area, organisations have created a 'Greenprint' that measures and maps the contribution of the region's natural resources and their impact on the economy, ecosystems, and communities.[22] In São Paulo, the Forestry Institute has published a book on ecosystem services located in the Green Belt Biosphere Reserve, which gives the public and policymakers information on the significance of ecosystem services, threats created by development, and recommendations for addressing those issues.[23] The environmental benefits provided by greenbelts can enhance resilience in the climate and biodiversity crisis, which is increasingly important for the future of cities and suburban centres.

Conclusion

As discussed within this chapter, the functions and land uses (planned or currently occurring) within the urban periphery of greenbelts have profound implications for urban and suburban centres (Figure 5). The cases examined here highlight how cities and their peripheries are interlinked in symbiotic relation.[24] Greenbelts are often connected to larger agricultural and natural systems, which provide critical functions for cities and suburban centres. With population growth, greenbelts are typically under threat from new housing development and infrastructure services. However, greenbelts are also central to residents' wellbeing due to the benefits they provide, including food production, recreational spaces, and climate change mitigation measures.

While greenbelts are increasingly central in environment and land-use planning policy discourse, government officials face challenges on how to effectively manage these complex peripheral centralities. The protection and enhancement of greenbelts is important for urban regions amid the global pressures of climate change, food and water scarcity, and extended urbanisation. As regions move closer to environmental tipping points, greenbelts can be an important planning tool for managing development pressures more effectively. Therefore, it is essential that policymakers and the public protect and enhance greenbelts, so that they can continue to provide the valuable assets needed for future generations.

Acknowledgements

The funding for this research was provided by The Greenbelt Foundation (Toronto, Canada).

Endnotes:

1 Erickson, D. L. The relationship of historic city form and contemporary greenway implementation: A comparison of Milwaukee, Wisconsin (USA) and Ottawa, Ontario (Canada), *Landscape and Urban Planning, 68* (2–3), 2004, pp. 199–221.

2 Taylor, L. The future of green belts, in: M. Scott, N. Galant, and M. Gkartzios (eds.). *Routledge companion to rural planning.* First edition. Routledge, 2019, pp. 458–468.

3 Macdonald, S., Chellew, C., and Hertel, S. *Greenbelts Around the World Responding to Local and Global Challenges.* Greenbelt Foundation, 2022; https://www.greenbelt.ca/global_greenbelts (accessed February 1, 2025).

4 Amati, M. (ed.) *Urban green belts in the twenty-first century.* Ashgate, 2008; Sturzaker, J. and Mell, I. *Green belts: Past; present; future?* Routledge, 2017.
5 Sturzaker and Mell, 2017, *op. cit.*
6 Amati, 2008, *op. cit.*
7 Macdonald, S., Monstadt, J., and Friendly, A. Rethinking the governance and planning of a new generation of greenbelts, *Regional Studies, 55* (5), 2021, pp. 804–817.
8 Ibid.
9 Ibid; Stoker, G. Governance as theory: Five propositions, *International Social Science Journal, 50* (155), 1998, pp. 17–28.
10 Phelps, N. A., Maginn, P. J., and Keil, R. Centring the periphery in urban studies: Notes towards a research agenda on peripheral centralities, *Urban Studies, 60* (6), 2023, pp. 1158–1176.
11 This paper borrows from research conducted for Macdonald, Chellew and Hertel, 2022, *op. cit.*
12 Functions that restore, conserve, or improve the management of natural areas to protect against environmental degradation and climate change are referred to as nature-based solutions.
13 Macdonald, Chellew, and Hertel, 2022, *op. cit.*, p. 110.
14 Buxton, M. The expanding urban fringe: Impacts on peri-urban areas, Melbourne, Australia, in: B. Maheshwari, R. Purohit, H. Malano, V. Singh, and P. Amerasinghe (eds.) *The security of water, food, energy and liveability of cities. Challenges and opportunities for peri-urban futures.* Springer, 2014, pp. 55–70; Victoria Planning Authority. (n.d.). *Key facts on Melbourne's urban growth boundary.* Victoria government; https://vpa.vic.gov.au/metropolitan/more-information/urban-growth-boundary-key-facts/#:~:text=In%202012%20the%20State%20Government,2017%2D2050%20at%20Policy%202.1 (accessed February 1, 2025).
15 Lua, J., Liua, C., and Buxton, M. The Impact Of Urban Growth Boundaries In Melbourne On Urban Sustainable Development, *Engineering Heritage Journal (GWK), 5* (1), 2021, pp. 34–41.
16 London Green Belt Council. 'Safe under us'? The continued shrinking of London's local countryside, 2022; https://londongreenbeltcouncil.org.uk/wp-content/uploads/2022/08/220821-Safe-Under-Us-report.pdf.
17 Ibid.
18 Lloyd Swail Consulting. *The Impacts of Linear Infrastructure Development on the Greenbelt.* Greenbelt Foundation, 2020; https://www.greenbelt.ca/linear_infrastructure_report.
19 Gray, T. Top reasons why building Highway 413 is a very bad idea, *Environmental Defence*, October 9, 2023; https://environmentaldefence.ca/2023/10/09/top-reasons-why-building-highway-413-is-a-very-bad-idea/ (accessed October 14, 2024).
20 Ibid.
21 London Green Belt Council, 2022, *op. cit.*
22 Bay Area Greenprint (n.d.); https://www.bayareagreenprint.org/ (accessed February 1, 2025).
23 Rodrigues, E. A., Victor, R. A. B. M., Pires, B. C. C., and de Luca, E. F. (eds.) *Servicos ecossistemicos e bem-estar humano na Reserva da Biosfera do Cinturao verde da Cidade de Sao Paulo.* [Ecosystem services and human well-being in the Sao Paulo Green Belt Biosphere Reserve] Instituto Florestal [Forestry Institute], 2020.
24 Phelps, Maginn, and Keil, 2023, *op. cit.*

A
gen
cy

A
gen
cy

The Dam Headquarters as a Symbol of Ecomodernism

Zachary Dark

> ... in the old days the army would walk back into the city in a grand parade, carrying and displaying the spoils of war in a triumphal procession. these days they just build new buildings. a few years ago the ribbon was cut to open a new downtown headquarters for manitoba hydro. everyone was there, and they were all shaking hands. and smiling. you think: 'maybe it will help to rejuvenate winnipeg's downtown!' you think: 'they made it using the ecologically latest features and materials!'... you think: 'maybe it'll be beautiful?!' but you really doubt it.[1]

Introduction

In 2009, Manitoba Hydro (a provincially owned electricity utility in Manitoba, Canada) opened its new headquarters on the edge of downtown Winnipeg. Manitoba Hydro Place was designed to be exceptionally energy-efficient, and the award-winning building is now considered an exemplar of environmentally minded, sustainable architecture. However, Manitoba Hydro's (MH) hydroelectric facilities have also caused massive socio-environmental degradation in northern Manitoba, disproportionately affecting Indigenous communities and land-based modes of living. At the same time, Manitoba Hydro Place (MH Place) is embedded in the 'revitalisation' of Winnipeg's downtown, aimed at attracting white-collar workers and intensified private investment. Sitting at the intersection of these two dynamics, MH Place forms an important point of connection between the provincial core, its northern periphery, and the various new centralities produced through Manitoba's hydroelectric infrastructure network.

Hydroelectric Ecomodernism in Manitoba

Following Maria Kaika's examination of dams as symbols of modernisation, I argue that MH Place functions as a symbol of *ecomodernisation*. Kaika uses the Marathon Dam (near Athens, Greece) to demonstrate the functional and symbolic character of infrastructure. Functionally, the dam linked Athens to modernity through the provision of a reliable water supply, while symbolically it connected modern Greece to its ancient glory through its location and classical architectural elements. The dam was *modern* in that it appeared to demonstrate human emancipation from natural constraints (whose destruction was to be celebrated, not mourned). However, despite this apparent liberation, such infrastructures actually demonstrate the inextricability of socio-environmental relations: 'now water not only *could*, but also *had* to be tamed ... in order to sustain the city's growth and expansion over space and in time'.[2] Ecomodernism is premised on a similar illusion.

This philosophy of incremental reform places its faith in technological solutions to socio-environmental problems.[3] This approach serves to sidestep political questions regarding the conditions under which technology is developed and deployed, the relations which govern the inputs required for 'green growth', and the global distribution of environmental benefits and harms.[4] Hydroelectricity was a key modernising technology in twentieth-century Canada, and, in the context of increasingly severe climate change, renewable hydroelectricity is now envisioned in *ecomodernising* terms as an important part of Canada's (supposedly) imminent low-carbon society.[5] MH positions itself as a key actor in provincial decarbonisation efforts, and these 'green' credentials feature prominently in promotional material aimed at attracting new private investment to the province.[6]

The construction of hydroelectric infrastructure entails the creation of new centralities (through massive concentrations of labour, capital, and materials) in certain parts of Manitoba's peripheral regions. MH's hydroelectric dams and water control structures have reshaped many of the province's major river and lake systems, and in so doing have harmed northern Indigenous people by displacing communities, impacting local social structures, and undermining land-based economies.[7] In particular, the huge influx of non-local construction workers that accompanies dam construction (i.e. 'man camps')—and the more permanent transformation of northern towns by rotating MH personnel and logistics operations—has had particularly significant impacts, bringing racism, sexual violence, and other social problems into northern Indigenous communities.[8] MH's operations—which are connected to a long line of colonial incursions reaching back to the fur trade—have contributed to the reshaping of Manitoba's northern periphery by imposing new colonial centralities on the Indigenous nations whose territories encompass the region. Through Indigenous resistance to MH's operations, numerous formal compensation and cooperation agreements have been created. Indeed, MH has begun to develop hydroelectric projects in partnership with First Nations, although the efficacy of these partnerships has been critiqued.[9]

Manitoba Hydro Place

It is in this broad context that MH constructed its new headquarters, MH Place. Built on the edge of downtown Winnipeg, occupying a prominent location on Portage Avenue (a major urban artery and a historically important retail street), the twenty-two-storey office building utilises an impressive array of both passive and active building systems. These include green roofs, geothermal climate control, operable windows, an indoor waterfall (to regulate temperature and humidity), programmable lighting systems, and building features which maximise natural light and solar gain, thus consuming far less energy than comparable buildings. Envisioned by MH executives as a 'world-class, signature building',[10] MH Place was intended to 'be a contemporary and distinctive "signature" design that celebrates the importance of Manitoba Hydro to the Province and that enhances the overall image of the downtown'.[11] While the potential energy-efficiency and environmental impact were key considerations in the site selection process, so were the site's visibility to the public and its suitability for an iconic new building. Praise for the building continued

Figure 1. Manitoba Hydro Place. Source: Photo by Jaxon Schleicher, 2022

for years after its opening, and MH Place was framed in the Winnipeg press as part of a wave of internationally significant architecture in the city.[12] MH Place was the 'first large-scale office tower in North America' to achieve the Leadership in Energy and Environmental Design (LEED) organisation's prestigious 'platinum' certification for sustainability. Since its completion, the building's architect has used MH Place as *the* exemplar of sustainable architecture for domestic and international audiences.[13] The building's sustainability credentials are at the core of its public profile. Indeed, through its iconic headquarters, MH projects an image of environmental and social responsibility despite the impacts of its northern operations and its broader role in reshaping downtown Winnipeg.

From its inception, MH Place was envisioned as a pillar of a new phase of accumulation in the provincial core. During the time the building was being planned, the hegemonic view of Winnipeg's downtown was of an area in uncontrolled decline, where inner-city social ills stifled economic activity and pushed suburbanite citizens (and their discretionary spending power) away.[14] From this standpoint, the city's core area (including Portage Avenue) was 'an individual, personal disgrace to all the citizens of Winnipeg' which, if left unaddressed, threatened the viability of the downtown area—and Winnipeg overall—as a location for leisure and business.[15]

This dominant view of Winnipeg's downtown clearly shaped the development of MH Place. Potential sites were assessed in terms of their ability 'to promote realistic, value-added developments ... that will enhance design opportunities and the downtown area in general'.[16] Leveraging public resources to facilitate private accumulation was an explicit development goal during this period, and the increased value of properties near MH Place has been approvingly highlighted in news coverage.[17] From the beginning of its design process through to the present day, MH Place has been consistently linked with a push to 'revitalise' Portage Avenue and the wider downtown.[18] Part of this 'revitalisation' process involves a remaking of the citizen in downtown Winnipeg. MH Place consolidated approximately 2000 workers from previously dispersed, suburban office buildings, thereby recentralising its white-collar workforce. Sites were evaluated based on the potential of employees to contribute to the downtown economy, and MH Place offers limited retail and dining facilities in order to encourage workers to patronise existing downtown businesses.[19] MH Place also includes a number of publicly

Figure 2. The solar chimney is one element in MH Place's low-energy building systems. Source: Photo by Jaxon Schleicher, 2022

The Dam Headquarters as a Symbol of Ecomodernism

Figure 3. Iconic architecture. Source: Photo by Jaxon Schleicher, 2022

Figure 4. MH Place in its downtown setting. Source: Photo by Jaxon Schleicher, 2022

accessible spaces and has hosted a popular downtown farmers' market since 2013. As a representative of the area's business association describes it:

> [D]owntown Winnipeg is never going to be what it was in the 1970s ... . But that doesn't mean it can't be something else, right? To those people who claim to hate downtown, I'd love to invite them down here on market day, when hundreds of people are milling about on their coffee breaks and lunch hours, buying cookies and whatnot to take back to the office ... it's so heartwarming to see such a buzz of activity.[20]

These intertwined dynamics demonstrate the fundamentally colonial processes that link the Manitoban core and its periphery through MH Place, as well as the peripheral centralities generated through the province's wider hydroelectric network. Accumulation in Winnipeg is predicated on dispossession in northern Manitoba. The intentional, hyper-visible recentralisation of white-collar workers in Winnipeg's downtown occurs in tandem with the less visible development of temporary construction camps and permanent dams. MH's undermining of Indigenous economies in northern Manitoba and the revanchist approach to downtown development in Winnipeg are connected through the broader dynamics of displacement and urban migration of Indigenous people in the twentieth century.[21] As Robert Wavey, a former First Nation leader, asks:

> The price [of hydroelectric development] has been paid by the most vulnerable. So when you see people on the streets, or in the North End, what's their story? Where did they come from? Why are they here? How many of them are here because of what happened up north?[22]

Conclusion

Hydroelectric generation requires massive material and capital investments in Manitoba's far north, a complex system of long-distance power lines, converter stations, a local distribution network, and a headquarters building to oversee it all. Despite the historical and ongoing socio-environmental degradation embodied in this network, MH Place projects a very different image to the people of Winnipeg. The spectacle of the building, much like the spectacle of the Marathon Dam, claims a mastery over nature. While the dam appears to harness an external nature for human use, MH Place exemplifies an ecomodernist vision wherein 'humanity should dwell [and work!] in an austere and antiseptic techno-sphere, dematerialized and drawing on phantom technologies that lessen human impact on the biosphere to the lowest possible level'.[23] In both instances, while these infrastructures rely on claiming to 'liberate' humanity from nature, they simultaneously 'signal the city's perpetual dependency on the production of (new) nature in order to sustain its life, its form, and its metabolism'.[24]

Infrastructure networks link colonial repression and anti-colonial struggle across space.[25] MH Place serves to sanitise colonial socio-environmental harms in Manitoba's periphery *through* its symbolism in the provincial metropolis. It exemplifies an ecomodernist vision in which the clean, green, and renewable technology of hydroelectricity exists above the social relations that shape it, and in which the remaking of Winnipeg's downtown as a space of middle-class consumption and leisure will bring prosperity for all. As climate crisis discourses become more urgent, and as transportation and other sectors become increasingly electrified, MH's renewable electricity production stands to benefit from its inclusion under the umbrella of 'sustainability'. This is not to say that energy and resource-efficient buildings are undesirable, nor that downtown public spaces and farmers' markets are to be condemned. Rather, it is the political function of these technologies and techniques that must be critically examined. For Manitoba Hydro Place, the representational and functional qualities of the building neatly coalesce, lending a new face to existing socio-environmental relations.

Figure 5. The network linking core, periphery, and peripheral centralities.
Source: Photo by Jaxon Schleicher, 2022

Endnotes:

1 Kulchyski, P. *Aboriginal rights are not human rights: in defence of indigenous struggles.* ARP Books, 2013, p. 156.

2 Kaika, M. Dams as Symbols of Modernization: The Urbanization of Nature Between Geographical Imagination and Materiality, *Annals of the Association of American Geographers, 96* (2), 2006, p. 295 [original emphasis].

3 Foster, J. B., Clark, B., and York, R. *The ecological rift: capitalism's war on the earth.* Monthly Review Press, 2010.

4 Ajl, M. *A people's Green New Deal.* Pluto Press, 2021, pp. 54–55.

5 Netherton, A. *From Rentiership to Continental Modernization: Shifting Policy Paradigms of State Intervention in Hydro in Manitoba, 1922–1977.* PhD Dissertation. Carleton University, 1993; Manitoba Innovation, Energy and Mines. *Manitoba's Clean Energy Strategy*, 2012; https://www.gov.mb.ca/sd/environment_and_biodiversity/energy/cleanenergy.html; Canadian Energy Strategy Working Group. *Canadian Energy Strategy*, 2015; https://www.gov.mb.ca/mr/energy/pubs/canadian_energy_strategy.pdf.

6 Department of Economic Development and Training. *Manitoba's Strategic Advantages, Government of Manitoba*; https://www.gov.mb.ca/jec/mbadvantage/index.html; Economic Development Winnipeg. *Energy & Environment*; https://www.economicdevelopmentwinnipeg.com/uploads/document/02606_edw_energy_envrionment_sector_brief_2020_screen.t1583168400.pdf.

7 Waldram, J. B. *As long as the rivers run: hydroelectric development and native communities in western Canada.* University of Manitoba Press, 1993; Martin, T. and Hoffman, S. M. (eds.) *Power struggles: hydro development and First Nations in Manitoba and Quebec.* University of Manitoba Press, 2008; Manitoba Clean Environment Commission. *A Review of the Regional Cumulative Effects Assessment For Hydroelectric Developments on the Nelson, Burntwood, and Churchill River Systems*, 2018; http://www.cecmanitoba.ca/cecm/hearings/pubs/Regional_Cumulative_Effects_Assessment/FinalReport/RCEA_Design_Web_Accessible_May24.pdf.

8 Manitoba Clean Environment Commission, 2018, *op. cit.*; Kulchyski, P. and Neckoway, R. *The Town That Lost Its Name: The Impact of Hydroelectric Development on Grand Rapids*, Manitoba, 2006; https://www.policyalternatives.ca/sites/default/files/uploads/publications/Manitoba_Pubs/2006/Grand_Rapids.pdf.

9 Buckland, J. and O'Gorman, M. The Keeyask Hydro Dam Plan in Northern Canada: A Model for Inclusive Indigenous Development?, *Canadian Journal of Development Studies, 38* (1), 2017, pp. 72–90; Kulchyski, P. A Step Back: The Nisichawayasihk Cree Nation and the Wuskwatim Project, in: T. Martin and S. M. Hoffman (eds.) *Power struggles: hydro development and First Nations in Manitoba and Quebec.* University of Manitoba Press, 2008, pp. 129–414.

10 Bob Brennan quoted in Santin, A. A Peek into the Future, *Winnipeg Free Press*, April 25, 2003.

11 Manitoba Hydro. *Manitoba Hydro Place Head Office—Guiding Principles*, Manitoba Hydro [Archived]. n.d.(a); https://web.archive.org/web/20120604093258/http://www.hydro.mb.ca/corporate/mhplace/vision.shtml.

12 Bellamy, B. City of architectural delights, *Winnipeg Free Press*, May 26, 2014; Cupoli, V. The Right Building for Where It Stands, *The Globe and Mail*, January 11, 2011; https://www.theglobeandmail.com/report-on-business/industry-news/property-report/the-right-building-for-where-it-stands/article4263253/.

13 Kuwabara, B. *Manitoba Hydro Place–a Model for Extreme Climate Responsive Design* (Conference Presentation [Video Recording], Chicago), October 22, 2009; https://www.youtube.com/watch?v=t6-54FJhn1c; Kuwabara, B. *Every Building Implies a City* (Public Lecture, Online Presentation), October 20, 2021; https://www.youtube.com/watch?v=ntjefruSVnI; KPMB Architects. *Manitoba Hydro Place*, 2020; http://www.kpmb.com/project/manitoba-hydro-place/.

14 CentreVenture Development Corporation. Heart of Gold: Strategic Plan 2007–2009, January 15, 2006, pp. 10–12; https://clkapps.winnipeg.ca/DMIS/Documents/DocExt/CUSTOM/CP-AM-2972.pdf.

15 Ibid., p. 12.

16 Manitoba Hydro. *Manitoba Hydro Place Head Office—Site Selection Criteria*, Manitoba Hydro [Archived]. n.d.(b); https://web.archive.org/web/20120604085847/http://www.hydro.mb.ca/corporate/mhplace/site_selection.shtml.

17 Cupoli, 2011, *op. cit.*; Kirbyson, G. Hydro unveils new building, *Winnipeg Free Press*, September 30, 2009; CentreVenture, 2007, *op. cit.*; Toews, O. *Stolen City: Racial Capitalism and the Making of Winnipeg.* ARP Books, 2018, pp. 228–277.

18 Cash, M. APTN boosts rebirth of Portage Commercial Real Estate, *Winnipeg Free Press*, July 4, 2011; Mayes, A. A Sneak Peek at Hydro Headquarters, *Winnipeg Free Press*, April 28, 2004; Kirbyson, G. Five-Storey Building to Rise on Theatre Site, *Winnipeg Free Press*, February 18, 2004; Waldman, B. Former Hydro HQ unplugged: With move to downtown building almost complete, Taylor Avenue site coming to market, *Winnipeg Free Press*, September 7, 2021.

19 Mayes, 2004, *op. cit.*; Manitoba Hydro, n.d.(b), *op. cit.*

20 Suzanne Ainley quoted in Sanderson, D. Down(town) on the farm, *Winnipeg Free Press*, July 7, 2019.

21 Toews, 2018, *op. cit.*, p. 129.

22 As quoted in Martin, M. Power Surge, *Winnipeg Free Press*, March 23, 2019.

23 Ajl, 2021, *op. cit.*, p. 47.

24 Kaika, 2006, *op. cit.*, p. 295.

25 Kipfer, S. *Urban Revolutions: Urbanisation and (Neo-)colonialism in Transatlantic Context.* Brill, 2022, chap. 4.

Peripheral Centralities in Val d'Europe: The Logics of Assemblage between Disneyland Paris and New Town Principles of Planning

Julien Aldhuy, Sophie Didier, and Loïc Vadelorge

Introduction

This photographic essay aims to document the ongoing transformations of the Val d'Europe sector in the New Town of Marne-la-Vallée, located in the eastern periphery of the Paris metropolitan area.[1] Val d'Europe is composed of six *communes* (municipalities joined in the Val d'Europe Agglomération), today totalling 50,000 inhabitants. It can be understood as the ongoing production process of a double-headed centrality: one of these centralities takes the form of a fully-fledged urban project, programmed in the development of the outermost sector of the New Town of Marne-la-Vallée. At the same time, the area hosts a touristic centrality dominated by the Disneyland Paris cluster of theme parks and tourist amenities whose influence extends to the production of the local landscapes, informing the processes and characteristics of the sector's general development as well as its real estate promotion.

Like all New Town developments designed in Greater Paris in the early 1960s, Val d'Europe is identified in current regional planning documents as one among several 'new urban centres'. For 1960s planners, these centres had to be peripheral, because there was no question of them offering all the various amenities available in Paris ('neither the Sorbonne nor the Comédie française', as stated in the 1965 *SDAURP*[2]). That said, they had to offer sufficient levels of services, amenities and public infrastructure (including hospitals, shopping centres, train stations, sports facilities, high schools and, after 1991, universities), to cover vast functional areas with the broader aim of organising (and thus creating centrality for) the ongoing Parisian peri-urban growth.

The presence of the Walt Disney Company in this French-style planning perimeter (itself a legacy of the *Trente Glorieuses* growth-driven era following World War II) represents both a historical innovation in the process of implementing French New Towns and a potential disruption of its classic planning tradition. Locating a tourism cluster at the centre of the Val d'Europe perimeter in the 1980s engaged other forms of centrality than those envisioned originally. And yet this cluster doesn't summarise the entire project as it took shape from the 2000s onwards, when the development of Val d'Europe as a more ordinary city began. It is therefore paramount to investigate the impact of Disney's theme parks on the emergence of an atypical peripheral centrality for Val d'Europe.

If the influence of Disney's parks is undeniable in Val d'Europe's urban space, departing from experimental initiatives implemented in other centralities at the same time (particularly in Île-de-France New Towns, such as Carré Sénart), then the urban landscape more generally testifies to the resistance of the above-mentioned French-style urbanism. This dimension has so far been largely overlooked by early scholarship investigating the urban form of Val d'Europe, which tended to be more interested in the introduction of architectural pastiche and New Urbanism in the Île-de-France context. This research focused more on the circulation of Disney-style planning than on its relationship to traditional local planning practices.[3]

On a very small perimeter of 3,000 hectares (and, for this particular photo-essay, on a 6-kilometre radius from the Val d'Europe RER station), one can distinguish several configurations of centrality for this new agglomeration—spanning the centre to the periphery—which underline its eminently composite character. The five following vignettes aim to render the complex combination in the perimeter of these centres and peripheries.

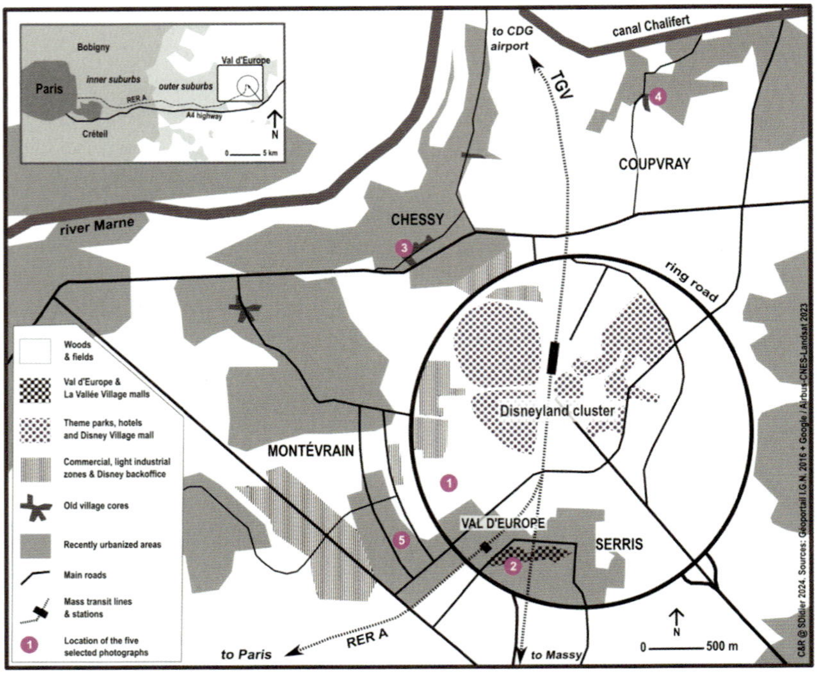

Figure 1. Location of the five photographs in the Val d'Europe perimeter.
Source: C&R S. Didier, 2024

The Ring Road as Border for the Heart of the Val d'Europe Urban Project (location: Chessy, corner of Rue Haddock and Boulevard du Grand Fossé)

The perfectly circular ring road that encircles the heart of the Val d'Europe perimeter represents a first in terms of road design in the development of French New Towns. It is visible on the map (Figure 1) and on the left and right hand sides of the panoramic photograph (Figure 2). The perfect circle—initially drawn as the starting point for planning—strongly separates the central zone, pointing to the invention of an urban-style density linked to the touristic project—from its peripheries, which are dedicated to suburban housing, the dominant form of peri-urban development characteristic of France between the 1970s and 1990s. However, a whole swathe of land in the centre of the ring is not yet urbanised. As a never-ending construction site since 2001, when the urbanisation phase of the sector was launched, the area located inside the ring road formally adheres to the logics of French-style planning. Although New Towns were originally conceived as territories where exceptional planning rules applied (*Opération d'Intérêt National*, i.e. 'development of national importance'), they nonetheless respected the principles of the 1967 land orientation law specifying the code for land use (*COS, Coefficient d'Occupation des Sols*) and joint development (*ZAC, Zone d'Aménagement Concerté*). One can clearly see the trace of this in the photograph. The centrality at the heart of the project imposes verticality and the supremacy of collective housing safeguarded by the *COS* rules. Likewise, the gatherings of cranes separated by vacant lots produce a patchwork of urbanisation that is a direct product of the *ZAC* zoning. The second centrality is nevertheless more ambiguous in that one can glimpse, almost in the centre of Figure 2, the Hollywood Tower of the Walt Disney Studios Park. This discreet presence in the landscape is, above all, protected in landscape terms by a visibility code, operating on the entire internal perimeter of the ring. Here, one can read the priority towards landscape control negotiated in the 1980s by the Walt Disney Company with the public developer. Consequently, the height limit of the buildings overall increases from the tourist 'centre' (Hollywood Tower) to the 'periphery' (the ring road), contrary to the principles generally applied in *ZAC*s. Finally, on the far left of the photograph, near a business park, one can see the presence of a stormwater management pond intended to reduce the risk of flooding due to the progressive artificialisation of the land. This pond also doubles as a birdwatching spot (in anticipation of future walks taken by future residents?), in keeping with the objectives of quality of life, access to green space and outdoor recreation, which were originally central to the philosophy of New Town programming.

Val d'Europe Shopping Centre (location: Serris)

The second photograph (Figure 3) illustrates a classic element of centrality present in the New Town design, namely the shopping centre. This centre, however, is unique in Seine-et-Marne owing to its size with nearly 200 shops and thirty restaurants spread over a commercial area of 100,000 square metres. Opened in 2000, it takes the form of a second-generation shopping centre, accessible both by road and by mass transit (the western entrance is directly accessible on foot

Figure 2. The Ring Road, panoramic view. Source: Photo by Julien Aldhuy, Sophie Didier, and Loïc Vadelorge, 2022

Figure 3. Val d'Europe shopping centre. Source: Photo by Julien Aldhuy, Sophie Didier, and Loïc Vadelorge, 2022

Figure 4. Chessy town centre, panoramic view. Source: Photo by Julien Aldhuy, Sophie Didier, and Loïc Vadelorge, 2022

from the Place d'Ariane, where the main RER A exit is located). On the road side, the shopping centre is bordered by a large multi-storey parking lot, which may seem slightly anachronistic considering that the time of its construction coincided with the Rio Earth Summit. On the city side, meanwhile, the shopping centre opens onto squares designed along resolutely urban references (Place de Toscane to the east, Place d'Ariane to the west), multiple references to the European architectural past (from Piazza Navona to Paxton's Crystal Palace, via Haussmannian buildings and nods to the Viennese Secession). Notably, these were produced in partnership between architects commissioned by the Walt Disney Company and architects commissioned by the French public planner. The shopping centre itself is almost a kilometre long, pastiching Parisian commercial architecture and the (now defunct) structures designed by Victor Baltard for Les Halles de Paris during the Second Empire.

From Chessy to Coupvray: Town Centres 'far, far away' from Disneyland Paris

The traditional planning of a French New Town operates a distinction between the New Town area itself (*ZAN, or Zone d'Agglomération Nouvelle*)—which is the responsibility of the public planning institution—and the inter-communal system imposed on the municipalities by the legislator (see the Boscher law of 1970, Rocard law of 1983 and Chevènement law of 1999) for the area outside the New Town (beyond the *ZAN*), which is the responsibility of the municipalities. This principle was strengthened by the decentralisation laws implemented after 1982, resulting in an administrative patchwork that is clearly visible in the urban landscapes surrounding the Val d'Europe ring road. If the presence of suburban-style detached housing contributes to unifying the periphery, as well as ensuring the maintenance of several town halls a few kilometres away from the commercial centre (such as Montévrain and Coupvray, to name just two), one cannot help but be struck by the morphological differences of these village centres that make up the inter-municipal political territory of Val d'Europe. Historically speaking, the 1987 agreement between the French state, the regional and departmental authorities and the Walt Disney Company created (on paper, at least) an incredible disjuncture between a powerful, multinational company and the relatively modest influence of elected officials from *communes* that were still 'rural' at the time of its signing. Yet, each centre has managed to successfully preserve its personality, and over time a clear socio-spatial differentiation has emerged between them.

Take Chessy, for example, where the point of contact with the heart of Val d'Europe is built around open areas based on a representation of the local rural heritage (a redesigned village square welcoming commercial activity, an old farmhouse currently undergoing heritagisation, the woods and park of the local castle ensuring the invisibility of the Disney parks). This is to the general benefit of a residential area where brand-new townhouses, often semi-detached with small gardens, would otherwise predominate. The 'middle and small middle classes'—that is, the target demographic of this transitional space between the urban centre and the outer, peri-urban area—are clearly accepted and solicited here. In 2019, the *commune*'s makeup was 25% executives and members of the higher intellectual professions.[4]

Figure 4 shows the central village square of Chessy, redeveloped around the church, an old nineteenth-century café, and the *foirail* converted into a parking lot. Around it, businesses have similarly moved 'upmarket' (wine shop, English learning centre), seemingly following the trend towards renewal.

In Coupvray, however, the situation is radically different. The town centre seems somehow out of time in Val d'Europe, far from the shadow of Disneyland Paris. There is no continuity with the ring road here, even though the *commune* straddles a quarter of the total central perimeter. The village centre, now bereft of shops, seems stagnant, and is organised around the classic triptych of French rural centralities: the church, the town hall and the Great War memorial. In Figure 5, one can see a small real estate programme that has been built next to a large 1930s house: here, again, those few shops located at the base of residential buildings seem to be little frequented, and the design of public space appears rudimentary. The rising popularity of centralities other than local ones certainly plays a role here, in particular those commercial centralities more oriented towards the northeast and the medium-sized town of Meaux, way outside the perimeter of the New Town.

Figure 5. Coupvray town centre. Source: Photo by Julien Aldhuy, Sophie Didier, and Loïc Vadelorge, 2022

Figure 6. Montévrain 2nd centre, panoramic view. Source: Photo by Julien Aldhuy, Sophie Didier, and Loïc Vadelorge, 2022

Montévrain *Écoquartier*: a *Banlieue* for Val d'Europe?

What remains, then, is an intermediate space undergoing profound change. The area immediately attached to the ring road takes the form of an improbable *banlieue* with a still-uncertain status. The examples of Chessy and Montévrain differ significantly here, suggesting the limitations of planning in the area. In Montévrain, whose town centre is quite far from the core perimeter, the junction with the ring road has taken the form of an *écoquartier*, i.e. an extensive group of collective housing with twenty-first century sustainable development standards (green malls, drainage ditches, use of wood as decorative material, etc.)

The eco-district is organised around a local shopping centre, new schools, an annex of the town hall and some local services (nursery, post office, etc.). Figure 6 shows an urban landscape that could be found in any urban periphery in northwestern Europe—i.e. small apartment buildings, a car park, and a small supermarket. Montévrain is not administratively part of Val d'Europe's inter-municipality. The influence of the Walt Disney Company in the production of this eco-district appears to be non-existent at first glance, even if the park and the eco-district are geographically close. That

said, the commercial centrality and transportation infrastructure of the Marne-la-Vallée–Chessy hub are obviously decisive in accounting for the urbanisation challenge represented by this new peripheral density. One could thus characterise it as a kind of *banlieue* for Val d'Europe: this eco-district suggests a form of polarisation in the urbanisation process, embraced by the municipality, which accepts the doubling of its own development between a traditional town centre and an eco-district physically separated from it and connected to Val d'Europe. This situation is somewhat reminiscent of the history of French housing projects (*Grands Ensembles*), which in most cases worked as peripheral developments for existing old centres (Les Sablons in Sarcelles, Le Val Fourré in Mantes-la-Jolie, etc.).

Conclusion

In the early 1960s, a group of architects proposed the creation of an 'alternative Paris' to solve the problems of rapid population growth in the Paris region. This hypothesis was quickly discarded and gave way to polycentric urban planning, which the five Parisian New Towns embodied in the last decades of the twentieth century. Presented for a long time as a specific project owing to the unprecedented deal between a multinational company and the central state, Val d'Europe today appears as a peripheral centrality relatively in keeping with the expectations of New Towns. The current densification of the interstices of the core perimeter as well as its immediate periphery are perfectly in line with the state's desire to make the phenomenal cost of infrastructure (RER, TGV) profitable. This is congruent with other (and older) New Town experiments such as Saint-Quentin-en-Yvelines or Evry-Sénart.

The touristic infrastructure and the architectural standards imposed by the Walt Disney Company do, indeed, draw a specific landscape (in Serris in particular) that has no equivalent in the other New Towns, which have never focused their urban development solely on tourism. However, the current urban scale of development in this territory can no longer be interpreted as exclusively influenced by the Walt Disney Company. While this undoubtedly suggests a French way to engage this type of public–private partnership, it also makes clear the rapid transformation of these peri-urban areas as well as the challenges for interpretation and practice they raise.

Endnotes:

1 This essay was written as a follow-up to the Graduate Programme Urban Futures workshop 'Histoire et devenir du Val d'Europe' (LABEX Futurs Urbains). We wish to acknowledge the contribution of the three master's students who participated in the workshop: Ikram Bouchenine, Roshni Mohammed Ghouse and Wilfried Pingault.

2 *SDAURP: Schéma Directeur d'Aménagement et d'Urbanisme de la Région Parisienne*, was the master plan document of the 1960s at the metropolitan level.

3 Chabard, P. Val d'Europe: de la ville nouvelle au nouvel urbanisme, in: C. Orillard and A. Picon (eds.) *Marne-la-Vallée, de la ville nouvelle à la ville durable.* Parenthèses, 2012, pp. 167–179; Picon-Lefebvre, V. Euro Disneyland: la ville des loisirs, in: Orillard and Picon, 2012, *op. cit.*, pp. 143–165.

4 INSEE; https://www.insee.fr/fr/statistiques/2011101?geo=COM-77111#chiffre-cle-1.

From Oil Refinery to Green Park: The Quest for Autonomy and Peripheral Centrality

Frédéric Mercure Jolette, Clarence Hatton-Proulx, and Sophie L. Van Neste

Introduction

For Jan Nijman, a suburb must be conceived as 'a transitional space', meaning a space that includes relational and evolutionary dimensions.[1] Nijman argues that we must stop seeing suburbs as fixed entities placed in an asymmetrical dependence with the city centre. Rather, the suburbs must be seen as evolving and autonomous spaces, which also form part of an urban region. Following Nijman, our hypothesis is that it is impossible to understand the formation and evolution of peripheral centralities—and, moreover, the political struggles in which they are involved—if we disregard their quest for autonomy.[2]

With good reason, suburban claims to autonomy have always been questioned.[3] From an empirical viewpoint, suburban growth is often seen as the result of a metropolitan dynamic tied to state policies and a globalised economy.[4] Technological development, transport infrastructure, and heavy industry are key factors that cannot be entirely controlled by local elites. Yet this chapter shows that their claim to autonomy matters. Even when representations of suburbia are out of step with material reality, they are often still operative in the thinking and action of local leaders—in how residents, businesses and industries are attracted, and in metropolitan politics.[5]

The quest for autonomy can also produce paradoxical effects. Indeed, in some cases, the means used by suburban elites to achieve autonomy can produce a feedback loop that shapes development patterns in a way that limits local political capacity. This is not to say that autonomy doesn't exist, but simply that it remains limited and dependent on the tools and resources used locally, and above all that it evolves over time. Our case study shows that the quest for autonomy is a determining factor in the formation and evolution of what we call, again following Nijman, a transitional centrality.

Anjou—a former suburb that was merged against its will with the City of Montréal in 2002—is a typical post-World War II suburb, whose development was boosted by the oil industry. Perhaps more importantly, Anjou's quest for autonomy led to a functionalist planning approach and an emphasis on economic growth, which in turn produced a form of path dependency. It did not, however, prevent the municipality from undertaking serious reforms after the decline of oil refining in Greater Montréal and the emergence of environmental awareness in the 1980s. Rather, this initial functionalist planning steered Anjou in a certain direction. Thus, the case of Anjou is interesting not only because it allows us to question the discursive importance of suburban autonomy, but also because it highlights the current struggles around the retrofitting of what was once seen as one of the most prosperous peripheral centralities in Montréal. Furthermore, it challenges the idea that post-war functionalist suburbia is a fixed urban form, or that functionalism is an obstacle to change.[6]

Anjou: a Peripheral Centrality in Montréal's Petroleumscape

Post-World War II North American suburbs like Anjou are part of what Carola Hein calls a global petroleumscape.[7] Over the last 200 years, the introduction of oil has permanently altered the urban landscape. Not only has it radically changed modes of transportation, which have in turn changed the way cities are inhabited, but oil as a resource and commodity has also transformed the landscapes where it is extracted, transported, refined, and consumed.

Both commuter town and industrial site, Anjou's landscape has been profoundly transformed by oil. Indeed, the founding of the city in 1956 took place in Montréal's 'golden age' of petroleum. At the time, Montréal was Canada's main oil refining hub, while the whole metropolitan region was entering a phase of suburbanisation that saw residential growth shift to the outskirts thanks to mass motorisation.

Anjou's founders tried to take advantage of this situation—and, above all, the construction of a new refinery on the Island of Montréal by British Petroleum (BP)—to build a multi-functional and self-sufficient model city.[8] This desire for distinction and autonomy immediately translated into an extensive use of urban planning instruments. Anjou adopted a hyper-functionalist urban plan (see Figure 1). The city was divided by two highways into four quadrants, each of which had a dominant function: light industry; heavy industry; residential; and, commercial. At its heart sits a huge interchange linking two major thoroughfares that bisect the Island of Montréal, facilitating swift access to Anjou by cars and trucks (see Figure 2).

In parallel, the establishment of BP—which owned about 12% of Anjou's surface area—kickstarted the construction of an industrial park, which in just twenty-five years became the third largest on the Island of Montréal. Moreover, the contract with BP provided the municipality with the liquidity it needed to build urban infrastructure and to grow rapidly. Accordingly, its population grew from 2,140 in 1956 to 33,395 in 1971. During this time, the local elite celebrated the presence of industry on its territory, which was carefully separated from single-family homes by a major highway. Soon after, in 1968, a shopping mall was built just a stone's throw from the interchange. With its huge parking lot and multiple stores, Les Galeries d'Anjou was the largest shopping centre in the province. Customers came from all over the region to enjoy this new apex of consumer society.

The result of this multi-functional suburb was the emergence of a new peripheral centrality dependent on oil and metropolitan growth, with a shape largely inherited from functionalist ideas. However, visions of progress can be short-lived and Anjou's development model quickly hit a wall. It was challenged by the closure of important industries and by new forms of peripheral centrality, built further off the Island of Montréal. So, despite the apparent land-use determinism in which they were engaged, changes in economic context and metropolitan dynamics forced Anjou's leaders to review their city's development faster than anticipated. Their quest for autonomy and centrality then led them to invest in new urban planning ideas.

Retrofitting Suburbia: a Short-lived Centrality?

While single-family residential growth was bound to reach a limit due to the amount of land available, the rapid closure of the BP refinery was more surprising. In 1982, rather than continuing to expand

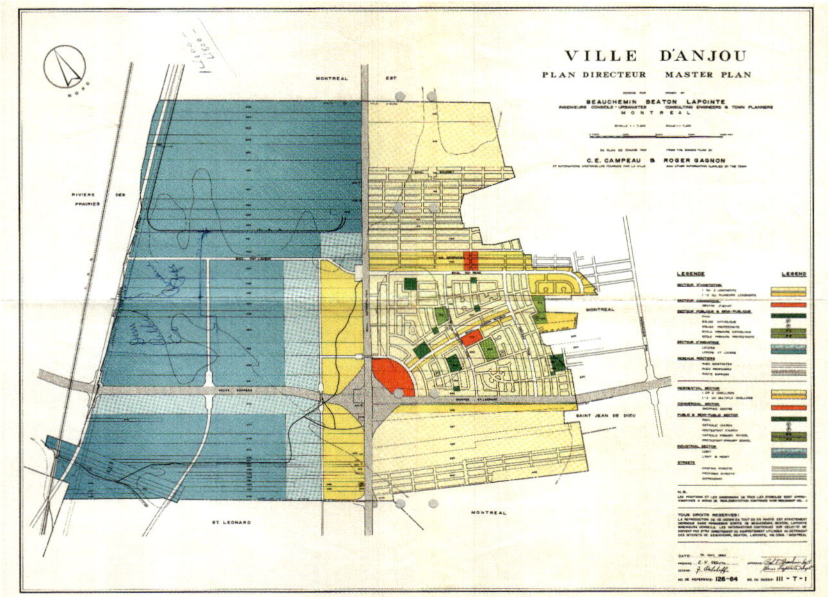

Figure 1. Anjou's master plan, 1960. Source: Archives de Ville d'Anjou

Figure 2. Aerial view of the highway interchange separating Anjou into four quadrants, 1976. Source: Photo by Henri Rémillard, courtesy of Bibliothèque et Archives nationales du Québec

its facilities as anticipated, BP was the first refinery in Montréal to announce its closure. As growth steadily migrated towards distant suburbs, Anjou's centrality—and perhaps even its viability as an autonomous municipality—were placed in jeopardy. Indeed, historically, the province of Québec has continually intervened to merge the financially troubled suburbs with the central city of Montréal.

Anjou was thus suffering from the leapfrog effect of urban development. And, less than twenty-five years after its foundation, the question of redesigning was already on the agenda. Building on the work of Ellen Dunham-Jones and June Williamson, Roger Keil has pointed out that 'much of the politics and governance of the suburban today relates to the idea of "fixing the suburbs"'.[9] But this urge to retrofit takes different forms depending on local context, resources available, and path dependency. As Glennon Sweeney and Bernadette Hanlon note, it often implies a desire to remain competitive in a changing metropolitan environment.[10]

Compared with its neighbours like Montréal East (where refineries and industry took up much more space and where there was little urban planning), Anjou's functionalist planning acted as an advantage, since its commercial and residential sectors were less affected by industrial pollution.[11] In the early 1980s, the newly elected local administration relied on planning to renew the city's image and consolidate its peripheral centrality. The idea was to break with the oil-based industrial past and assert the city's innovative, green character. To do so, the city council set in motion a series of reforms. Anjou created an environmental department dedicated to the beautification of its territory, and aimed to create a new, denser downtown area near the Galeries d'Anjou, with office towers and residential buildings. Mayor Jean Corbeil also reiterated the request for a subway station that would be located precisely in the new downtown area but—given his strained relations with the central city—all he received was empty promises. The downside of this quest for autonomy was a smaller share in metropolitan transit infrastructures.

Anjou also had to redevelop its industrial sector, starting with the enormous swathe of land left behind by BP. The city council favoured the development of a 'high-end' industrial park with a golf course. Anjou's political elite wanted to welcome a new type of industry in line with the tertiarisation of the economy: electronics, computers, and high technology. Anjou's initial master plan was never questioned. Residential or commercial functions were not considered and, if a recreational function was envisioned, it was only as an instrument to renew the industrial function and promote economic growth.

Accordingly, a golf course was built in the 1990s. The project for a high-end industrial park, however, was compromised since Anjou had difficulty attracting 'high-tech' companies. Instead, following a trend common to many North American suburban areas, the borough became a major logistics centre thanks to its proximity to two major highways. Anjou today hosts several massive delivery warehouses and Amazon is planning to build an additional warehouse on a huge stretch of land formerly owned by Shell, which straddles Anjou and Montréal East.[12]

Thus, despite the hopes of the 1980s, heavy industry has not been replaced by high-tech companies, but rather by logistics warehouses. While gasoline is no longer produced in Anjou, it is still consumed in massive quantities by trucks and cars—mainly belonging to workers and inhabitants for whom the deficient state of public transit makes alternative commuting options unfeasible. Still, the densification of the Galeries d'Anjou area has been quite successful. High-rise apartments and corporate headquarters, for instance, were built around Anjou's main boulevard (see Figure 3), to which a bicycle path was added. Some see this redevelopment as continuous with the emergence of a new form of viable community[13], though one with very little interactivity with the neighbouring industrial park (from which it is still separated by design).

Continuity, Change, and Anticipation in a Transitional Centrality

Like many other North American inner-ring suburbs, Anjou was only for a short time—maybe fifteen years at best—the embodiment of an up-to-date peripheral centrality, with its affluent commuters and indefinite economic growth.[14] However, even if Anjou is no longer what it once was, it remains an important second-tier peripheral centrality in the grand scheme of Montréal's metropolis. Local elites also retain the idea that their community is different from the central city, and they seek to preserve this difference through urban redesign and new business development. This case shows how important it is to understand peripheral centralities as transitional spaces, even more so since the formation of peripheral centrality is usually based on anticipations of progress that may well prove misleading or become outdated.

Figure 3. View of the surroundings of the Galeries d'Anjou mall.
Source: Photo by Axel Drainville, 2019, courtesy of Flickr

Figure 4. Wasteland near Anjou's golf course.
Source: Photo by Renard Frak, 2021, courtesy of Flickr

In Anjou, even the golf course was a short-lived option, and is now the site of an important political struggle for land protection. Over the last two decades, the Montréal Metropolitan Community and the central city have been actively seeking to protect green open spaces. Protecting the Metropolitan Golf Club's land is justified for the ecosystem benefits it provides at the metropolitan level. Moreover, the land north of the golf course is now owned by the City of Montréal and is officially designated as a nature park. But it remains virtually inaccessible to the public and to Anjou residents.

A ghost park, sited beside warehouses and a golf course waiting to be something else, hardly looks like a persistent centrality.[15] But it is fertile ground for a clash of visions over progress and future centrality, especially in light of the central city's desire to be a leader in nature-based solutions for climate change adaptation. On the one hand, the central city believes that this site could become one of the most important nature parks on the whole Island of Montréal. On the other, local authorities see it as an opportunity to accommodate new warehouses and consolidate the economic centrality that Anjou has always sought to embody.

Conclusion: The Contemporary Politics of Peripheral Autonomy

While there are now many metropolitan policies in Canada aimed at reshaping suburban development through densification and the protection of green spaces, Jill L. Grant has shown that not all localities comply straightforwardly with these policies.[16] It is important to understand how and why this resistance is expressed, even more so in a suburb like Anjou, which has always prided itself on being at the cutting edge of urban planning. Our case study shows that, for Anjou leaders, the implementation of prohibitive zoning on the land of the Metropolitan Golf Club rehashes a familiar narrative: it is a central city-driven measure that does not respect local autonomy. Their opposition is thus explained not only by the promotion of economic development, but by a historical defence of local autonomy and a representation of their suburban community as an innovative centrality. In other words, past dreams of autonomous peripheral centrality are not easily put aside.

Figure 5. View of Anjou's golf course. Source: Photo by Clarence Hatton-Proulx, 2021

Endnotes:

1 Nijman, J. *The Life of North American Suburbs: Imagined Utopias and Transitional Spaces.* University of Toronto Press, 2020.

2 A similar claim is made in Bérubé, H. *Des sociétés distinctes: Gouverner les banlieues bourgeoises de Montréal, 1880–1939.* McGill-Queen's University Press, 2014.

3 Dilworth, R. *The Urban Origins of Suburban Autonomy.* Harvard University Press, 2005.

4 Ekers, M., Hamel P., and Keil R. Governing Suburbia: Modalities and Mechanisms of Suburban Governance, *Regional Studies, 46* (3), 2012, pp. 405–422.

5 Mercure Jolette, F., Hatton-Proulx, C., and Van Neste, S. L. Mobilizing Suburban Stereotypes: The Case of Ville d'Anjou (1956–1973), *Journal of Urban History, 50* (1), 2024, pp. 98–122.

6 Scott, J. C. *Seeing Like a State: How Certain Schemes to Improve the Human Condition Have Failed.* Yale University Press, 1999.

7 Hein, C. (ed.) *Oil Spaces: Exploring the Global Petroleumscape.* Routledge, 2021.

8 Mercure Jolette, Hatton-Proulx, and Van Neste, 2024, *op. cit.*

9 Keil, R. *Suburban Planet: Making the World Urban from the Outside In.* Polity, 2017, p. 192; Dunham-Jones, E. and Williamson J. *Retrofitting Suburbia, Updated Edition: Urban Design Solutions for Redesigning Suburbs.* Wiley, 2011.

10 Sweeney, G. and Hanlon B. From Old Suburb to Post-Suburb: The Politics of Retrofit in the Inner Suburb of Upper Arlington, Ohio, *Journal of Urban Affairs, 39* (2), 2017, pp. 241–259.

11 Hatton-Proulx, C., Mercure Jolette, F., and Van Neste, S. L. L'héritage contrasté de l'âge d'or du pétrole: histoire et évolution des paysages de l'est de Montréal, *Recherches sociographiques*, to be published.

12 Dubuc, A. *Anjou accueillera les plus grandes installations d'Amazon au Québec.* La Presse, 2021; https://www.lapresse.ca/affaires/entreprises/2021-10-08/anjou-accueillera-les-plus-grandes-installations-d-amazon-au-quebec.php.

13 Kiti, M., Sénécal, G., and Hamel, P.-J. La collectivité viable et son double: penser le paysage d'une banlieue péricentrale et dépendante de l'automobile. Le cas d'Anjou, in: L. K. Morisset and P. Dieudonné (eds.) *Patrimoines pour le XXIe siècle: Regards du Québec et de la Bretagne.* Nota bene, 2006, pp. 137–155.

14 Hanlon, B. *Once the American Dream: Inner-Ring Suburbs of the Metropolitan United States.* Reprint Edition. Temple University Press, 2012.

15 ICI.Radio-Canada.ca, Zone Politique. *Les parcs-nature fantômes de Montréal ouverts au public, à condition de les trouver*, Radio-Canada, 2017; https://ici.radio-canada.ca/nouvelle/1061070/parcs-nature-fantomes-montreal-ouverts-pas-amenages-terrains-payes-acquis.

16 Grant, J. L. Contested Spaces: Suburban Development in Halifax and Other Midsized Canadian Cities, in: Nijman, 2020, *op. cit.*, pp. 328–347.

Jakarta's Suburban Reverie

Dinar Ramadhani

Introduction

For many Indonesians, Jakarta represents the 'American Dream', a place where people can achieve prosperity and improve their quality of life. When someone comes to Jakarta, they aspire to earn higher incomes and thus provide a better life for themselves and their family. This aspiration is not without reason. In 2021, despite seventeen years passing since the stipulation of regional autonomy laws aimed at boosting economic growth outside Jakarta, 70% of Indonesia's money circulation and economic activities were still centred in this city[1]. This situation is supported by the concentration of both foreign and domestic investments in the capital, as evidenced by the increase in real estate development and speculative urbanism in Jakarta[2].

The premise that Jakarta is the city of hope still resonates strongly. The development in Jakarta and its surroundings contributes to the high migration flow in this agglomeration area. The Department of Population and Civil Registration of Jakarta recorded an increase in migration into Jakarta during the 2020–2022 period, before a decline in 2023 owing to migrants spilling over into Jakarta's outskirts, including Bogor, Depok, Tangerang, and Bekasi[3]. The massive economic activity taking place on the urban fringe—such as property, retail, and shopping malls—tends to attract migrants. Furthermore, the recent improvement in the quality of public transportation makes daily trips to Jakarta much easier for commuters.

Beginning in 1980, several new towns have been built around Jakarta which ranged in size from 500 to 6000 hectares[4]. After the economic crisis that hit Indonesia in 1998, only about three-fifths of these projects still survive[5]. From the developers' viewpoint, new towns in Jakarta Metropolitan Area (JMA) aim to: 1) comply with people's desire to live in a quiet, modern, and safe environment; 2) provide investment opportunities for the developers; and, 3) gain a financial profit[6]. The new town resembles those in Western societies, with exclusive residential areas in gated communities and standardised automobile thoroughfares[7].

BSD City is a satellite town located in Greater Jakarta, Indonesia, which has now entered into a phase of being a self-sustaining city[8]. The development of this city, which is run by a prominent private developer in Indonesia, marked the massive privatisation of land caused both by the aggressive movement of the private sector in expanding the business and the redistribution of power and authority from public to private sector in land development decisions[9]. After decades as a dormitory town, BSD City has evolved into a hub of opportunity with a robust economic base, assuming a new role in the national landscape. In early 2024, the President of Indonesia announced BSD City's designation as a national strategic project, focusing on education, biomedicine, and digital industries, spanning an area of 59.6 hectares[10]. BSD City exemplifies the concept of peripheral centralities: it has successfully transformed from a domesticated town, once intended as a mere residential suburb, into an economically and politically relevant periphery connected to the urban core of Jakarta. This chapter examines the challenges and complexities of BSD City's development from an urbanism perspective, considering its development as the new centre in Jakarta's periphery.

Architecture and Urban Form

BSD City was first referred to as Bumi Serpong Damai (BSD) and was initiated in 1984 by Ciputra Group, a prominent private developer, on a large uninhabited rubber plantation. Ciputra held a land permit for up to 6000 hectares. The first phase of the development (between 1989 and 1996) included 29,565 housing units in total, which consisted of 15,000 small-sized units, 11,000 middle-sized units, with the remainder reserved for large-size units[11]. At that time, the main target market of BSD was middle- to low-income families, reflected in the humble design and affordable price of the housing units in

BSD[12]. Ciputra is renowned for its commitment to (and consistency in) developing housing for all economic classes[13]. Under Ciputra Group management, the residential clusters were named after Indonesian and Sanskrit languages, including Giri Loka, Puspita Loka, Griya Loka, Anggrek Loka, Nusa Loka, and Kencana Loka. The first shopping centre in BSD, named BSD Plaza, was also constructed in the 1990s.

Following the economic crisis in 1997, ownership was transferred from Ciputra to the Sinar Mas Group which then rebranded BSD as BSD City[14]. With its aggressive approach, Sinar Mas applied a new strategy which aimed to develop BSD City as a modern and high-tech self-sufficient city, implementing an integrated eco-friendly concept throughout[15]. In line with this vision, the target market shifted to prioritise middle-upper class families, offering safe, comfortable environments and modern housing clusters in gated communities. These subsequent developments in BSD adopted foreign names, such as The Icon, Sevilla (Spanish), De Latinos (Latin), Freja Haus (Nordic), Tabebuya (Japanese), Barcelona and Madrid Shophouse (Spanish), and Eonna (Korean), among many others. The transfer of ownership between Ciputra and Sinar Mas has resulted in the diverse urban landscape we see in BSD City today, which features various international as well as local themes in its newer parts.

The style, design, and layout of buildings and public spaces make a significant contribution to any city's identity. In the case of BSD City, the urban façades create a confused impression, adopting wildly varying architectural styles. Each shopping block and housing cluster–as well as iconic or institutional buildings, including shopping malls, offices, and the university campus–look entirely distinct. This morphological and architectural hybridity resembles the notion of the 'blendscape'[16]. The eclectic landscape of BSD City and its neighbouring new town, Gading Serpong, inspired a group of talented youth to create a short film titled *Tour de Serpong*, which won the Europe on Screen Short Film Pitching Project (SFPP) 2020[17]. The movie tells the story of Anton, who aspires to attend university in Paris but is scammed by a scholarship agent. He ultimately ends up in Serpong, where he finds a semblance of 'Paris' just by looking at the eclectic buildings around him.

This 'internationalised' trend in the city's physical design is well-known in new towns across Greater Jakarta–not only in BSD City, but also in Alam Sutera, Pantai Indah Kapuk, Gading Serpong, and others. These new towns feature designs reminiscent of residential areas in advanced countries. Many are indeed designed and planned by expatriate architects and urban planners with limited knowledge of local planning, architecture, and culture[18]. Relph categorised the new town as a 'placeless' place in part because of its lack of character[19].

Single-Family Zoning and its Impacts

Urban planning affects how the city works more generally. As shown in Figure 1[20], the planning decisions have economic, social, and environmental impacts on urban form, land use, and travel behaviour. The development of BSD City began in response to concerns about urban sprawl. Ciputra, recognising the potential of a large, inactive rubber plantation located approximately thirty-six kilometres from Jakarta's city centre, envisioned building a satellite town to support Jakarta. The government agreed to give the development permit to Ciputra in the 1980s, resulting in BSD City having the characteristics of sprawl growth. According to Brody[21] the characteristics of sprawling development include: 1) low-density and single-family dwellings; 2) automobile dependency even for a short trip; 3) spiralling growth outward from the existing urban centres; 4) leapfrogging patterns of development; 5) strip development; and, 6) an undefined edge between urban and rural areas.

This planning decision has several impacts on the urban form. Based on the information on its marketing website, BSD City has sixty-five single-family housing projects in total and only four high-rise apartment projects, which classifies this city as having low density. This sprawl characteristic is further emphasised by the toll roads serving as the main access points to BSD City. By 2022, at least four toll roads connected BSD City to adjacent areas, including Jakarta, Tangerang, Bekasi, and Soekarno–Hatta International Airport. Meanwhile, the BSD City area has only two commuter line stations: Rawa Buntu and Cisauk.

Connectivity within the city itself is still highly reliant on the automobile. Most of the main roads in BSD City consist of three-lanes in each direction, separated by a line of trees. This condition encourages residents to rely on motorised vehicles even for short trips. In addition, single-family zoning is applied in BSD City, reflecting the

Figure 1. Froggy Floating Castle, which features a design reminiscent of Disneyland. Source: Photo by Dinar Ramadhani, 2024

Figure 2. The roof of 'Barcelona Shopping Line' adopts a classic European architectural style. Source: Photo by Dinar Ramadhani, 2024

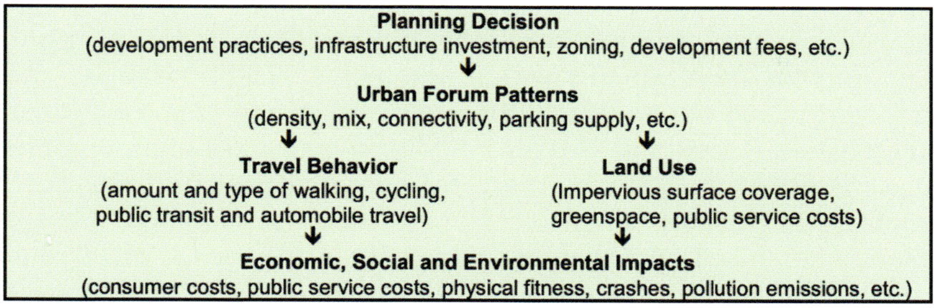

Figure 3. The impacts of planning decision on the city. Source: Litman, 2004

Figure 4. Three-lane roads in each direction are found in most areas of BSD City. Source: Photo by Dinar Ramadhani, 2024

utopian idea of stable neighbourhoods composed of single-family houses that are separated from other city activities. This zoning policy restricts development within residential neighbourhoods and has aggravated the housing affordability crisis and increased social segregation in the city. This also results in high rates of automobile use and emissions[22]. Furthermore, the non-motorised infrastructure, such as pedestrian sidewalks and bike lanes, are hard to find. Though there was a bike boom that began in 2020 during the COVID-19 outbreak, this trend has not resulted in the provision of proper bike lanes. Thus, cycling has remained something of a hobby, rather than a permanent option for mobility.

The sprawl has impacted the economic, environmental, and social facets of the city. The high dependency on automobiles generates additional cost for developers in providing parking lots and hits consumers with parking fees. Vehicle emissions and reduced green coverage—due to road and parking lot construction—both lead to environmental issues, such as urban heat islands and floods. A study[23] covering the Tangerang Selatan area, which includes BSD City, revealed that the region experienced a significant temperature increase in 2020 attributed to land development. In November 2022, reports indicated that BSD City had been hit by floods[24] (despite its marketing as a flood-free city).

On another note, BSD City continues to experience social segregation as a result of the development of gated communities. Ghazi Falah[25] stated that spatial segregation in Greater Jakarta can be categorised as 'self-segregation' or 'voluntary segregation'[26] since the middle and upper classes select their residential neighbourhoods for reasons of security as well as certain lifestyle perks. Another study[27] found that Indigenous kampong residents living in BSD City area now feel out of place and no longer recognise their native surroundings in the new urban landscape.

Conclusion

Despite being built entirely from scratch in the 1980s, BSD City is perpetuating the failures seen in most older cities, particularly in the U.S., where urban sprawl and car dependency dominate the landscape. The early signs of potentially alarming outcomes have already emerged, ranging from social segregation to rises in temperature, air pollution, and flooding. The development phase of BSD City is still underway, thus it is important to pay close attention to these issues in the next phases of its growth.

As a case study of peripheral centrality, BSD City demonstrates how a suburb that was once a 'bedroom community' has developed into an independent region that now plays a significant role at the national level. Having been fully managed by a private developer from the earliest stages of its development, this case study exposes tensions around several problematics that still warrant further discussion—among them the spread of enclave urbanism resulting in social and economic segregation, as well as issues of urban governance, particularly in terms of affordable housing, infrastructure, and public service provision.

Endnotes:

1 Nugroho, J. Indonesia's Lessons in Capital Relocation, *Nikkei Asia*, 2023; https://asia.nikkei.com/Editor-s-Picks/Tea-Leaves/Indonesia-s-lessons-in-capital-relocation (accessed April 27, 2024).

2 Herlambang, S. et al. Jakarta's Great Land Transformation: Hybrid Neoliberalisation and Informality, *Urban Studies, 56* (4), 2019, pp. 627–648.

3 Singgih, V. Arus Balik: Jumlah Pendatang Baru di Jakarta Pasca-Lebaran Diperkirakan Turun – Mengapa Jakarta Kehilangan Daya Tariknya?, *BBC News Indonesia*, 2024; https://www.bbc.com/indonesia/articles/cx7dnn864z1o (accessed April 28, 2024).

4 Firman, T. New Town Development in Jakarta Metropolitan Region: A Perspective of Spatial Segregation, *Habitat International, 28* (3), 2004, pp. 349–368.

5 Firman, 2004, *op. cit.*

6 Leisch, H. *Structures and Functions of New Towns in Jabotabek.* Paper presented to the workshop of Indonesian Town Revisited, The University of Leiden, December 6–8, 2000.

7 Leisch 2000, *op. cit.*

8 Firman, T. and Fahmi, F. Z. The Privatization of Metropolitan Jakarta's (Jabodetabek) Urban Fringes: The Early Stages of 'Post-Suburbanization' in Indonesia, *Journal of the American Planning Association, 83* (1), 2017, pp. 68–79.

9 Firman and Fahmi 2017, *op. cit.*
10 Nugroho, M. R. A. Terungkap! Alasan Jokowi Tunjuk BSD Masuk Proyek Strategis Nasional, *CNBC Indonesia*, March 27, 2024; https://www.cnbcindonesia.com/market/20240327163241-17-526061/terungkap-alasan-jokowi-tunjuk-bsd-masuk-proyek-strategis-nasional (accessed May 31, 2024).
11 Fadhilah, A. N. ABCD Tentang BSD City, *huni.id*, 2022; https://www.huni.id/blog/abcd-tentang-bsd-city (accessed December 4, 2022).
12 Mega. BSD 101, *BSD City*, 2021; https://bsd-city.com/bsd/ (accessed December 4, 2022).
13 Alexander, H. B. Menyoal 'Terjungkalnya' Ciputra Group di Tangan Sinarmas Land Group Halaman All, *KOMPAS.com*, September 7, 2015; https://properti.kompas.com/read/2015/09/07/070000521/Menyoal.Terjungkalnya.Ciputra.Group.di.Tangan.Sinarmas.Land.Group?page=all (accessed December 4, 2022).
14 Alexander 2022, *op. cit.*
15 Mega. BSD 101, *BSD City*, 2021; https://bsd-city.com/bsd/ (accessed December 4, 2022).
16 Maginn, P. J. and Anacker, K. B. *Suburbia in the 21st Century: From Dreamscape to Nightmare?* Routledge, 2022, pp. 1–22.
17 Alexander, H. B. and Ruhulassin, M. F. Terinspirasi Kawasan Gading Serpong, Film Ini Tampil di Eos 2021, *KOMPAS.com*, September 30, 2021; https://www.kompas.com/properti/read/2021/09/30/183000921/terinspirasi-kawasan-gading-serpong-film-ini-tampil-di-eos-2021 (accessed May 31, 2024).
18 Firman, T. New Town Development in Jakarta Metropolitan Region: A Perspective of Spatial Segregation, *Habitat International, 28* (3), 2004, pp. 349–368.

19 Relph, E. *Place and Placelessness.* Pion Books, 1976.
20 Litman, T. *Evaluating Transportation Land Use Impacts.* Victoria Transport Policy Institute, 2004.
21 Brody, S. The Characteristics, Causes, and Consequences of Sprawling Development Patterns in the United States, *Nature Education Knowledge, 4* (5), 2013, p. 2.
22 Ewing, R. et al. *Growing Cooler: The Evidence on Urban Development and Climate Change.* Urban Land Institute, 2007.
23 Prastiwi, A. D. et al. Urban Heat Island di Kota Tangerang Selatan, *Jurnal Geosaintek, 8* (2), 2022, p. 182.
24 Hambali. Diguyur Hujan Deras, Jalan di BSD Serpong Terendam Banjir, *SINDOnews Metro*, November 8, 2022; https://metro.sindonews.com/read/935653/170/diguyur-hujan-deras-jalan-di-bsd-serpong-terendam-banjir-1667905888 (accessed May 31, 2024).
25 Falah, G. Living together apart: Residential segregation in mixed Arab–Jewish cities in Israel, *Urban Studies, 33* (6), 1996, pp. 823–857.
26 Greenstein, R., Sabatini, F., and Smolka, M. Urban Spatial Segregation: Forces, Consequences, and Policy Responses. *Land Lines Newsletter of the Lincoln Institute of Land Policy*, November 2000; UNCHS (United Nations Centre for Human Settlements). *The State of the World Cities Report 2001.* Nairobi, 2002.
27 Mulyasari, D. A. and Sihombing, A. Feeling of Being Out of Place: A Case Study of Kampung in Bumi Serpong Damai, Indonesia, *WIT Transactions on Ecology and the Environment*, 2011.

T
ech
nologies

T
ech
nologies

From Central Peripheries to Peripheral Centralities: Housing, Uneven Infrastructure, and Urban Inequalities in Canada's Waterloo Region

Brian Doucet and Emma McDougall

Introduction

In the Waterloo Region (Ontario, Canada), gleaming new Light Rail Transit (LRT) vehicles glide up and down the region's central spine every ten minutes. At first, they seem out of place in this typical mid-sized urban area, which is situated one hundred kilometres west of Toronto. Home to a rapidly growing population of approximately 620,000, most of the Waterloo Region is decidedly car-oriented. This is unsurprising given most of the population lives and works in areas constructed after World War II, when the assumption dictating land use, density, and mobility patterns was one of automobility. Suburban strip malls are the main retail hubs, sprawling subdivisions are where most of the population resides, and tech and industrial parks are major employment clusters. Older, more centrally located parts of the region experienced decades of economic and social decline.

These are trends which have dominated the geographies of mid-sized cities across North America[1]. However, in Waterloo, the LRT's arrival is reshaping the geographies of the peripheral and the central. After decades of suburbanisation, a new centrality is emerging along the transit route (and not just in the old downtowns), creating a linear spine of density near stations well beyond the traditional urban core. This both reinforces and spatially extends what is considered to be 'urban' in a highly suburban community.

This chapter explores shifting ideas of the peripheral and the central through the arrival of higher order transit, which has offered a once-in-a-generation opportunity to proactively shape *where* new growth and development take place. It draws on several pieces of research, all exploring the relationship between transportation and neighbourhood change. This includes partnership-based research with local housing advocates that helps us to better understand how low-income residents navigate more than CAD $4,000,000,000 worth of investment along the line, and the subsequent gentrification and displacement threatening centrally located yet socially peripheral communities. This chapter presents an overview of research including interviews with over forty local residents, all with lived experiences of poverty, homelessness, or housing precarity. In compiling their testimony, it aims to assemble and analyse not only their individual experiences, but their knowledge of the kinds of change taking place within their communities. This work was done in partnership with the Social Development Centre Waterloo Region and sought to render visible experiences, processes and patterns that remain undetectable in statistical analysis, as well as discourses that are not part of the mainstream narrative about the changes taking place along the new transit corridor[2].

Peripheral Centrality in Downtown Kitchener

Kitchener is one of three cities that make up the Waterloo Region. Like many mid-sized cities, downtown's once dominant position has been eroded over several decades. Long gone are the days when major national department stores and high-end fashion chains sought addresses on King Street. The suburban shopping malls which opened in the 1960s and 1970s sucked the retail life out of downtown. Deindustrialisation also took its toll, as factories began closing in the 1980s. Once a hive of industrial activity, the advent of free trade and a series of recessions eliminated most manufacturing downtown, though there remain many peripheral factories, warehouses, and logistics sites.

Around downtown, many of the early twentieth century residential neighbourhoods also fell into steep decline as mansions were subdivided into multi-tenant houses, providing cheap rent to those on unemployment or disability support. At its lowest point, during the early 2000s, downtown Kitchener played a very peripheral role within the region, save for a few administrative and cultural functions. However, as downtown became more economically peripheral,

Figure 1. The Countryside Line dividing the City of Waterloo and Wilmot Township. Source: Photo by Brian Doucet, 2024

Figure 2. Repurposed factories and new condominium construction in downtown Kitchener. Source: Photo by Brian Doucet, 2022

Figure 3. A new 138-unit condominium development on King Street West in Kitchener. Source: Photo by Brian Doucet, 2022

Figure 4. A renovated apartment on Weber Street in downtown Kitchener. Source: Photo by Brian Doucet, 2019

it also became central to the region's growing marginalised populations. In addition to low-end, primarily market-based housing, a cluster of non-profits emerged beginning in the early 1980s. These organisations catered primarily to the needs of a growing unemployed class and, more recently, a large homeless population. This support function is now juxtaposed with a new centrality that is developing due to the LRT. Starting at one suburban shopping centre and ending at another, the line runs through downtown Kitchener.

Beyond its contribution to the expanding transportation network, the LRT was conceived as a growth management tool, with the goal of limiting sprawl and encouraging new development within the existing urban footprint. As a planning and land-use tool, the LRT has been incredibly successful, working to shift where the bulk of new development takes place[3]. An emerging skyline of residential towers accompanies many of the LRT stops in downtown Kitchener and the neighbouring City of Waterloo.

To achieve this density, the LRT works in collaboration with the Countryside Line, a growth boundary around the region's cities and towns. Hard boundaries between subdivisions and farmland hold (more or less) firm, while along the LRT line, new condominiums and apartment towers are sprouting up where low-rise structures, long-abandoned factories and parking lots stood for decades.

A New City Emerges, but for Whom?

This renewed centrality within the urban core is focused on a new (middle-class) urbanity based around the tech sector, trendy lifestyles, and non-car dependency. Mobility includes not only the LRT, but enhanced walking and cycling infrastructure, aspects of an urban lifestyle that are valued by residents living in central neighbourhoods, forming a distinct part of their urban identity[4].

However, there is a concern that despite increasing transportation accessibility, these areas will become less accessible for those on lower incomes. Gentrification of older housing and new condominium developments do not exist in a vacuum, and the loss of affordable housing is a major concern. Some of this loss happens through 'demoviction'—when residential units are demolished to make way for new development. When interviewed in 2021, Kate, a resident with lived experience of poverty and housing precarity, succinctly stated: 'They knocked down eight or nine houses for that. And then they'll put up condos that the people in the houses couldn't possibly afford'. Another resident, Mike, also commented on what this development/loss means:

> It used to be a much older apartment building, smaller as well. It was an affordable place to live... It was a place you could live if you were on Ontario Works (OW), financial assistance or you only worked part time; you could definitely afford to live in this place. Looking at it now, the rent has got to start at around CAD $1,200/month. It's just one more place in my city where I can't afford to live anymore; a lot of people couldn't afford to live at. It's upsetting.

While demovictions do occur, 'renovictions' are far more common. A renoviction occurs when tenants are evicted under the guise of renovations. In most cases, they are unable to return once the renovations are completed, despite their right to do so. Kathy's description of how tenants were forced out of an apartment near City Hall is typical of dozens of small and medium-sized apartments throughout the downtown core:

> The apartments were all old, but they were cheap, heated and everything. My friend lived up there and he was told that all the tenants had to be out within two months' time, that the place was being renovated. [The landlord] had to do all the apartments up. They all had to be renovated all over. So everybody, not just him, everybody in the place moved. And there were three floors... Well they said they were going to do it up, and you can move back in but the rent would be very, very high. The landlord told him the new people that took it over, that rent's up high now. And they've got security at the bottom to get in, brand-new elevator in the place. All the places are done up with new appliances and everything—doubled its price.

Juxtaposed with Kathy's experiences, the co-owners of the building were quoted in the local newspaper after the renovations were completed. Here, they discuss how projects such as this are part of a new downtown: 'The uptake has been unbelievable. We put them on the market about a month ago. The whole top floor is leased. The second floor is two-thirds leased and we are starting to lease on the first floor, which isn't finished yet. ... We are finding a cross-section of people that seems to be growing who don't even have vehicles anymore'.[5]

Rethinking the Periphery beyond the Urban Core

Across Canada and beyond, poverty is increasingly concentrated within inner suburban areas largely constructed in the decades after World War II, particularly in large cities. Sandwiched between gentrifying neighbourhoods downtown and newer suburban areas on the spatial fringes, the inner suburbs are positioned as the 'antithesis' of the urban core, and are 'framed as a space filled with decay, where life is short, undesirable, unexciting, and devoid of any real culture'.[6] The Toronto-based author and placemaker, Jay Pitter, described the inner suburbs as *forgotten densities*, where substandard and inadequate housing intersect with a lack of transportation options, over-policing, and predatory businesses[7].

But even here, when new transit is built, gentrification and displacement tend to follow. Along the LRT corridor, there is a huge incentive to 'reposition' ageing apartment buildings[8] given their new 'centrality' within the region's transportation infrastructure network. Tenants we interviewed spoke of profit squeezing by landlords that contributed to deteriorating living conditions. Cutting back on maintenance, ignoring tenants' concerns, unsafe buildings, and outright harassment are common for those residing in inner suburban apartments, particularly for minority tenants. Eviction Prevention WR, a programme established by the Social Development Centre Waterloo Region, calls this 'forced eviction': when 'landlords harass people to the point where they feel so unsafe, that they feel like they have no other option but to leave'.

There were also many stories of renovictions not dissimilar to those happening in the gentrifying downtown core. In Sam's inner suburban building, situated not far from the LRT:

> They manage to bully people to get out. And the initial thing said that they had to update the plumbing and the electrical and they were going to redo the exterior. And then I said, "Well, how long do I need to be out of the apartment, so I could make plans?" And they said, "Between 8 and 18 months".

The pressure to redevelop ageing, low-rise housing near stations in the inner suburbs is immense. The LRT alters the relative position of these peripheral areas by placing them prominently within the region's transportation infrastructure. It connects these peripheral localities to premier infrastructure[9], lending them a new centrality.

(Auto)mobility as a Defining Boundary between the Central and the Peripheral

Morphology and infrastructure intersect to define emerging fault lines that centre around mobility options in different parts of the city.[10] The LRT corridor is emerging as a distinct place which is denser and less car-oriented than the vast areas surrounding it.

The LRT is doing what it is intended to do: namely, limiting sprawl at the fringes of the region by providing the incentive to create a dense new city along its route. The new urbanity that is emerging along the line is extending beyond downtowns areas into parts of the inner suburbs served by the line. Access to different transportation infrastructure becomes the new fault line as downtowns revive and some peripheral areas become more central. Urban residents also feel that their urbanity is validated by the LRT and see greater lifestyle connections to big cities such as Toronto, rather than their suburban neighbours a few kilometres away.[11]

In Kitchener, the marketing for two recent housing projects (both by the same developer) speaks to the relationship between mobility, morphology, and infrastructural centrality. In one project, situated on the site of a former factory near downtown Kitchener, the logo features a bicycle. Named after a popular recreation trail, the development's marketing materials evoke an urban lifestyle that is entirely distinct from the suburban experience: 'Your people are already here enjoying life.'

Figure 5. An LRT train running through a neighbourhood of older apartments near the end of the line in Kitchener. Source: Photo by Brian Doucet, 2022

Just a few kilometres away, another project frames mobility in terms of accessibility by car: 'Stay in touch with Kitchener–Waterloo through conveniently located city traffic arteries—shopping at Fairview Mall, swimming at the local pool or jump onto the 401 for an eagerly anticipated day trip in or outside the region'.[12]

Conclusion: Housing, Uneven Infrastructure, and Urban Inequalities

While new middle-class and urban housing options emerge, building and maintaining affordable housing near good transit remains one of the biggest challenges facing contemporary cities. Investing in higher order transit is one of the few truly transformational policies a local government can develop. But transit does not exist within a vacuum; the Region of Waterloo was very proactive in shaping *where* new growth would take place. However, questions about *what kind of housing and for whom* were left almost entirely to the market to determine, leading to a large supply of small condominiums primarily bought by investors[13].

To ensure that these new centralities are spaces accessible to everyone, governments at all levels need to be more proactive in restricting speculation in the housing market, reintroducing rent controls, incorporating inclusionary zoning in new developments, and using publicly owned land to create the types of housing that the market is unwilling or unable to build[14]. Without implementing measures such as these, the geographies of the peripheral and central will continue to shift, but who has access to the best infrastructure (and all the benefits that provides) will remain socially and spatially unequal.

Endnotes:

1 Grant, J., Walks, A., and Ramos, H. *Changing Neighbourhoods Social and Spatial Polarization in Canadian Cities.* University of British Columbia Press, 2020.

2 See https://www.waterlooregion.org/mapping-of-displacement.

3 Doucet, B. The 'hidden' sides of transit-induced gentrification and displacement along Waterloo Region's LRT corridor, *Geoforum, 125*, 2021, pp. 37–46.

4 Ellis-Young, M. and Doucet, B. From 'big small town' to 'small big city': Resident experiences of gentrification along Waterloo region's LRT corridor, *Journal of Planning Education and Research, 44* (1) 2021; McDougall, E. and Doucet, B. Polarized Paths: 'Selling' Cycling in City and Suburb, *Tijdschrift voor economische en sociale geografie, 113* (2), 2022, pp. 179–193.

5 As quoted in Pender, T. Tech surge in Kitchener core prompts conversion of office space to apartments, *Waterloo Region Record*, May 7, 2016.

6 Sriskandarajah, A. The two Torontos: Young people navigating the core-inner suburb socio-spatial divide, *Canadian Journal of Urban Research, 30*, 2021, p. 48.

7 Pitter, J. Urban Density: Confronting the Distance Between Desire and Disparity, *Azure Magazine*, April 17, 2020.

8 August, M. and Walks, A. Gentrification, suburban decline, and the financialization of multi-family rental housing: The case of Toronto, *Geoforum, 89*, 2018, pp. 124–136.

9 Graham, S. and Marvin, S. *Splintering urbanism: networked infrastructures, technological mobilities and the urban condition.* Routledge, 2002.

10 Filion, P. Enduring features of the North American suburb: Built form, automobile orientation, suburban culture and political mobilization, *Urban Planning, 3* (4), 2018, pp. 4–14; Sewell, J. *The Shape of the City: Toronto's struggles with modern planning.* Toronto: University of Toronto Press, 1993; Walks, A. Stopping the 'war on the car': Neoliberalism, Fordism, and the politics of automobility in Toronto, *Mobilities, 10* (3), 2015, pp. 402–422.

11 Ellis-Young and Doucet, 2021, *op cit.*

12 Reid's Heritage Homes, 'Spur Line Common'; https://www.reids heritagehomes.com/site/spur-line-common-waterloo (accessed June 15, 2021); Reid's Heritage Homes, 'Welcome to The Ridge' (Lackner Ridge web page); https://www.reids heritagehomes.com/site/lacknerridge-condos-kitchener.

13 Outhit, J. Less than 25% of Waterloo Region's new condos are owner occupied, *Waterloo Region Record*, February 15, 2023.

14 Doucet, B. The 'hidden' sides of transit-induced gentrification and displacement along Waterloo Region's LRT corridor, *Geoforum, 125*, 2021, pp. 37–46.

Peripheral Centrality or Resource Periphery? Eastern Germany amid the Boom of Transnational Investment in Green Technologies

Hannes Langguth

Introduction

In 2018, the Chinese firm Contemporary Amperex Technology Co., Limited (CATL) announced a €1,800,000,000 investment in a new electric vehicle (EV) battery cell gigafactory, near Arnstadt in Thuringia (Germany). This is just one of many instances of large-scale transnational investments in green technology projects and associated infrastructures, predominantly in Germany's eastern states. Other examples include Intel and TSMC's multi-billion-euro semiconductor factories in Magdeburg (Saxony-Anhalt) and Dresden (Saxony), Tesla's 'Gigafactory' in Grünheide (Brandenburg), and LEAG's attempt in the Lusatia region (Brandenburg) to transform lignite-fired thermal power plants into Germany's largest green energy storage system.

The recent rise of green technology projects demonstrates the European Union's shift towards climate neutrality and diversified supply chains in a post-COVID landscape, which has in turn sparked a major investment surge in formerly peripheralised regions in Europe, including Eastern Germany. In addition to the ample space and proximity to renewable energy sources, many of these regions offer relatively low labour costs and favourable EU investment policies. As Eastern Germany experiences structural shifts, like the decline of the traditional automotive supply industry and the transition away from former coal-mining areas, the latest investments are accompanied by the promise of repositioning the region as a future-oriented 'peripheral centrality'.[1] According to the grand narratives of local policy officials and business representatives, the region will now take the form of a technological frontier, leading to new concentrations of employment, value creation, infrastructure development, and transnational connectivity in the context of Europe's broader green transition.

Eastern Germany's Chronic 'Left-Behindness' as Fertile Ground for Transnational Capital

After reunification in 1989/90, the new East German federal states were promised investments aimed at modernising and enhancing the environmental standards of the GDR's former key industries. However, what followed was the exact opposite. Instead of economic prosperity, industries were either quickly downgraded to the status of extended workbenches for mainly West German firms or even partially abolished. In the post-reunification era, for instance, the chemical industry—one of the most important industrial hubs of the former GDR—lost 150,000 of its original 180,000 workers, making it a prototype of the Treuhand's industrial 'sell-out' across the new federal states at the time. As a result, during the two decades that followed, industrial sector recovery took significantly longer than initially anticipated, with unemployment rates remaining persistently high for years and well above the national average. The migration of well-educated individuals to more prosperous regions in West Germany resulted in a substantial brain drain, especially felt in the loss of young citizens. Additionally, low birth rates exacerbated the population decrease, turning many regions into a downward spiral of continual socioeconomic deterioration, urban shrinkage, and infrastructural decline.[2]

The post-reunification period and ongoing peripheralisation have increasingly excluded regions and their actors from local economic and social resources, further limiting their influence on political decision-making.[3] This is evident in the developments around Arnstadt, Thuringia, which are reflective of many post-industrial regions in Eastern Germany. Despite facing sizeable economic challenges in the late 1990s, the promise of significant growth under a new market economy continued to fuel ambition. Following the transfer of a 'ready-made state'[4] from West to Eastern Germany, extensive land restructuring and institutional reforms were

Figure 1. Children playing between car wrecks during the closure and decline of the former GDR's chemical industry in Bitterfeld-Wolfen, Saxony-Anhalt in 1993. Source: Photo by Detlev Konnerth, courtesy of IMAGO

implemented. As public funds dwindled and municipal roles were diminished, local municipalities sold vast lands to the newly formed State Development Corporation of Thuringia. This corporation, operating as an extension of the Thuringian Ministry of Economic Affairs, was granted the authority to negotiate directly with investors. It not only increased the exclusion of local municipalities from setting investment conditions for industrial development, as seen recently with the Chinese firm CATL in Arnstadt, but also led to the persistent presence of large industrial parks and related infrastructure systems, which endure far beyond the erratic, short-term cycles of economic upheaval and profit-making.

Despite making significant economic and democratic progress, Eastern Germany has yet to achieve the expectations of West German living standards, even thirty-five years post-reunification. Economic, demographic, and socio-cultural differences not only persist but are, contrary to general expectations, becoming more pronounced.[5] Nearly 30% of Eastern German workers are employed in low-wage sectors—twice the national average—contributing to a widening wealth gap. Only 2% of Germany's inheritance tax revenue comes from the new federal states. Additionally, East Germans are underrepresented in top-level jobs, holding just 2% to 5% of these positions despite comprising 20% of Germany's population. Demographic trends worsen these disparities; Eastern Germany has a higher proportion of people over sixty-five years old and continues to face a sharp decline in birth rates and population post-reunification, unlike the more stable figures observed in the West. In Thuringia, projections indicate that only fifty young workers will enter the labour market for every one hundred retirees.[6] Even with positive economic developments, this demographic decline fosters increasing frustration and insularity for those left behind, making the region less attractive to newcomers from other areas or abroad.[7]

Persistent inequalities between the former West and East German states illustrate a chronic 'left-behindness' in Eastern Germany, which goes beyond the economic performance of the respective regions to include broader political and socio-spatial processes of restructuring.[8] At the same time, these conditions have created a fertile ground for new transnational capital, resulting in Eastern Germany's heavy dependency on foreign transnational investment over the past three decades. This pertains to large industries in particular, forcing the respective regions to maintain associated infrastructure systems through continuous new inflow of capital and debt.

The Boom of EV Battery Cell Gigafactories and China's Global Resource Peripheries

The rise of transnational investment in green technology projects across formerly left-behind regions is exemplified by the current boom in EV battery cell gigafactories. As of August 2023, fifty-eight of these large-scale projects have either been announced, are currently under construction, or are already operational. Geographically, these projects primarily appear in regions of Central, Eastern and Southern Europe, as well as in neighbouring countries such as Great Britain and Turkey (see Figure 2). Spurred by the European Battery Alliance policy—and several funding rounds targeting large-scale clean tech manufacturing projects under the European Innovation Fund—new gigafactory clusters have emerged rapidly across Eastern Germany, the east of Hungary, the southwest of Spain, and the north of France. All of these are formerly peripheralised regions with relatively low labour costs, and boasting a close proximity to the production sites of major European car manufacturers.

However, despite efforts to diversify global supply chains, the European EV sector remains heavily dependent on importing green technologies, including the associated expertise and resources, from East Asia, particularly China.[9] China's technological leadership in the field is self-evident: as of spring 2024, six of the top ten global EV battery cell manufacturers are Chinese corporations, alongside three Korean firms and one Japanese. Although China's outbound investment in the EV industry experienced a sharp decline due to global restrictions during the COVID-19 pandemic, it has recovered swiftly and now forms the mainstay of the country's economic engagement in Europe. The quick recovery focuses primarily on greenfield investments in new EV battery cell gigafactories, with many either under construction or already operational by the end of 2023.

Notably, CATL's large-scale development on the edge of the small town of Arnstadt is the first ever Chinese EV gigafactory in Europe. Built between 2019 and 2023, this is not only the firm's first manufacturing facility outside mainland China but also the largest single investment in the history of the Free State of Thuringia, with

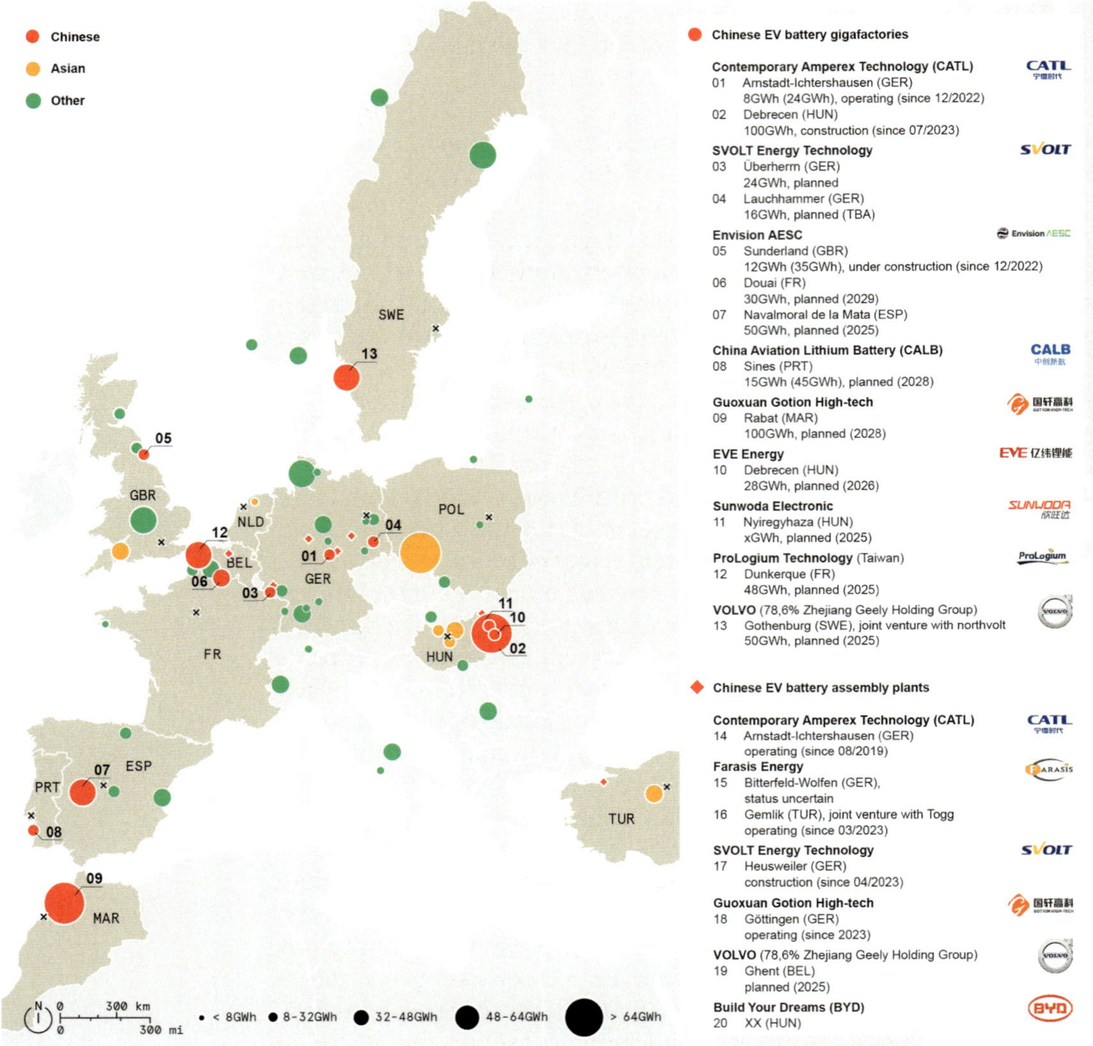

Figure 2. Overview of EV battery cell gigafactories (Chinese, Asian, Other), which are currently in planning, under construction, or already implemented in Europe and neighbouring countries. Source: Graphic by Hannes Langguth, August 2023, based on battery-atlas.eu (PEM RWTH Aachen University, 2022) and own research; no claim of completeness

investment exceeding €2,000,000,000. CATL is by far the largest EV battery cell manufacturer, with a global market share of 38% as of August 2023. In Arnstadt, they have established a highly automated, windowless industrial complex on a thirty-four-hectare western extension of the Erfurter Kreuz industrial park, measuring some 540 metres in length and 220 metres in width. Concurrently, CATL acquired a vacant office and module assembly complex, established a joint research centre with the Fraunhofer Institute for Ceramic Technologies and Systems (IKTS), and planned a new Rail Logistics Centre with Deutsche Bahn Cargo. They have also utilised Opel's freight station in nearby Eisenach and leased warehouses in Erfurt-Vieselbach and Magdeburg-Sülzetal, Saxony-Anhalt.

Tracing CATL's extensive commitment across the entire EV value chain, we can trace the formation of a 'global supply chain empire'[10] that aims to connect the firm's operations in mainland China to various resource peripheries. From this perspective, the region around Arnstadt becomes a strategic investment location that not only enables CATL to secure profitable access to the European EV market but also to spatially 'fix' domestic overaccumulation through geographic expansion.[11] Drawing on Henri Lefebvre's relational account of capitalist urbanisation—as a socio-spatial process leading to the formation of 'urban zones' (implosions) and 'urban fabrics' (explosions)—urban theorists have depicted such far-reaching networks of global value creation and accumulation as material and immaterial metabolic systems.[12] According to them, these systems serve the world's urban centres at the expense of ever-expanding operational landscapes constructed at a 'planetary' scale.

What does this actually mean for the Arnstadt region? To what extent is the region becoming an integral component in a system that extracts and generates value while reproducing uneven geographies of labour and environmental degradation? Conversely, how significantly do the developments surrounding new green technology clusters contribute to future economic and infrastructural centrality, potentially alleviating the region's chronic 'left-behindness'?

Figure 3. Drone image of CATL's EV battery cell gigafactory on the western extension of the Erfurter Kreuz industrial park at the northern outskirts of the small town of Arnstadt, Thuringia. Source: Photo by Marcus Glahn, 2024

Between Peripheral Centrality and Resource Periphery: Evidence from Arnstadt, Thuringia

The distinction between concentrated (cities, city–regions) and extended (hinterlands, operational landscapes) forms of urbanity, as encompassed by the planetary urbanisation thesis, falls short in two significant aspects. Firstly, as Lefebvre's notion of the urban revolution suggests, 'implosion' and the creation of 'centrality' can (crucially) evolve across non-urban places distant from urban centres.[13] Secondly, as Keil[14] elaborates, 'explosion' in the context of extended urbanisation is characterised by its numerous, disjunctive elements (e.g. suburbs, industrial parks, resource extraction sites), also operating its own dynamics and variations involving multiple implosions and explosions. Framing recent green technology developments as forms of extended urbanisation thus implies recognising emerging centralities (implosions) in previously neglected places, such as economic growth and employment. However, it also requires acknowledging the emergence and/or reinforcement of multi-scalar dependencies (explosions) triggered by centrality, including associated dynamics of socio-spatial peripheralisation and exclusion.

The relationship between evolving centrality and multi-scalar dependency is exemplified by three issues related to CATL's developments in Arnstadt, most prominently addressing the issue of value creation and extraction. While CATL's historic investment has partially spurred the local EV industry by attracting Chinese suppliers like KEDALI, SK Automation, and Wuxi Lead Intelligent, the regional benefits remain mixed. Around 1,500 jobs have been created, increasing the local population. However, half of these employees are Chinese engineers and office workers who are temporarily posted onsite for facility and supply chain setup. The rest are mainly assembly and logistics workers, mostly hired through temporary agencies. Additionally, local municipalities see little immediate tax revenue since CATL can write off its massive investment over twelve years. Meanwhile, the real estate market has inflated, and property prices have surged. Profiteers are primarily international investors, especially from China, who have recently acquired numerous properties in Arnstadt and nearby villages. Such outward-oriented value extraction 'constrain[s] "*in-situ* value retention"',[15] thus highlighting a persistent contradiction in developing large industries through transnational capital.

Moreover, the current developments in Arnstadt align with the temporality of profit-making, where speed in planning and implementation is crucial for securing market advantages. This has created a significant gap between the substantial investments made for CATL's EV gigafactory and the broader social-infrastructural needs of the local area. Although the gigafactory—situated in an isolated, island-like location at the northern outskirts of the town—boasts centrality in terms of connectivity to highways, freight transport, and logistics hubs, its production facilities and logistics infrastructures are designed solely to ensure the preservation of CATL's resource imports and supply chain efficiency. Meanwhile, public transport options for workers are scarce. Instead, buses chartered by CATL's Chinese subsidiaries transport workers between the factory and the surrounding villages and town, further marginalising local public transport infrastructure. Due to CATL's lack of extensive logistics infrastructure planning, local residents and municipalities must now bear the increased traffic volume, having to fund road expansions themselves. A failed freight station project, intended for use by multiple local firms, further complicates the situation, as CATL was unwilling to commit to a minimum volume of imported and exported goods. What remains are large built infrastructures mostly disconnected from local life, developed with insufficient transparency and without public involvement.

The third issue concerns the short-term cycles of value extraction and creation that are greatly mismatched with the long-term lifespan of the newly built infrastructures. This trend was already evident in the short history of Germany's new federal states. One prescient example is the German state-driven solar boom, which was expected to trigger an industrial renaissance over a decade ago but left behind vacant production buildings now utilised by CATL in Thuringia and other green technology investors in Saxony-Anhalt and Brandenburg. However, in light of ongoing competition between East Asian and Western EV battery cell manufacturers (as well as tense relations between China and the EU), the future of CATL's presence in Arnstadt remains highly uncertain. At the end of 2023, CATL announced it would no longer pursue the originally planned three-phase expansion of the gigafactory, opting instead to build a new gigafactory three times larger in Debrecen, Hungary. Due to an overvalued EV market and a lack of orders, CATL furloughed many employees in Arnstadt in early 2024. This demonstrates that rapid

Figure 4. Bus belonging to a Chinese subsidiary from Eastern Europe chartered by CATL, transporting workers between the new EV battery cell gigafactory and the accommodation (mostly rented by Chinese agencies) in the surrounding villages and small towns. Source: Photo by Marcus Glahn, 2024

Figure 5. Goods are transported exclusively by lorry in the region, leading to a significant increase in traffic and a burden on local residents. Source: Photo by Marcus Glahn, 2024

market-driven investment is accompanied by the possibility of rising infrastructural 'zombies' whenever profitability wanes and capital is withdrawn.[16]

Conclusion

In conclusion, the recent surge of transnational capital into green technology projects in Eastern Germany presents a paradoxical development. While it introduces perceived economic opportunities for previously left-behind regions, it also brings 'multiple and risky attempts to forge new global-local relations ... without any assurance of success'.[17] The example of Arnstadt illustrates the significant influence of historically evolved conditions, emphasising the role of host-state institutions. Post-reunification restructuring of land ownership and institutional agency allowed state bodies to channel investment into new 'infrastructural frontiers', aiming to attract foreign capital to the region.[18] This led to entrenched and long-lasting path dependencies on single industries, compelling regional actors to leverage globally connected infrastructures and emerging markets within an increasingly multipolar world order.[19] However, this results in unequal social, economic, and spatial developments, which connect to and partly amplify the region's dynamics of peripheralisation.

This chapter thus highlights that the emergence of new economic and industrial centralities is inherently linked to their site-specific histories, driving transnational connectivity but hindering other forms of much-needed socio-infrastructural development within the region. For this reason—whether in the analysis of green technology expansion or beyond—any future examinations should aim to engage a site-specific, multi-scalar, and temporally attuned understanding of peripheral centralities.

Endnotes:

1 Phelps, N. A., Maginn, P. J., and Keil, R. Centring the periphery in urban studies: Notes towards a research agenda on peripheral centralities, *Urban Studies, 60*, 2023, pp. 1158–1176; https://doi.org/10.1177/00420980221135418.

2 Lang, T. Shrinkage, Metropolization and Peripheralization in East Germany, *European Planning Studies, 20*, 2012, pp. 1–8; https://doi.org/10.1080/09654313.2012.713336.

3 Kühn, M., Bernt, M., and Colini, L. Power, politics and peripheralization: Two Eastern German cities, *European Urban and Regional Studies, 24*, 2017, pp. 258–273; https://doi.org/10.1177/0969776416637207.

4 Rose, R. and Haerpfer, C. The impact of a ready-made state: East Germans in comparative perspective, *German Politics*, 1997; https://doi.org/10.1080/09644009708404466.

5 Mau, S. *Ungleich vereint: warum der Osten anders bleibt.* Suhrkamp, 2024.

6 André, T., Behr, M., Philippus, U., and Reuß, A. Das Thüringen-Paradox: Thüringen droht tatsächlich eine 'zweite Wende' – aber anders als von manchem erhofft, *ifo Dresden berichtet, 27*, 2020, pp. 17–24.

7 Schmalz, S., Hinz, S., Singe, I., and Hasenohr, A. *Abgehängt im Aufschwung.* Campus, 2024.

8 MacKinnon, D., Béal, V., and Leibert, T. Rethinking 'left-behind' places in a context of rising spatial inequalities and political discontent, *Regional Studies, 58*, 2024, pp. 1161–1166; https://doi.org/10.1080/00343404.2023.2291581.

9 MERICS. *Net-zero Europe risks a heavy dependence on China*, 2022; available at: https://merics.org/en/comment/net-zero-europe-risks-heavy-dependence-china (accessed December 22, 2023).

10 Khanna, P. *The Future Is Asian.* Simon & Schuster, 2019.

11 Harvey, D. Globalization and the 'Spatial Fix', *Geographische Revue: Zeitschrift für Literatur und Diskussion, 3*, 2001, pp. 23–30.

12 Brenner, N. The Urban Revolution?, in: N. Brenner (ed.) *Critique of Urbanization: Selected Essays.* Birkhäuser, 2016, pp. 192–211; https://doi.org/doi:10.1515/9783035607956.

13 Vogelpohl, A. Städte und die beginnende Urbanisierung. Henri Lefebvre in der aktuellen Stadtforschung, *Raumforschung und Raumordnung, 69*, 2011, pp. 233–243; https://doi.org/10.1007/s13147-011-0105-3.

14 Keil, R. Extended urbanization, 'disjunct fragments' and global suburbanisms, *Environmental Planning D, 36*, 2018, pp. 494–511, p. 500; https://doi.org/10.1177/0263775817749594.

15 Gansauer, G., Haggerty, J. H., Smith, K .K., Haggerty, M. N., and Roemer, K. F. Can infrastructure help 'left behind' places 'catch up?' Theorizing the role of built infrastructure in regional development, *Cambridge Journal of Regions, Economy and Society, 17*, 2024, pp. 393–406, p. 396; https://doi.org/10.1093/cjres/rsad032.

16 Carse, A. and Kneas, D. Unbuilt and Unfinished: The temporalities of infrastructure, *Environment and Society, 10* (1), 2019, pp. 9–28; https://doi.org/10.3167/ares.2019.100102.

17 Wiig, A. and Silver, J. Turbulent presents, precarious futures: Urbanization and the deployment of global infrastructure, *Regional Studies, 53*, 2019, pp. 912–923, p. 921; https://doi.org/10.1080/00343404.2019.1566703.

18 Schouten, P. and Bachmann, J. Infrastructural frontiers: Terrains of resistance at the material edge of the state, *Geoforum, 136*, 2022, pp. 219–224; https://doi.org/10.1016/j.geoforum.2022.06.002.

19 Schindler, S., DiCarlo, J., and Paudel, D. The new cold war and the rise of the 21st-century infrastructure state, *Transactions of the Institute of British Geographers, 47*, 2022, pp. 331–346; https://doi.org/10.1111/tran.12480.

Distribution at the Periphery: Inland Ports and Regional Infrastructure

Julie Cidell

Introduction

Logistics facilities in metropolitan regions around the globe must strike a balance between locating close to centres of population—thereby minimising travel to market/consumers—and locating on the edges where little congestion and plentiful land exist. The Chicago region, which has long depended on its access to hinterlands and distant markets along a network of road, rail and water infrastructure, exemplifies this tension well. On the southwestern edge of the urbanised area is the core of an intermodal complex that has transformed suburban development in this region. This is the continent's largest inland port—as large as the coastal ports of Vancouver, Canada, and Le Havre, France, in terms of containers handled per year[1]—and it deftly illustrates the ways in which infrastructure can make the peripheral central.[2]

The CenterPoint intermodal complex that comprises this inland port is sited here (Figure 1) for two reasons: flows and land, or mobility and fixity. The corridor to the southwest of Chicago has been a conduit for flows of people and goods for centuries: first waterborne, then by rail and then by road. At the same time, the military history of the region preserved a large swathe of undeveloped land beyond the metropolitan fringe, while providing intensive transport infrastructure that reinforced existing networks.[3] As suburban development has spread closer to this location, a new kind of land use has appeared: massive distribution centres and intermodal yards, generating conflicts between rural landowners and commercial developers that connect back to the city centre in surprising ways.

Military Peripheries

During the early years of World War II, the U.S. built a series of ammunition factories across the Midwest. Two of these were built in 1940 well beyond the suburban fringe of Chicago, later combined and renamed the Joliet Army Ammunition Plant (JAAP). The factories had to be far enough from settlements that military security and safety could be ensured, while close enough to the metropolitan area to enable a reasonable commute for its workforce. Out of many possible sites, this one was chosen because the federal highway Route 66 ran between the two factory sites, and three major rail lines existed either on or adjacent to those sites.

The arsenal produced ammunition for World War II as well as wars in Korea and Vietnam. It remained closed from the mid-1970s to the mid-1990s, when a reuse plan was approved consisting of three main components: the Midewin National Tallgrass Prairie, managed by the U.S. Forest Service; U.S. Army training lands; and, the first major intermodal centre in the U.S. interior. The intermodal centre was sited where TNT and other explosives had been stored for the purpose of making bombs, shells, and mines, which was also where the heaviest concentration of rail tracks were within the site. Today, containers arrive at CenterPoint on BNSF trains from the West Coast before being loaded onto trucks and travelling to distribution centres throughout the inland port area (Figure 1).

Figure 1 also shows the site's relationship to Chicago. This is where some, but not all, of the intermodal activity is directed. There are Amazon fulfilment centres and other warehouses that serve the Chicago market, but there is also the 1,000,000-square-foot Walmart distribution centre that serves the entire Midwest. Most of the truck traffic to and from this site heads north on federal and state highways but some of it goes east or west, connecting with other routes to St. Louis, Memphis, and Indianapolis. Nevertheless, this intermodal centre and the inland port more broadly remain part of the legacy of the transportation corridor that linked the Great Lakes to the Mississippi River, thus connecting Chicago and its military production to the world. Though existing on the outskirts of the metropolitan area, the centre nonetheless drove urban and regional patterns of logistics and distribution.

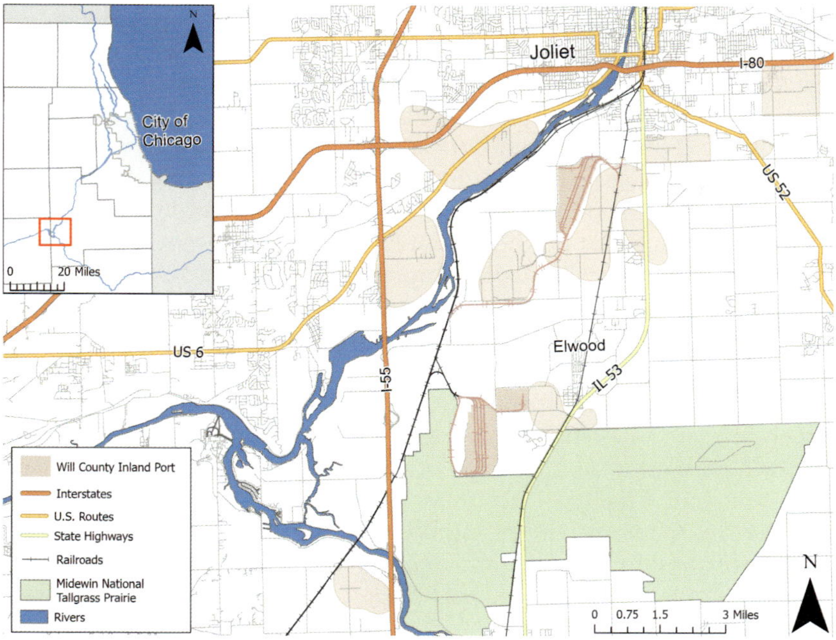

Figure 1. Will County inland port. Source: Map by Gabrielle Capone

Figure 2. Informal offsite container storage. Source: Photo by Julie Cidell, 2007

Conflicts with the Local

Of course, while the goal of logistics is to keep shipping containers and the freight they carry in constant motion, this aim is not always achievable (Figure 2). Even before the pandemic and its associated supply chain crises, there were often pauses in the flow of goods. Drivers might not be available; chassis that hold containers behind truck cabs might be in short supply; stores might not be ready to receive goods; or inflow might simply exceed outflow. Containers are allowed to stay in the BNSF intermodal yard for only three days before their shippers are charged by the day, leading some shippers to look for cheaper alternatives within the peri-urban landscape.

In urban port settings like Los Angeles, the images of colourful containers stacked high enough to tower over nearby neighbourhoods have caught the attention of activists, planners, and legislators. In peri-urban Chicago, the impromptu yards in which containers pause briefly before continuing their journeys are much lower density. Enterprising farmers offer space on their land for short-term container storage at a lower cost than the intermodal yard. Figure 2 shows the kind of interstitial storage space that has appeared around this inland port. The parked recreational vehicle indicates that this space was already used for informal storage before the advent of the intermodal yards, although the security fence around the containers suggests the space is becoming more formalised. These containers are parked on chassis because the cranes do not exist here to load and unload them as in an intermodal yard. These containers all appear to be functional, but there are other impromptu yards nearby with damaged or dented containers, which will likely sit for much longer before being recycled.

Just as in urban settings, however, nearby residents often object to the transformation of the rural landscape into a container yard.[4] In rural areas, there are usually no restrictions on what a landowner can park on their property, no matter how unsightly it might be. In peri-urban settings, however, there can be a push for aesthetic requirements from new residents who have moved away from denser suburban settings. Municipalities that are closer to the suburban side of the suburban–rural fringe have implemented requirements for berms, sidewalks, and plantings around elements of the inland port. In other places, the unincorporated land on which development sits means there are no such requirements, and functionality takes priority.

While container pauses can create aesthetic difficulties for rural residents and peri-urban municipalities, their mobility can create even greater problems because of their large number and rapid growth. Figure 3 illustrates a roadway to the south of CenterPoint, with traffic backed up from a freight train passing down the main Union Pacific line between Chicago and St. Louis. The mixture of FEUs, TEUs, bobtails, pickup trucks and cars in the image illustrates the conflicts that occur between users of the intermodal facility and residents and travellers in the surrounding rural area.

CenterPoint is technically located within the Chicago metropolitan area because it sits within Will County, one of the six core counties of the region, and parts of it even fall within the urbanised area as designated by the U.S. Census. But this is a rural setting. The roads that connect CenterPoint to the region's interstate highways were and are largely two-lane roads. A mile west of CenterPoint, the Interstate 55 exit had to be moved a mile to the south to provide additional queuing space on the exit ramp because lines of trucks were backing up onto the highway itself. The trucks heading east and west to other interstates pass along rural roads that are made to carry a few cars an hour, not dozens of fully loaded trucks. Because the responsibility for road maintenance falls on unincorporated townships, there are scarce funds available to strengthen or even repair the roads.

There are also the literal conflicts between rural drivers and semi-trucks. The small town of Elwood, located at the eastern exit of CenterPoint, persuaded the state to close a grade crossing over the Union Pacific line because of trucks frequently breaking through the railroad gates, including one incident where a passenger train almost hit a truck stopped on the tracks.[5] Local residents are extremely worried not only about the long lines of trucks blocking their usual routes, but the increasing number of crashes between semi-trucks and cars, some of which have been fatal.

A proposed project to alleviate the stress on rural roads, the Illiana Expressway, would have connected the CenterPoint site to the eastern interstates via a privatised toll road. Nevertheless, most local residents opposed the project because it would have commandeered farmland and the emissions and noise problems would remain. The expressway was not approved by CMAP, the Chicago Metropolitan

Figure 3. Trucks leaving the intermodal facility wait at a rural train crossing. Source: Photo by Julie Cidell, 2016

Agency for Planning (the organisation which spends federal transportation dollars within the region), because it was too peripheral to the metropolitan area, both in geographical terms and because any congestion improvements it provided would be a drop in the bucket compared to major bottlenecks elsewhere in the region. There are now plans for a private toll bridge over the Des Plaines River that would allow for a northern exit from the intermodal complex directly onto Interstate 80. However, there would still be considerable truck traffic on rural roads from current developments, not to mention the prospect of future expansion.

Future Logistics Centralisation on the Urban Periphery

From its beginnings as a component of the JAAP reuse plan, logistics development at the southwestern edge of the Chicago metropolitan area has exploded. The tiny municipality of Elwood has struggled to deal with increased traffic and crime stemming from the intermodal yards, although it has benefitted from tax revenue on newer developments that it has been able to annex. To the north, the city of Joliet is a rust belt town that has fought to replace the jobs lost to 1970s and 1980s deindustrialisation. Joliet sprawled south-westward in the 1990s to annex land for a riverboat casino, and north-westward across county lines in the 2000s to annex standard suburban residential development; it is now spreading southward to secure space for future speculative logistics development.

This southward annexation could include a new project on the northern edge of the Midewin National Tallgrass Prairie. The developer NorthPoint has plans for 4000 acres of new logistics development, more than doubling the volume of intermodal facilities that were developed out of the JAAP reuse plan. Local residents are strongly opposed to the plan because of the further increase in truck traffic on rural roads and, since 2017, an organisation called Stop NorthPoint has been fighting against this development. Their work is pictured in Figure 4.

While Stop NorthPoint has produced various maps and diagrams, this one is particularly interesting. It takes the footprint of the proposed development and places it over downtown Chicago. First of all, this shows just how large the projected space is, stretching three times the length of the central business district known as the Loop. Juxtaposing the footprint of NorthPoint's proposed development with the built-up area of Chicago is a reminder of how much land is under discussion here. At the same time, this image asks us to consider how rural land is so often thought of as 'empty' and unending, especially by urban dwellers. It also demands that we think about the multiplicity of land uses taking place within that footprint in an urban context, as compared to the solitary land use of logistics within the proposed development–itself a new kind of land use for most peri-urban governments.

Finally, and perhaps more subtly, the image demonstrates the ties between the peripheral and the urban. NorthPoint would be the same speculative kind of logistics development that has characterised

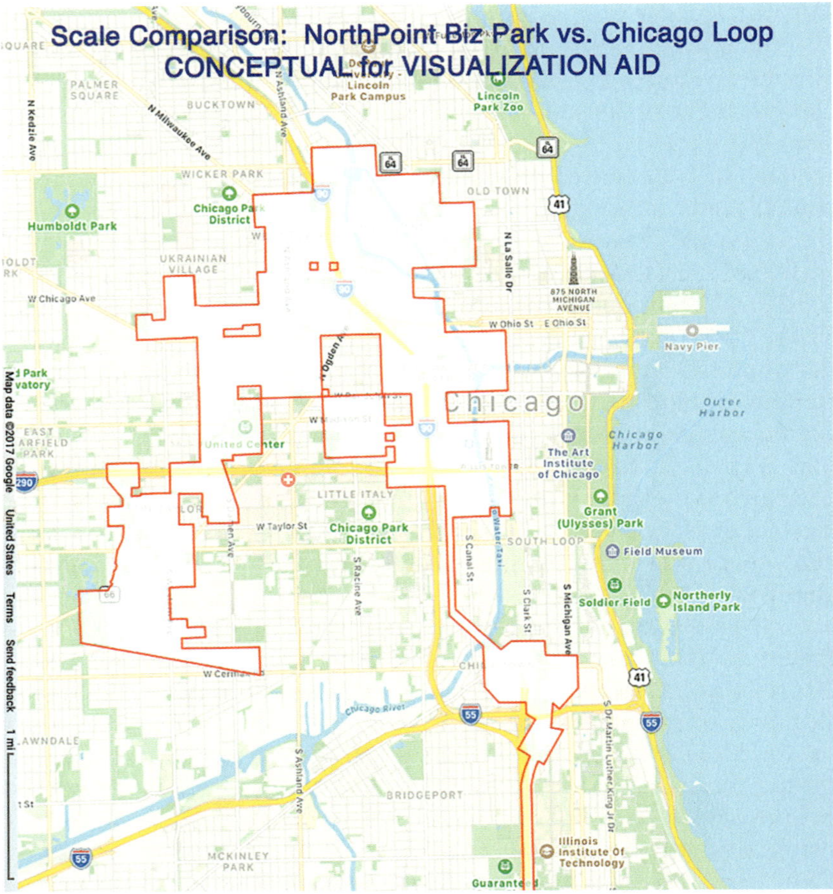

Figure 4. Map from Stop NorthPoint comparing the footprint of a proposed development to the City of Chicago. Source: https://www.stopnorthpoint.com/about/the-project

the millions of square feet built in this inland port in the last decade, most of which is Chicago-focused. Consumers in the neighbourhoods covered by the outline of NorthPoint's development will be acquiring goods that travel through that site, unaware of the displacement of farmland and the increased congestion and traffic that will result. Of course, the image does *not* show the urban distribution centres that also bring traffic and pollution to central city neighbourhoods, especially in the predominantly Latinx areas just to the south of the NorthPoint outline on the north bank of the Chicago River. These inner-city sites are the other side of the ongoing tug-of-war between central and peripheral settings for twenty-first-century logistics.[6]

Conclusion

Although the JAAP closure provided a unique opportunity for what was at that point a relatively unknown type of land use—namely, intermodal facilities—it has since transformed the rural area just beyond the southwestern suburban development edge of Chicago. Truck traffic heading to and from the site has heavily impacted nearby farm roads, and the short-term storage of shipping containers illustrates a new version of the tension between the ability to do what you want with your own property and neighbours' aesthetic objections. The local effects of a global transportation system are clear here, especially as proposed expansions are fought by neighbours concerned about the growing problems of safety and pollution.

At the same time, these images demonstrate the close connections between this peri-urban development and the very epicentre of the urban. Expansion opponents invite us to consider these two side by side, in mapping NorthPoint's development footprint onto the heart of Chicago. It is the connections between this rural site and the stores and homes of consumers that pose the current problems, ranging from farm roads ill-equipped to handle truck traffic to bottlenecks where expensive new bridges or highways might have to be built. This inland port might not have a coastline to hinder its immediate expansion, but it may nonetheless end up being constrained by its hinterland connections and clashes with traditional residential-led suburban development. As more of the North American economy comes to rely on fast, reliable freight transportation, conflicts like these will continue to shape the consumption patterns of some residents and the quality of life of others—whether on the edge of the metropolitan area or at its centre.

Endnotes:

1 WCCED (Will County Center for Economic Development). *Transportation assets*, 2023; https://willcountyced.com/site-selection/transportation-assets/.

2 Phelps, N. A., Maginn, P. J., and Keil, R. Centring the periphery in urban studies: Notes towards a research agenda on peripheral centralities, *Urban Studies, 60* (6), 2023, pp. 1158–1176.

3 Cidell, J. Canals, containers, and corridors: Bringing river geomorphology to North America's largest inland port, *Journal of Transport Geography, 115*, 2024, p. 103819.

4 Cidell, J. Flows and pauses in the urban logistics landscape: the municipal regulation of shipping container mobilities, *Mobilities, 7* (2), 2012. pp. 233–246.

5 Lafferty, S. Dangerous rail crossing in Elwood ordered shut, *Chicago Tribune*, January 16, 2015; https://www.chicagotribune.com/2015/01/16/dangerous-rail-crossing-in-elwood-ordered-shut/.

6 Acosta-Cordova, J. *The freight hub of North America: environmental justice issues in Chicago created by the movement of goods.* Colloquium presentation to the Department of Geography and GIS, University of Illinois Urbana-Champaign, May 22, 2023.

Time Out of Space: Data Centres on the Periphery of the Greater Toronto Area

Steven Logan

Introduction: Reading the Periphery

In his attempt to better understand the extremes of Los Angeles's architecture, the UK-based architectural theorist Reyner Banham learned the local language: 'the language of design, architecture, and urbanism in Los Angeles', he wrote, 'is the language of movement'. And so, to 'read Los Angeles in the original', Banham learned how to drive.[1] In her work on FlexSpace, Ute Lehrer wrote that the Swiss periphery was best and most easily apprehended via train. Most suburban, non-residential construction happens along major arteries—be that commuter-train lines or highway interchanges. Like Banham, Lehrer exchanges a static way of seeing for vision in motion, on the train or in a car, because 'the diffuse space which we encounter in the new peripheries cannot be grasped by traditional ways of seeing'.[2] I found myself in a similar situation when I decided to explore the data centres of the in-between landscapes located on Toronto's periphery. Car or commuter train? Helicopter? Denied access to a Google data centre in Oklahoma, artist John Gerrard hired a helicopter to 'tour' the infrastructure from above.[3]

The landscape of data centres on the periphery troubles ways of seeing because on the ground *there is nothing to see*. Not literally of course, but the buildings are tucked away and never recognisable as such. With their featureless façades, a warehouse of Barbie dolls could easily be a warehouse of server racks. Although anonymity may be the data centre's defining feature, each facility forms a nodal point in the multi-scalar infrastructure of the suburb which stretches time and space, extending beyond the city and the periphery into the region and the globe.[4] How does one 'see' all of this?

I have long given up on driving in the city, and I was not opting for a helicopter trip, so I decided to read the landscape in a different language altogether—namely, that of the bicycle—traversing it using a vehicle whose movement is significantly hampered by this inhospitable terrain. Attempting to negotiate this in-between landscape on two wheels is a task akin to the Situationists using a map of London to navigate the streets of Paris—absurd yet somehow revealing. On a bike, vulnerable and unprotected on roads occupied by trucks as well as the SUVs and minivans of the suburbs, the machinic landscape reveals its jarring temporal and spatial scales. Working against the grain and against the scale, the bicycle—that quintessential mode of city transportation—offers a juxtaposition of rhythms: it is human-powered with all the limits that entails when pitted against machines that increasingly sideline the human in the pursuit of technological leaps across space and time. This is the suburb as machinic landscape.

Anonymous Architecture

In 2020, the Greater Toronto Area (GTA) was the second-fastest-growing data centre market in North America, albeit a distant second to Northern Virginia, which has housed the infrastructure of the internet since its inception and is home to the world's largest concentration of data centres. The purpose-built data centre often exists on the periphery of cities or in small cities and towns—Facebook made Prineville, Oregon an early peripheral centrality—and has become the focus of urban land and infrastructure researchers. In their 2013 exhibition, *Networked Nation*, the LA-based Center for Land Use Interpretation (CLUI) drew attention to the new phenomenon of dedicated data centres emerging in office parks in converted or new buildings, clustering in the suburbs and small towns to take advantage of cheap land and access to power. It was a new kind of 'physical information architecture',[5] wrote the CLUI: the building as a machine, whose core feature was anonymity. 'Architecture without architecture', as the critic Karel Teige referred to the austere industrial architecture of the early twentieth century. Architecture in this case does not consist in the outward display of the architect's genius, but rather works here in a double sense: the layout of the buildings, per se, flanked by the architecture of infrastructure, server, and web application. When Microsoft or Cisco refers to data centre architecture, this is architecture optimised to house machines; it bears little or no resemblance to the exterior of the building, where architecture 'shows' itself to the world.

Tom Sieverts describes the in-between city as 'an anonymous space with no visual quality'.[6] Sieverts did not have data centres in mind, but it is a more than apt description both for the logistical landscapes where data centres are located, and for the buildings themselves. These buildings house the servers of some of the economy's most powerful players in finance, insurance, and banking. In his introduction to *Machine Landscapes: Architectures of the Post-Anthropocene*, artist Liam Young writes of the data centre: 'a building of extraordinary meaning that sits at the core of what it means to exist today, but at the same time turns its back on any expression of that significance'.[7] The aesthetic form of the data centre is distinctly anaesthetic.

Cycling through these landscapes on a brilliant autumn day was my own attempt to bring an aesthetic to the anaesthetic, to see up close and *unmediated* buildings that serve as the backbone for our very mediated existences. As Sieverts writes, 'only the sensitivity to its great non-aesthetic side, which truly represents the result of innumerable "emotionless" rational decisions, can stake out the way to a different handling of the *Zwischenstadt*'.[8] I was also taking further inspiration from Banham, who wrote somewhere that he would never write about a building that he did not visit himself.

The Machinic Landscape

Data centres redefine the suburb not as a place of residence, an appendage to the city, but as part of the infrastructural suburb of energy and computation that defies its peripheral location in its centrality to data processing, transmission, and storage. Whether its primary inhabitants have been humans or machines and data, the suburb has always been a machinic landscape of gas plants, manicured corporate office parks, highways, climate-controlled shopping malls, and Amazon and Walmart fulfilment centres.[9] The idea can be traced back to Le Corbusier's mantra that a house is a machine for living in, which was itself inspired by industrial architecture, and inaugurated on the ground with the mass production of apartment blocks in the Soviet Union and socialist Eastern Europe—facilitated by cranes and prefab slabs of concrete. Similarly, the architecture of post-Fordism is the architecture of the warehouse, the skyscraper, and the container.

And while the prefab apartment blocks were built to house people, the buildings that occupy today's periphery have become increasingly inhospitable to humans, designed not for people but for the care, cooling, and protection of rack upon rack of servers, or for the efficient movement of the automated robots in Amazon warehouses. These are 'architectures and infrastructures of a system not built for us, but whose form, materiality and purpose is configured to anticipate the logics of machine vision and habitation'.[10] With their primary focus on keeping machines cool, they are best seen as controlled environments: 'enclosed and engineered socio-technical spaces that create specialised "microclimates" for food production, but also ecological protection and human occupation'.[11] Here the atmospheric control is not about enabling plant or human occupation, but managing and controlling servers in the interests of protecting data and their global interests. These controlled environments ensure the life and maintenance of machines, so that humans can access the world from the comfort of their own phones.

Welcome to the Desert of the Real

Although the focus of the literature on media infrastructures (both popular and academic) has been on the 'hyperscale' data centres of the most visible corporations—Google, Amazon, Facebook, and Microsoft[12]—the Greater Toronto Area (GTA) is blanketed by a host of global players in co-locationed data centres whose anonymity is compensated by names that evoke the cyberspace of an early William Gibson novel: Equinix, Centrilogic, TMX, EdgeConneX (Figure 1), and Cyxtera (Figure 2). The actual data centres themselves are identified by codes that begin with YYZ, making them the informational counterparts to Toronto's airports. And, much like their neighbouring container facilities, they are 'the fringe that enables the centre'.[13]

The director of Centrilogic's Canadian facilities described data centres to my students in *Matrix*-like fashion: they are everywhere. You pass by them every day and will likely never notice them. I was assured there were at least seven or eight data centres along one minor street in Markham, although rarely if ever are they visible as a data centre with the signature air conditioning units on the roof—I found at least one of them on my bike tour, run by one of North America's largest data centre companies, Digital Realty (Figures 3 and 4). You would never notice the data centre that my students and I walked through because it took up one floor in a nondescript office building in Mississauga, adjacent to the city's most iconic residential towers (Figure 5).

Tucked away on the manicured corporate campus of the former headquarters of IBM Canada, on the border of the inner suburbs of Scarborough and Markham, is a key node in the financialisation of the periphery. Although the former IBM campus, with its carefully manicured lawns and vast parking lots, is a classic example of postwar corporate suburbanisation,[14] the complex houses probably one of the most important data centres in Toronto. Somewhere among the cluster of 1980s-era corporate architecture are the matching engines—servers that match buy and sell orders—of the Toronto Stock Exchange and the Montréal Stock Exchange, accessing the largest derivative markets in Canada. Live trading ended in 1997, and so no humans are involved in the actual buying and selling of stocks—it all 'auto-magically happens' here in Markham, as a director with the TMX Group that operates the data centre explained to me. The site was chosen in part because there are two feeds from the power grid, but the real advantage of co-location is not just about operating 24/7, but the ability to achieve a nanosecond advantage over competitors. Companies 'lose' one nanosecond for every extra foot of fibre-optic or copper cable. Co-location, or density for servers, makes the time between transactions virtually instantaneous. Markham is one of five nodal points that connect to the Nasdaq central data facility in Carteret, New Jersey: the other two nodal points are in New Jersey—Secaucus and Mahwah—and downtown Chicago and Toronto.

One of the GTA's largest data centres is in Vaughan, a burgeoning suburban centre built around the newly extended subway (metro) beyond Toronto's city limits. The data centre lies outside Vaughan's suburban centre, a sprawling 700,000 square feet nestled between the intersection of two of the region's 400 series highways—the 407 and 400—and an intimidating space to approach on a bicycle (see Figure 6).

The story of this building mirrors the history of the architecture of FlexSpaces and the general movement of industry away from the centre and into the periphery. The data centre is the former

Figure 1. EdgeConneX data centre in North York. Source: Photo by Steven Logan, 2022

Figure 2. Cyxtera (now Centersquare) data centre in Markham.
Source: Photo by Steven Logan, 2022

Figure 3. Digital Realty data centre in Markham. Source: Photo by Steven Logan, 2022

Figure 4. Digital Realty data centre in Markham. Source: Photo by Steven Logan, 2022

printing plant of *The Toronto Star*, which printed its papers from 1992 until 2016, when the paper closed the plant and outsourced its printing (getting rid of 220 unionised jobs, and sixty-five part-time staff). Previously, *The Star* had printed its papers at One Yonge Street, next to the shore of Lake Ontario and in the heart of Old Toronto. Like its counterpart in Montréal, *The Montréal Gazette*, both papers have outsourced their printing and both their plants have been converted into data centres: as Susan Leigh Star remind us, infrastructure is built on an already installed base.[15] While internet exchanges situated in downtown areas use conduits originally designed for telegraph and telex transmissions, such as 151 Front Street West in downtown Toronto or 60 Hudson Street in Manhattan, purpose-built data centres like the one in Vaughan reuse the spaces of newspaper printing, the infrastructural equivalent of the death of print.

Conclusion: Peripheral Energies

As I stood with my bike overlooking hydro fields, surrounded by some of the region's largest highways, an oil pipeline flowing underground, gazing at what used to be the printing plant of the country's largest newspaper, I felt with my body the scale and scope of periphery and centre come together in a confluence of transportation and communication modes. The bicycle may not have belonged, but I believe it gave me privileged access to the variegated rhythms of peripheral centralities.

If the monster home with its three-car garage epitomised the guzzling energy of the 1990s suburb, the energy-hungry data centres dominating the age of AI may define the suburb of the future. While the pandemic called attention to the energy demands of streaming, these pale in comparison to the energy demands of artificial intelligence as well as the increasing electrification of the cars sitting in those garages. The suburb of the future, as a peripheral centrality underpinning the world of AI and electric cars, will likely become the infrastructural flashpoint for the inevitable energy crises that arise. Then, the object of ire will no longer be *those other people* who live in the suburbs, but rather *all of us*, as appendages to the ever-expanding machinic landscape. Now, where is my bike?

Figure 5. Centrilogic data centre (in the building on the left), Mississauga. Source: Photo by Steven Logan, 2022

Figure 6. Digital Realty data centre in the former Toronto Star printing plant, Vaughan. Source: Photo by Steven Logan, 2022

Endnotes:

1 Banham, R. *Los Angeles: The Architecture of Four Ecologies.* Penguin Books, 1971, p. 23.

2 Lehrer, U. Images of the Periphery: The Architecture of Flex Space in Switzerland, *Environment and Planning D: Society and Space, 12* (2), 1994, p. 190.

3 Young, L. Where the internet Lives, John Gerrard: *Farm*, in: L. Young (ed.) *Machine Landscapes: Architectures of the Post-Anthropocene.* John Wiley & Sons, 2019, pp. 56–59.

4 Addie, J. P. Theorising Suburban Infrastructure: A Framework for Critical and Comparative Analysis, *Transactions of the Institute of British Geographers, 41* (3), 2016, pp. 273–285.

5 The Center for Land Use Interpretation, Networked Nation, *The Lay of the Land, 37*, 2014; https://clui.org/newsletter/winter-2014/networked-nation-0.

6 Sieverts, T. *Cities without Cities: An Interpretation of the Zwischenstadt.* Spon Press, 2003.

7 Young, L. Architecture without People: Neo-Machine, in: Young, 2019, *op. cit.*, p. 8.

8 Sieverts, 2003, *op. cit.*, p. 95.

9 LeCavalier, J. Human Exclusion Zones: Logistics and the New Machine Landscapes, in: Young, 2019, *op. cit.*, pp. 48–55.

10 Young, 2019, *op. cit.*, p. 10.

11 Marvin, S. and Rutherford, J. Controlled Environments: An Urban Research Agenda on Microclimatic Enclosure, *Urban Studies, 55* (6), 2018, pp. 1143–1162.

12 Edwards, D., Griffin, Z., Cooper, T., and Hogan, M. The Making of Critical Data Center Studies, *Convergence, 0* (0), 2024.

13 Manaugh, G. Where Tomorrow Arrives Today, in: Young, 2019, *op. cit.*, pp. 36–43.

14 Mozingo, L. *Pastoral Capitalism: A History of Suburban Corporate Landscapes.* MIT Press, 2011.

15 Star, S. The Ethnography of Infrastructure, *American Behavioral Scientist, 43* (3), 1999, pp. 377–391.

The Western Sydney Aerotropolis: A New Centre for Peripheral Sydney

Philip Graus, Robert Freestone, and Simon Pinnegar

Introduction

The recentralising of peripheral regions has a historical connection with airport development that is increasingly entangled with the rise of aviation as it enables globalisation. In the process, the production of urban space and the management of air space are intertwined through complex territorial governance. This is the case in Sydney, Australia. Greater Sydney's history as an aspirational polycentric city is a chequered one. The post-World War II period, when the notion of peripheral suburban centres first took hold, reveals a history of plans for outer suburban centres that were thwarted by poor governance, high costs of infrastructure, speculative pressures, and fluctuating political support. However, the parallel drive to develop a new international airport as an urban hub in outer Sydney represents the most ambitious attempt to restructure Greater Sydney as a truly polycentric metropolis. In this chapter, we outline the genesis, progress, and prospects for a case study in what Jean-Paul Addie terms 'aero-regionalism'.[1]

Post-World War II to 2014

Well into the post-World War II era, metropolitan Sydney essentially remained a monocentric urban region. Retail, industry, and community facilities followed the tentacular pattern of radial development to serve everyday needs in the unplanned diffusion of settlement.

The ebb and flow of continuity and disjuncture was reflected in a succession of metropolitan plans dating from the mid-twentieth century onwards.[2] Sydney's County of Cumberland Plan (Figure 1a) was designed to bring an end to the 'promiscuous urbanisation' of leapfrogging land speculation and ribbon development on the Cumberland Plain spreading westward.[3] The importance of multiple metropolitan centres was recognised, capturing the influence of Abercrombie's contemporaneous plan for London.[4] The proposal was to restructure the built-up area into community districts, enveloped by a permanent green belt, with rural satellite towns absorbing long-term growth. The 1947 Copenhagen Finger Plan inspired the succeeding 1968 Sydney Region Outline Plan (Figure 1b), which was made up of a series of radiating linear arms, interspersed by green, and punctuated by more strongly defined corridor-contained subregional centres.[5]

The policy of concentrating activity in accessible centres continued as a fixture in subsequent plans, which shifted away from overarching spatial imaginaries towards more incremental forms of urban management that guided—rather than strictly dictated—metropolitan form. The 1988 *Sydney into Its Third Century* strategy implemented a loose hierarchy of subregional centres sitting within blob forms, diluting the structured centres and bounded edges of Sydney's second plan two decades earlier.[6] Elsewhere, in the U.S., Jonathan Barnett expressed concern that planning and urban design had not kept up with the need to shape growth at the edges of cities, thereby creating amorphous megaregions.[7]

Sydney's western periphery continued to recede towards the Blue Mountains through the 1990s, with Parramatta emerging as Sydney's demographic centre—a 'city' with the status of a second metropolitan CBD. Even into the new millennium, metropolitan plans continued to embrace the global city, which was reflected spatially as a unitary 'global arc'. The revealingly named *City of Cities* strategy (2005) portrayed the arc as a suburban-encroaching economic corridor stretching though the Sydney CBD. The broader urban vision included an imaginary of five 'cities'.[8] Although the 2014 *Plan for Growing Sydney* lacked the overarching spatial clarity of *City of Cities*, it decisively extended the global arc westward, growing tentacles that reached out towards the northwest growth corridor and down to Sydney Olympic Park, thus cementing Parramatta's positioning as a key node in Global Sydney.[9] However, despite the projected shift

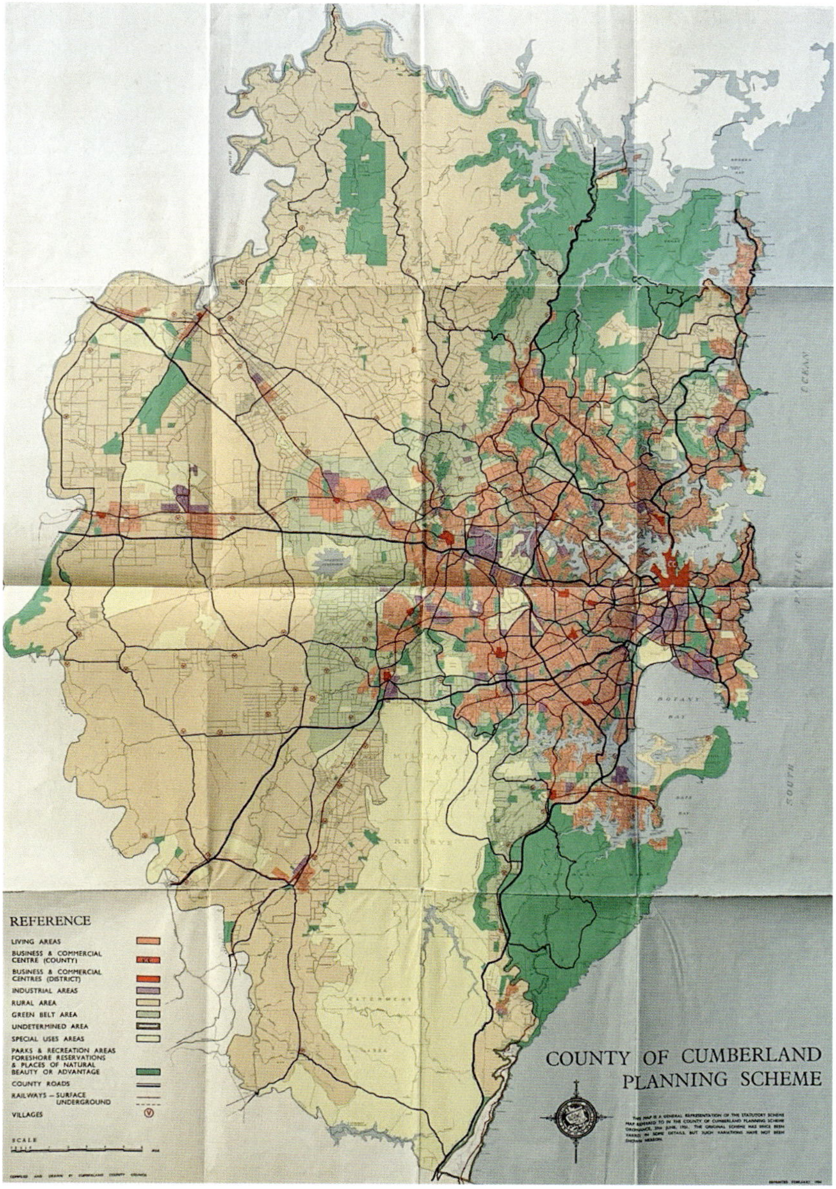

Figure 1a. 1948 County of Cumberland Plan. Source: State of New South Wales Department of Planning Housing and Infrastructure

of economic focus westward, the divide between a job-rich eastern Sydney (closer to the coast) and a largely residential western periphery remained stark, laying bare the relative failure of decades of polycentric thinking. Accordingly, the public, political, and planning divide between the 'two Sydneys' intensified.[10]

A Second Sydney International Airport

An account of Sydney's troubled fifty-year stop-start journey in planning and delivering a second international airport is reflective of the powerful push and pull of community, environmental, and political forces. Sydney's 1968 plan first identified the need for a second major airport, locating it outside the Cumberland Plain. Although aviation transport imperatives were a clear priority, political sensitivities stymied serious consideration for decades. Peripheral communities opposed the idea of either relocating or duplicating the noise and pollution associated with the existing Kingsford-Smith airport to western Sydney.

The 1988 metropolitan strategy (NSW Department of Environment and Planning 1988) identified a second major airport site in Western Sydney at Badgerys Creek, but the 1995, 1998, and 2010 metropolitan plans remained silent on this politically charged issue. With no concrete move towards the new airport, Badgerys Creek was mutedly designated as a 'potential' area for economic growth. While successive state governments remained uncommitted, the Australian Government progressively acquired 200 rural residential sites through the 1980s and 1990s. In 2014, the federal government finally committed to building the airport, delivering 'jobs and infrastructure' that signalled a fuller appreciation of Western Sydney. The 2014 metropolitan plan duly reinstated Badgerys Creek as an 'airport precinct'.

From this time onwards, growing concern around the lack of employment opportunities in Western Sydney shifted the strategic focus away from airport congestion and accessibility towards ensuring a more balanced metropolitan distribution of jobs. Arguments for the new airport—now seen as a high value job catalyst—strengthened alongside a shift in political sentiment as local councils and the Western Sydney Business Chamber saw the potential for a second international airport to generate significantly higher income jobs.[11]

In early 2015, John Kasarda, a leading international advocate for restructuring cities around airports, was commissioned by the Sydney Business Chamber and Liverpool City Council to prepare a report and present his findings at the Western Sydney Airport Conference. The presentation referred for the first time to a 'Western Sydney Aerotropolis', capturing popular and professional attention.[12] This reimagining of the Western Sydney periphery would inform a series of ambitious plans and initiatives.

A Metropolis of Three Cities

The 2018 *Greater Sydney Region Plan: A Metropolis of Three Cities* was made by the Greater Sydney Commission (GSC), established to lead Sydney's metropolitan planning in new directions.[13] It did this by instigating the most significant conceptual shift in Sydney's overarching polycentric form since the 1968 corridor plan jettisoned the Green Belt. The 2018 plan embraced familiar pro-growth and global city themes as the principal drivers but reimagined a metropolis of three distinct 'cities'—virtually eliminating the trope of peripherality (Figure 2).

Earlier plans optimistically assumed a 'trickle down' effect as the global economic arc radiated westwards from the eastern seaboard. More explicit aspirations of social equity and fairness underpinned this new plan's overarching metropolitan spatial form, which comprised three thirty-minute cities. The GSC Deputy Commissioner described the central vision as a 'rebalancing' of Greater Sydney. The intent was to dismantle the imaginary 'latte line' dividing eastern and western Sydney, both in terms of income and access to high value jobs and services.

The Western Parkland City

The Western Parkland City (WPC), envisaged as Sydney's third city, has thus evolved through the convergence of decades of planning dialogue about issues including: additional airport capacity, the neglect of the west, jobs deficit, strong regional sub-centres, aviation needs, disjointed governance and inadequate infrastructure funding, and environmental planning. Geographically, the WPC covers an area of

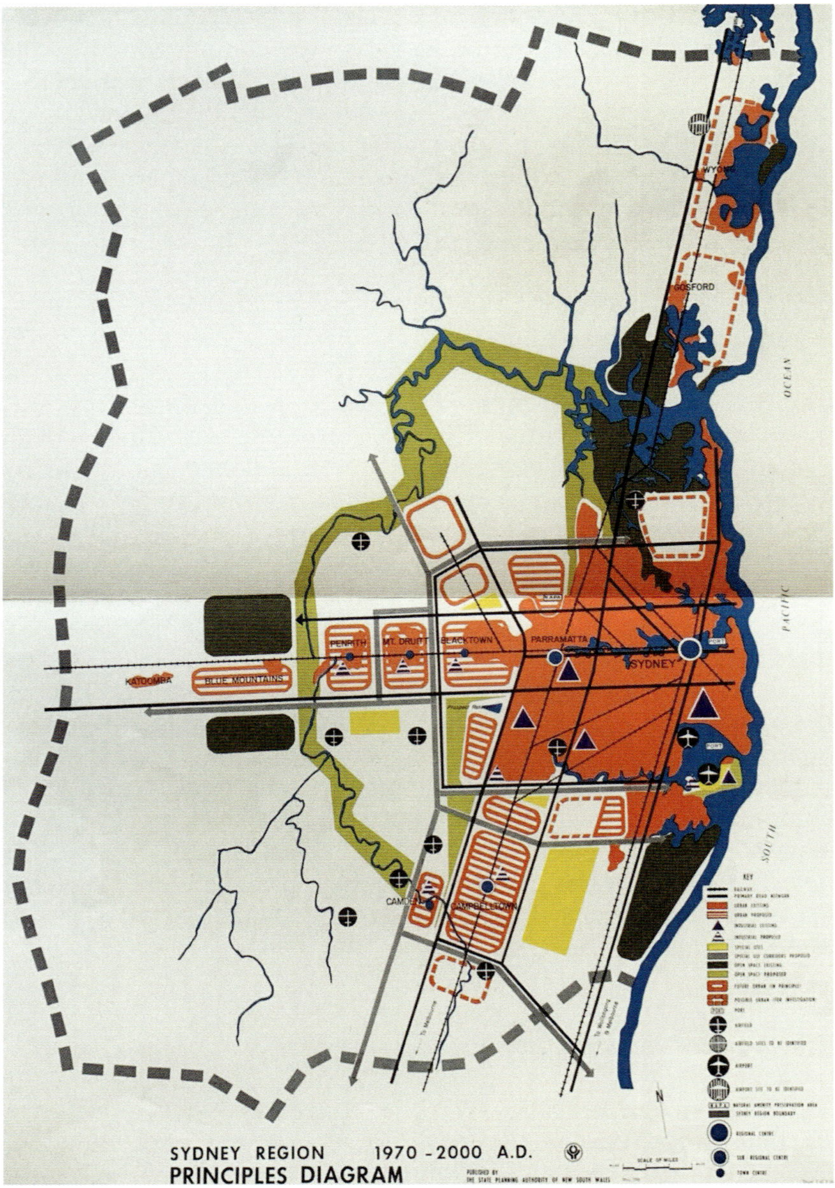

Figure 1b. 1968 Sydney Region Outline Plan. Source: State of New South Wales Department of Planning Housing and Infrastructure

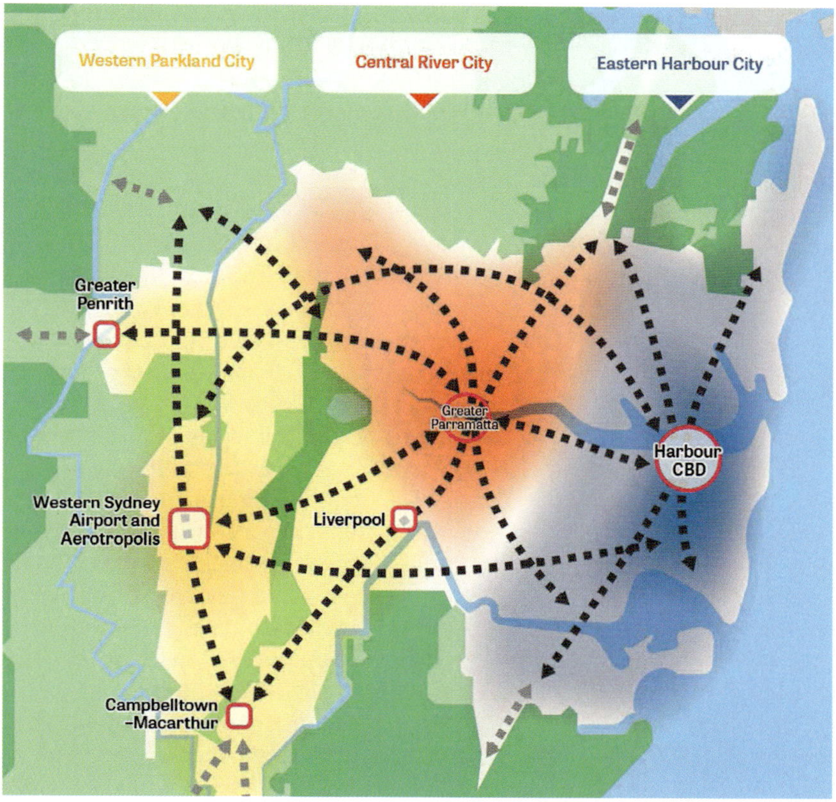

Figure 2. Metropolis of Three Cities spatial vision (2018 Greater Sydney Region Plan). Source: State of New South Wales Department of Planning Housing and Infrastructure

80,000 hectares encompassing large tracts of bushland, scenic hills, floodplains, gorges, rivers, and major waterways, farmland, suburban centres, and smaller villages. In the Indigenous Dharug language the major creek is called *Wianamatta*, meaning 'mother place'. The area more broadly is known as *Dyarubbin*, meaning 'major river', and has been the home of Aboriginal people for at least 50,000 years. The sixty-kilometre-long Wianamatta South Creek is a catchment of creeks and tributaries running the length of Western Parkland City.

The WPC had to be invented. The area at the western periphery of the Cumberland Plain was originally identified as 'Rural Background' in the 1948 plan but has incrementally transitioned to peri-urban. While the 1968 plan proposed linear expansion along transport routes to Penrith and Campbelltown (and speculatively extended northwest), the rest of the periphery was seemingly left alone. Over the next forty-five years, all the lands between the 'fingers' would be infilled with vaguely defined development blobs by successive metropolitan strategies which also implemented new notional centres that lacked a robust, overarching spatial structure.

The 2018 plan broke form with this practice by decisively reframing the WPC as a 'metropolitan cluster'. Here, the thirty-minute-city functions were distributed across a network of existing cities (sometimes referred to as the 'string of pearls' or 'ring of university towns'),[14] including Penrith, Liverpool, and Campbelltown alongside several new greenfield nodes. Ways of generating jobs had to be found and the 'big idea' was to harness the employment-creating centripetal power of an international airport, setting expectations of creating some 200,000 new jobs—many of them tied to global-facing sectors, including export-focused agribusiness, aerospace, defence, and advanced manufacturing. This was spatialised with more 'big thinking', instigated by the Australian Institute of Landscape Architects (AILA) in 2016, which called for a landscaped urbanism that would articulate the Wianamatta South Creek waterways as the 'central urban element' of the new city.[15] The metropolitan planners responded, recognising the potential for the waterway system to be the backbone of a 'cool and green' parkland city; they then added a north–south rail line to define the 'city' through parallel blue-green and transport infrastructures.

Landscape and urban design practice Tyrrell Studio identified still further opportunities for reimagining the shattered mosaic of fragmented landscapes and drainage corridors that remained after decades of opportunistic, largely uncoordinated development.[16] A landscape-led design approach accepts that, while it is impossible to slow down the city's continued growth, the residual deep network of green, blue, and ochre earth forms a unique open space and cultural framework for the future city. This was reflected in the Western Parkland City Structure Plan, which is defined by the Wianamatta South Creek Corridor, a planned transport network, Western Sydney Airport (WSA), and the 'aerotropolis' (Figure 3).

The Western Sydney Aerotropolis

Kasarda's concept of the aerotropolis—with cities organised around aviation—says little about greenhouse gas emissions but taps into globalisation as a growth generator, with new pre-planned airport complexes erected on metropolitan peripheries. In contrast to the placeless, congested, and environmentally unfriendly airports of the past, future forms could be markedly improved through the better integration of infrastructural, site, and regional planning. City airports will become airport cities.[17]

The planned 11,200-hectare Aerotropolis lies at the heart of the Western Parkland City, located on Commonwealth-owned land immediately adjacent to the 2000-hectare airport site (Figure 4). Its urban core has been named Bradfield, commemorating John Job Crew Bradfield, a leading engineer of the 1920s who delivered Sydney's Harbour Bridge. The 2018 region plan rests in large part on the Western Sydney International Airport and Aerotropolis urban precinct which, as the catalyst for a spatially restructured city, needs to generate globally significant jobs including advanced manufacturing, catering to a burgeoning population in the west—something previous plans have failed to do.[18]

The Western Sydney City Deal

The decades of disjunctures in Sydney's development—between planning and intent, visions and outcomes—can be attributed to a metropolitan governance deficit that is evident in most Australian cities.[19] Indeed, implementation of urban development has historically been a weak point. Concurrent with the establishment of the GSC, attempts to engineer improved alignment between federal, state, and local government interests culminated in the signing of the Western Sydney City Deal, a multi-million-dollar partnership. This package of financial and infrastructural obligations will facilitate integrating new citywide development with the airport's operations, currently due to commence in 2026. City deals are a new inter-governmental focus for federal urban policy and the Western Sydney City Deal (Commonwealth of Australia [2018]) is one of largest ever negotiated in Australia.[20]

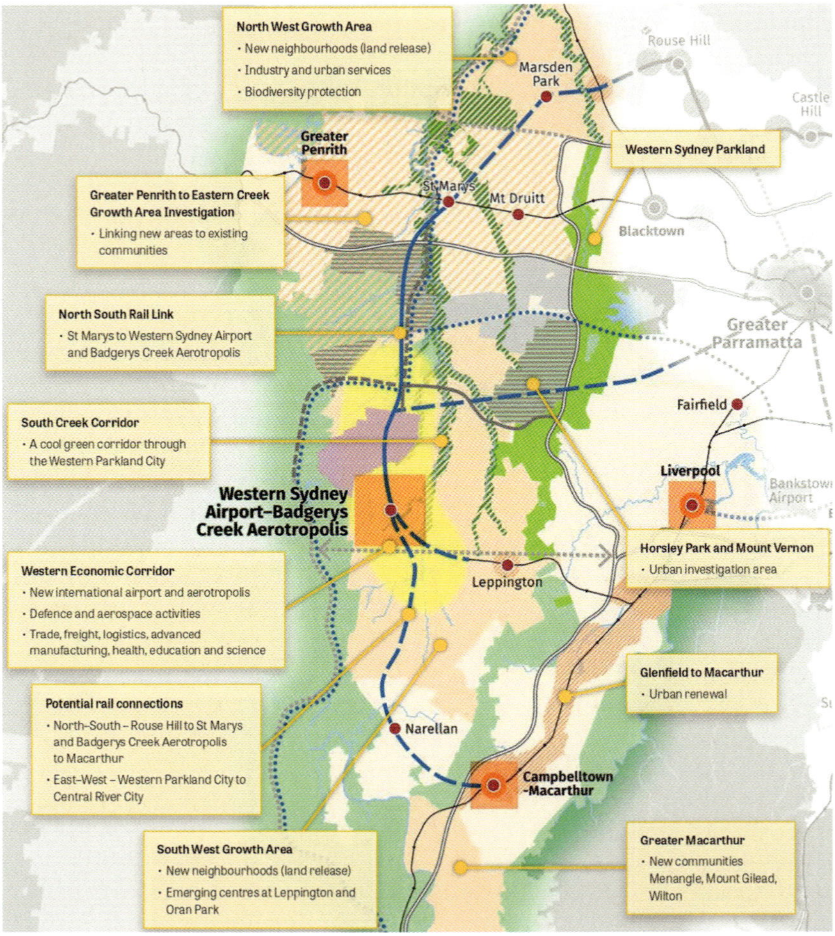

Figure 3. Western Parkland City Structure Plan (2018 Greater Sydney Region Plan). Source: State of New South Wales Department of Planning Housing and Infrastructure

Unlike other city deals, which tend to target singular projects, this one is closely linked to a metropolitan strategy aimed at entirely restructuring place, district, subregional and metropolitan geographies. The deal will enable the overarching planning and urban design framework of Western Parkland City. Its most significant funding elements are the construction of the airport and the first stage of a new metro rail line. Additionally, the deal includes thirty-eight commitments and brings together eight western Sydney councils in partnership with state and federal governments. The Wianamatta South Creek Corridor Rehabilitation Project is the first blue-green infrastructure project to be put on its Priority Project List, signalling its central role in shaping future urban form.

Intent and Outcomes

To what extent can a plan made by a metropolitan planning commission—albeit one enabled by a multi-billion-dollar city deal—deliver a 'city' in Sydney's western periphery? Can a new greenfield peripheral centrality based on a new airport, an Aerotropolis town centre, and associated development—located some sixty kilometres from Sydney's iconic harbour—effectively rebalance a functionally and socioeconomically lopsided metropolis, delivering a truly polycentric region as the culmination of decades of planning?

Already, the actions taken—and funding channelled—towards generating jobs in Western Parkland City far exceed those implemented for new urban sectors in previous strategies, and the airport's economic impact must be catalytic for Western Sydney. However, some critics have questioned the economic viability of creating globally significant jobs so far removed from Sydney's global CBD. There is also an enormous infrastructural and image deficit to overcome in terms of responding to the challenges of climate change. Notably, urban sprawl in Western Sydney has exacerbated the urban heat island effect, in one of the driest and hottest environments in metropolitan Sydney.

Conclusion: Progress and Prospects

Perhaps unsurprisingly, progress has been mixed. On the planning side, detailed development control plans for the Aerotropolis precinct have been completed. The master plan for Bradfield has also recently been approved.[21] The tri-level city deal partnership has continued. The infrastructure promised under the Western Sydney City Deal—including the stage 1 runway, terminal, and Metro (Figure 5)—are currently under construction and generally running on time.

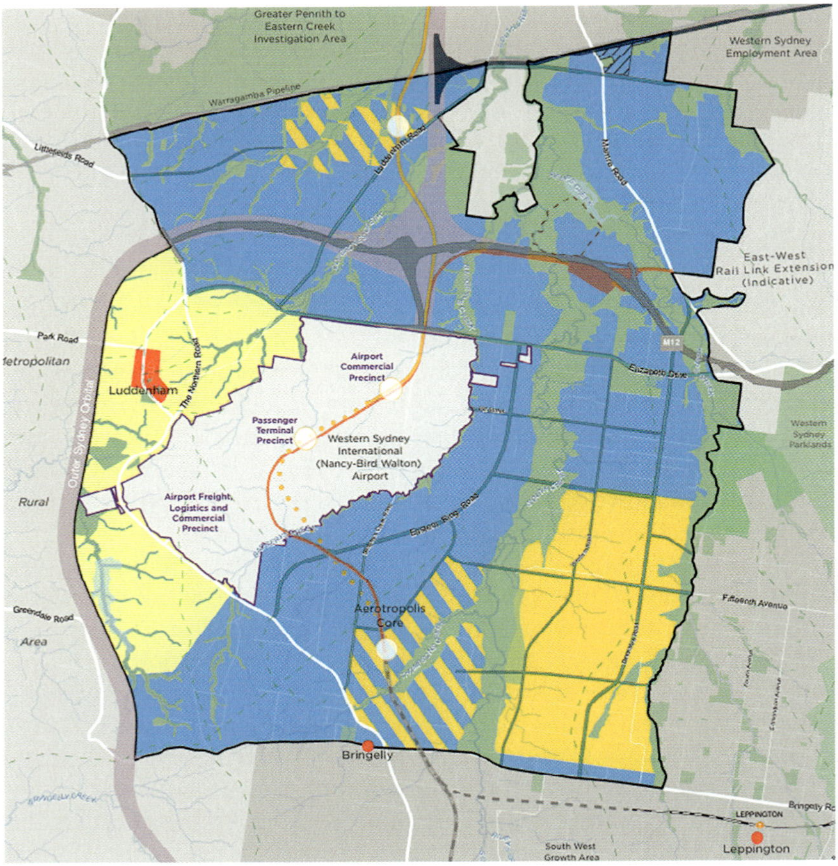

Figure 4. 2020 Western Sydney Aerotropolis Plan. Source: State of New South Wales Department of Planning Housing and Infrastructure

On a negative note, however, the GSC—briefly expanded to a regional role as the Greater Cities Commission, and updating the 2018 *Metropolis of Three Cities* into a far-reaching mega-regional vision[22]—was abolished in late 2023 along with its independent commissioners and absorbed into the planning body of the state of New South Wales. Similarly, the remit of the Western City Aerotropolis Authority—initially expanded as the Western Parkland City Authority—was also reabsorbed into the state planning body, rebadged as the Bradfield Development Authority, now focused on developing the Bradfield City Centre. Calls for the abolition of its independent board signal a further drive towards increased state control. Although the first advanced manufacturing building is under construction at the time of writing, calls from the private sector demanding less planning and more enabling of investment have grown louder, forcing the NSW Government to accelerate development ahead of the airport opening.

The centre/periphery pendulum has also firmly swung back towards Sydney's established geographies and nodes, with a renewed emphasis on catalysing transit-oriented development as a new government seeks to ramp up supply by building more 'homes where people want to live' and 'where infrastructure costs less' in the face of a housing affordability crisis[23]. To some extent, the future of the Western Parkland City hangs in the balance. Acknowledging the historic disjuncture between planning intent and outcome, the most compelling argument for creating a polycentric network of peripheral centres is that a 'business as usual' approach will only result in expanding an unstructured periphery lacking in jobs, covering the remaining Cumberland Plain with low-density residential development. After half a century of stop-start politicking and planning, the tri-level city deal represents a significant commitment to creating a new centrality oriented around a twenty-four-hour international airport, embedded in an ambitious regional plan that presents an unprecedented opportunity. The extent to which this grand vision (Figure 6) is deliverable remains an open question. Clearly, the *volte-face* precipitating the transformation of an entire region from a periphery to a sustainable centre still has a very long way to go and must overcome many obstacles along the way.

Figure 5. Rendering of Aerotropolis Core station, Aerotropolis. Source: Sydney Metro

Figure 6. Visualisation of Bradfield, 2020. Source: State of New South Wales Department of Planning Housing and Infrastructure

Endnotes:

1 J-P. D. Flying high (in the competitive sky): Conceptualizing the role of airports in global city-regions through 'aero-regionalism', *Geoforum, 55*, 2014, pp. 87–99.

2 Freestone, R. and Pinnegar, S. Sydney: Evolution towards a tri-city metropolitan region and beyond, in: M. Neuman and W. Zonneveld (eds.) *Routledge Handbook for Regional Design.* Routledge, 2021, pp. 263–283.

3 Cumberland County Council. *The Planning Scheme for the County of Cumberland.* Sydney, 1948.

4 Abercrombie, P. and Forshaw, J. H. *The County of London Plan.* Macmillan, 1943.

5 State Planning Authority of New South Wales. *Sydney Region: Outline Plan 1970-200A.D.* SPA, 1968.

6 NSW Department of Environment and Planning. *Sydney Into Its Third Century: Metropolitan Strategy for the Sydney Region.* NSW Government, 1988.

7 Barnett, J. *Designing the Megaregion: Meeting Urban Challenges at a New Scale.* Island Press, 2020.

8 NSW Department of Planning. *City of Cities: A Plan for Sydney's Future.* NSW Government, 2005.

9 NSW Department of Planning and Environment. *A Plan for Growing Sydney.* NSW Government, 2014.

10 Collins, J. and Poynting, S. (eds.) *The Other Sydney: Communities, identities and inequalities in Western Sydney.* Common Ground Publishing, 2000.

11 Searle, G. and O'Connor, K. Flawed Vision? Sydney's Three Cities Metropolitan Strategy, *Urban Policy and Research, 40* (4), 2022, pp. 369–388.

12 Kasarda, J. *A Western Sydney Aerotropolis: Maximising the Benefits of Badgerys Creek.* NSW Business Chamber, 2015.

13 Greater Sydney Commission. *The Greater Sydney Region Plan: A Metropolis of Three Cities.* NSW Government, 2018.

14 Greater Sydney Commission. *A Metropolis of Three Cities.* NSW Government, 2018, p. 107.

15 Australian Institute of Landscape Architects. *Letter: A master plan for Western Sydney: to NSW Planning Minister.* AILA, 2016; https://www.aila.org.au/.

16 Tyrrell Studio. *West District: Sydney Green Grid. Spatial framework and project opportunities.* Prepared for the Department of Planning and Environment in association with the Office of the Government Architect, 2017.

17 Kasarda, J. and Lindsay, J. *Aerotropolis: The Way We'll Live Next.* Penguin, 2011.

18 Searle and O'Connor, 2022, *op. cit.*

19 Tomlinson, R. Metropolitan governance is the missing link in Australia's reform agenda, *The Conversation*, April 4, 2016; theconversation.com https://theconversation.com/metropolitan-governance-is-the-missing-link-in-australias-reform-agenda-55872 (accessed February 3, 2025)..

20 Department of Infrastructure, Regional Development and Cities/NSW Department of Premier and Cabinet. *Western Sydney City Deal.* Commonwealth of Australia, 2018.

21 Western Parkland City Authority. *Bradfield City Centre Master Plan: Specific DevelopmentControls.* NSW Government, 2023.

22 Greater Cities Commission. *Discussion paper: The Six Cities Region.* NSW Government, 2022.

23 NSW Government. Transport Oriented Development Program; https://www.planning.nsw.gov.au/policy-and-legislation/housing/transport-oriented-development-program (accessed February 3, 2025).

S
ee
ing

Seeing

Centring the Inconspicuous: The Central Role of Peripheral and Alternative Global Spaces in Aspropyrgos

Astrid Safina

Introduction

The spatial effects of globalisation have been systematically studied under different approaches: as advances of Lefebvrian ideas of extended urbanisation,[1] as nodes that concentrate capital and flow in the form of global cities,[2] and as highly recognisable and orchestrated infrastructural forms.[3] However, many global spaces and transnational relations are much more inconspicuous and elusive than existing literature recognises since they operate within peripheral and marginal areas that frequently remain obscure to academic inquiry. Such peripheral areas, often regarded as 'off the map,'[4] need to be brought out of the shadows in order to overcome the urban centrality and geographical selectivity of urban studies.[5] Peripheries, marginal areas, small towns, rural areas, hinterlands, and new urbanities embedded within global dynamics (often in the background of our observations) represent a horizon to be further explored. These are 'black boxes'[6] yet to be uncovered and put at the centre of theoretical constructions since they may shed light on alternative urbanities.

Following the necessity of addressing the spatiality of globalisation beyond the evident and the central, this chapter argues that peripheries can be regarded as new containers of inconspicuous global spaces. In the process, they become alternative centralities of the contemporary urban condition. Thus, this contribution questions whether (and indeed how) peripheral spaces face such transformation, how they manage to reclaim a central role from their marginal locations, and how alternative ways of becoming global and central are emerging within their present and future transformations. The chapter does so by addressing and rendering visible the plurality of actors driving peripheral transformations, the imaginations they awaken, the narratives they spark, and the places that define them. To engage with such issues from the ground up, the contribution investigates the dynamics and urban forms—together with the actors and economies—in Aspropyrgos, an eclectic suburb located between the periphery of Athens and the massive commercial port of Piraeus, Greece.

The chapter is structured as follows. It first highlights the shifting condition of the Port of Piraeus and its hinterland, Aspropyrgos, by drawing on the relations and compromises between the two parts, as well as addressing the contrasting nature of formal and informal modes of globalisation on the ground. I then go on to address the variegated and fragmented urban forms in Aspropyrgos, exploring their interdependency, hierarchy, precarity, and invisibility. Finally, the chapter briefly unpacks some of the theoretical implications this poses for peripheries as they begin to occupy an increasingly central role.

From Piraeus to Aspropyrgos: Centring Peripheries under the Shadow of a Global Colossus

One hour west of Athens by road and north of the massive commercial port of Piraeus is the area of Aspropyrgos, an eclectic suburb of 30,000 people, where the frenetic movement of trucks, containers, and goods takes place on a daily basis. Despite this, Aspropyrgos has remained peripheral and marginal to both Athens and Piraeus. It is considered a local backyard;[7] hence, the activities, population, and spaces overspilling from both cities are concentrated there. As a result, Roma families, old public buses, abandoned emergency housing, waste yards, minor distribution centres, logistics villages, metal recycling facilities, scattered residential areas, and other 'undesirable' urban forms concentrate here and give it a distinct character.

Once an agricultural area, Aspropyrgos's current condition is linked to a massive industrial transformation that has attracted major and heavy industries to the area since the late 1980s. More recently, the area has been progressively transformed into a dislocated logistical centre due to the growing performance of Piraeus's port (see Figure 1).

Figure 1. Logistics and warehouse spaces scattered across the plateau of Aspropyrgos, connected through minor roads. Source: Photo by Astrid Safina, June 2022

Since 2010, this hub has been upgraded and expanded, becoming one of the world's biggest passenger ports (22,500,000 passengers per year), a major Mediterranean container port (5,300,000 TEUs in 2021), and a rising car transhipment centre (305,190 cars in 2021).[8]

Despite several expansions that have empowered the port in the last few years, local authorities maintain that it has reached maximum storage capacity and that additional space is required.[9] Aspropyrgos represents that available space. Even though it is located fifteen kilometres northwest of the port, severed from the rest of the region by the sea on one side and an arc of mountains on the other, the area is one of the few remaining spaces available in the Attica Region, with a plateau of over one hundred square kilometres of land yet to be developed.[10] Hence, Aspropyrgos provides the requisite landmass to expand the port's logistical infrastructure. However, it does so on its own terms. On the one hand, operations within the port are highly recognisable and self-contained within its perimeter, focusing mainly on transhipment; these operations are charactered by efficiency, standardisation, heavy infrastructure, specialised labour, maximum security, and hermeticism.

Operating on the periphery, however, Aspropyrgos offers an alternative logistic environment comprised of eclectic, apparently irrelevant spaces that–in between the cracks–enable a dense web of invisible operations that are now fundamental to global logistics chains. This observation is supported by statistics: for instance, in recent years, Aspropyrgos has steadily maintained over 650 industrial units;[11] over 35% of the active population is employed in manufacturing, transportation, and storage (the highest percentage in Attica);[12] and over 20% of the goods that enter through the Port of Piraeus spend their first hours and days in Aspropyrgos, before being moved on to Central and Eastern Europe by a complex network of container trucks.[13]

When addressing Aspropyrgos's hidden centrality from the ground, two main issues emerge: first, the distinctive heterogeneity and informality of its logistics spaces; and, second, the precariousness and invisibility of the networks through which these logistics operate. Regarding the first, the heterogeneity of the logistics is visible in the types of spaces, the socioeconomic conditions, and the activities taking place in the area. However, the word 'logistics' often remains too vague. It is necessary to break it down into its constituent shapes and forms, and to disentangle the many economies at work behind it.[14]

Figure 2. Signs of logistics operations in Aspropyrgos. Source: Photo by Astrid Safina, June 2022

Figure 3. Abandoned emergency housing property, belonging to the Ministry of Construction and Housing in Aspropyrgos. Source: Photo by Astrid Safina, June 2022

Figure 4. One of the many piles of containers on the plateau of Aspropyrgos. Source: Photo by Astrid Safina, June 2022

Figure 5. Container in a private yard in Aspropyrgos. Source: Photo by Astrid Safina, June 2022

For instance, the highlands on the plain of Aspropyrgos host what we might term 'traditional' large distribution centres, which occupy the area as large logistics platforms. These consist of international enterprises, such as Procter & Gamble and AstraZeneca—often related to refrigerated or high-standard products—with their own fleet of container trucks, specialised and standardised architecture, and a high degree of order and private security. A second group relates to minor warehouses, used as production sites by local entrepreneurs. These are primarily minimal cement structures, many the size of aircraft hangars, and protected by barbed-wire fencing. They rely on external local transportation services, do not relate to specific products, and might include minor manufacturing activities, such as glass cutting or pellet assembly. These spaces are characterised by many irregularities, including deregulation in the property market, unauthorised constructions, and non-compliant uses of the land. A third category relates to the service sector. Parking spaces for trucks, repair garages for trucks and containers, retail operations selling spare parts, and minor Greek transportation companies are scattered around the area. Finally, a fourth group relates to scrap metal operations and the many forms of shadow economy that, in the most opportunistic ways, capitalise on the continuous flow of raw material into the area. Mostly carried out by Roma, this practice targets electric cables, container parts, and metal pipelines.[15]

Despite its large distribution centres and isolated parking lots, the compendium of alternative global spatialities in Aspropyrgos is precariously connected. Unpaved roads, single-lane roads, and minor rural roads make up the area's mobility network. Moreover, heavy traffic, container trucks, smoke, and horns fill the daily lives of local people, even in the most remote locations. Several efforts have been made to change this situation, the most pertinent being a cargo railway connecting the Port of Piraeus with the Thriasio Logistics Centre, an intermodal hub located just north of the area which—owing to empty tenders and unsatisfactory concession agreements—remains essentially idle today. The result of this dormant logistical project is clearly visible; piles of containers have suddenly materialised on street corners, inside residential patios, in empty lots, and anywhere else they can fit. This reflects how, despite a lack of infrastructure, the logistical flows of the area manage to find a mode of circulation even in the most unanticipated of ways.

The highly diverse spaces of Aspropyrgos all share an important set of characteristics: namely, their ability to occupy the available interstices and cracks in an improvised, almost spontaneous way, as well as their capacity to operate within the possibilities offered by a highly unregulated space.[16] As a result, the peripheral spaces of Aspropyrgos reclaim their central relevance to the port by operating in a complex space ruled by spontaneity, deregulation, personal connections, and varying degrees of informality. These operational conditions result in a dense but flexible network of high-functioning yet simultaneously fragmented spaces, whose centrality to broader dynamics is perhaps difficult to recognise at first glance (since it does not fall within traditional canons of what we consider 'global' or 'central' in the context of contemporary urban forms).[17]

Instead, these apparently peripheral but highly central spaces are built and organised from below as it were, with the objective of claiming their own central role in developing global dynamics despite their 'outsider' status.[18] This centrality is based mainly on the interdependence of parts and on the continuous reconstruction and adaptability of spatial fragments. These characteristics give global peripheries such as Aspropyrgos a great level of dynamism and capacity for reaction that more recognisable urban centres rarely enjoy. Thus, places like Aspropyrgos can no longer be considered as passive, secondary spaces, resigned to an urban condition of disregard. By contrast, the many minor efforts and transformations that alter them, and the unanticipated forms of development they pursue, showcase how urban peripheries are reclaiming their own distinctive and differentiated centralities.

Conclusion

The study of alternative global spaces in Aspropyrgos—and their central role in the functioning of a global colossus such as the Port of Piraeus—highlights how former peripheries are moving centre stage, challenging not only the economic dominance of the 'centre' but the very system on which the established global order and centre–periphery relations have been operating.[19] Furthermore, reading such alternative spaces in detail, from the ground up, sheds light on how peripheries, in their attempt to retrieve a central role, do not follow the same direction as consolidated urban areas—nor do they replicate consolidated stereotypes of American suburbs, pastoral landscapes, or marginal and neglected urban fringes.[20] Instead, they pursue their own development path, often as innovative and improvised urban forms that exist in a complementary way to the large centres whose deficiencies they compensate for. Hence, they benefit from the shortcomings of urban centres, taking advantage of their peripheral flexibilities to transform and act as the 'solution' to problems created elsewhere.

From this perspective, then, it is necessary to explore the generative power of peripheries and the many possibilities they offer to our ever-evolving urban condition. Moreover, instead of adopting a traditionally negative lens that obscures any form of urban discovery, it is necessary to recontextualise peripheries by eroding existing biases, rethinking them in light of critical interpretations that connect them to broader urban issues. If the study of Aspropyrgos speaks to alternative ways of 'being global', looking at other peripheral suburbs across the globe could shed light on alternative ways of building urban relations, being central, and even alternative ways of 'being urban' within an era of global extended urbanisation.

Endnotes:

1 Brenner, N. and Schmid, C. Towards a new epistemology of the urban?, *City, 19* (2–3), 2015, pp. 151–182; https://doi.org/10.1080/13604813.2015.1014712.

2 Sassen, S. *The Global City: New York, London, Tokyo.* Princeton University Press, 2013.

3 Easterling, K. *Extrastatecraft: The Power of Infrastructure Space.* Verso Books, 2014.

4 Robinson, J. Global and world cities: A view from off the map, *International Journal of Urban and Regional Research, 26* (3), 2002, pp. 531–554; https://doi.org/10.1111/1468-2427.00397.

5 Angelo, H. and Wachsmuth, D. Urbanizing Urban Political Ecology: A Critique of Methodological Cityism, *International Journal of Urban and Regional Research, 39* (1), 2015, pp. 16–27; https://doi.org/10.1111/1468-2427.12105; Angelo, H. From the city lens toward urbanisation as a way of seeing: Country/city binaries on an urbanising planet, *Urban Studies, 54* (1), 2017, pp. 158–178; https://doi.org/10.1177/0042098016629312.

6 Brenner, N. and Katsikis, N. Operational Landscapes: Hinterlands of the Capitalocene, *Architectural Design, 90* (1), 2020, pp. 22–31; https://doi.org/10.1002/ad.2521.

7 Mavrakis, A. and Salvati, L. *Thriasio Plain – Greece: Diachronic multiple environmental issues and some proposals for possible recovery of the area.* International Conference on Changing Cities II: Spatial, Design, Landscape & Socio-economic Dimensions, June 22, 2015.

8 Piraeus Port Authority. *Piraeus Port Annual Financial Report*, 2021.

9 Hatzopoulos, P. and Kambouri, N. Piraeus Port as a Machinic Assemblage: Labour, Precarity, and Struggles, in: B. Neilson, N. Rossiter, and R. Samaddar (eds.) *Logistical Asia: The Labour of Making a World Region.* Springer, 2018, pp. 155–174; https://doi.org/10.1007/978-981-10-8333-4_8.

10 Mavrakis, A., Rontos, K., Chronopoulou, C., and Salvati, L. Population dynamics, industrial development and the decline of the traditional agro-forest landscape on the Mediterranean urban fringe: A case study in Greece, *International Journal of Sustainable Development, 19* (1), 2016, pp. 1–14.

11 Marmaras, I. The Newly Builts and the Aspropyrgos Zone: Illegality, Racism, Infrastructures, *Logistical Worlds No. 1: Piraeus*, 2014, pp. 29–39.

12 Maloutas, T. and Spyrellis, S. Inequality and segregation in Athens: Maps and data. *Athens Social Atlas*, 2019; https://www.athenssocialatlas.gr/en/article/inequality-and-segregation-in-athens/.

13 Piraeus Port Authority, 2021, *op. cit.*

14 Neilson, B., Rossiter, N., and Samaddar, R. *Logistical Asia: The Labour of Making a World Region.* Springer, 2018.

15 Lascari, A. The New Ikonion-Thriassion Rail Line, *Logistical Worlds No. 1: Piraeus*, 2014, pp. 29–39.

16 Safina, A. Formalità e informalità dentro il sistema logistico Pireo-Aspropyrgos, *TERRITORIO, 103*, 2022.

17 Choplin, A. and Pliez, O. The Inconspicuous Spaces of Globalization, *Journal of Urban Research, 12*, Article 12, 2015; https://journals.openedition.org/articulo/2905#tocto1n1.

18 Keil, R. Extended urbanization, 'disjunct fragments' and global suburbanisms, *Environment and Planning D: Society and Space, 36* (3), 2018, pp. 494–511; https://doi.org/10.1177/0263775817749594.

19 Mortenbock, P. and Mooshammer, H. *Informal Market Worlds: Atlas: The Architecture of Economic Pressure.* First edition. Nai Uitgevers Pub, 2015.

20 Ren, X. Suburbs and Urban Peripheries in a Global Perspective, *City & Community, 20* (1), 2021, pp. 38–47; https://doi.org/10.1111/cico.12505.

Rendering Density as a Public Good

Katherine Perrott

Introduction: A Suburb Rises

Dramatic densification is envisioned for Richmond Hill, a suburban city located in south central York Region at the extension of Toronto's subway system.[1] The grand vision includes more than thirty towers with between forty to eighty storeys, constructed around a new subway station in an area called the High Tech Transit-Oriented Community (TOC) (see Figure 1).[2] This chapter examines the visual representation and political rhetoric promoting this future densified suburban transit node, aiming to probe the continual remaking and reimagining of peripheral centralities. Distinct from images produced as part of direct condo marketing, which invite potential buyers to imagine themselves as residents,[3] these images were released years before selling or building the units. What is the purpose of the effort (and money) invested in this early-stage image production? What discursive work are these images doing?

The argument here is that the vision for the TOC strategically renders density as a 'public good' in order to secure broad-based support for densification as a solution to the housing supply crisis in the Toronto region, and to justify dramatic change in the spatialisation of capital. These arguments are based on analysis of place images contained in planning reports on the TOC project's engagement website, which were discussed in the recorded virtual open house.[4] Rooted in an interest in suburbanisation processes, this analysis views place images not just as discursive objects, but also as discursive moments in the overlapping and intersecting processes of capital's circulation and the production of spatial imaginaries. This chapter briefly establishes a theoretical approach, before moving on to discuss the area of study's built form and its political context. It then explores the role of images in generating public support for suburban densification and the extended urbanisation of place-image production.

Densification Aesthetics

Densification is not a neutral process. Rather, as Éric Charmes and Roger Keil have highlighted, different interests are favoured or disadvantaged.[5] Density is promoted as a form of sustainability in urbanist and environmental policy circles, fuelling growth in vertical form. The suburban public is not always swayed by arguments in favour of density, especially when it can feel like a community's collective quality of life, and household-level property values are being weighed against a big developer's profit margins. Densification in suburban contexts—including Richmond Hill—can be controversial and contested among local residents, who often express concerns about traffic, parking, insufficient amenities, wind, and shadow impacts.[6]

Faced with a sceptical, conservative suburban public, how does densification garner acceptability and indeed desirability in the public eye? Proponents and beneficiaries of densification must produce place images and 'vibes' that can be seen and felt as good. The most powerful ideology often operates aesthetically—what we come to know and feel through vision and other bodily senses. As Kanishka Goonewardena has explained, for ideology to be effective it 'must also be affective, that is to say aesthetic'.[7] Chris Philo and Gerry Kearns describe the aesthetic production of place image as a 'subtle form of *socialisation*' to convince people—even those who may be disadvantaged or disaffected—that a wider social good is being produced and 'that all sorts of "good things" are really being done on their behalf'.[8] Hillary Angelo argues that producing a shared understanding or social imaginary of a public good provides a logic for remaking urban space and shapes our orientation towards particular solutions.[9] With densification, the aesthetics producing shared understandings of progress are central yet overlooked aspects of theorising urbanisation.

Figure 1. Visual Rendering of the High Tech Transit-Oriented Community, Richmond Hill, looking south towards Toronto's skyline, punctuated by the CN Tower in the top-left corner. Source: Rendering by Frontop, courtesy of BPD Quadrangle

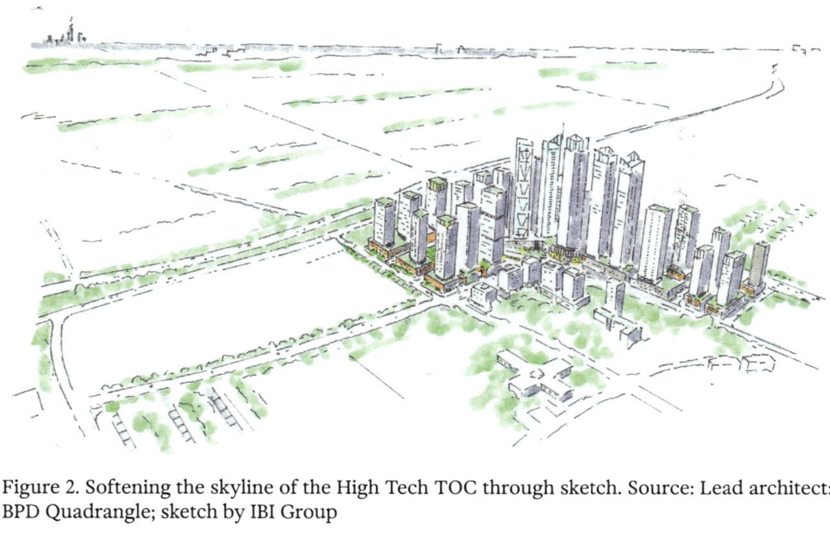

Figure 2. Softening the skyline of the High Tech TOC through sketch. Source: Lead architect: BPD Quadrangle; sketch by IBI Group

Richmond Hill: an Emerging Peripheral Centrality

The City of Richmond Hill is one of the suburban municipalities located in the metropolitan ring between Toronto and a greenbelt area that protects land for agriculture, ecosystems, and resource extraction. Housing development in Richmond Hill followed a suburban pattern typical for the broader region, with subdivision growth beginning in the 1950s, followed by an intense period of car-oriented expansion between 1981 and 2000 when over half of the housing stock was built out in a low-rise, detached housing typology.[10] Apartments in Richmond Hill have been (contentiously) regulated to heights under thirty storeys[11] and have been focused along Yonge Street, which connects the city southward to Toronto. The new subway extension will run under the Yonge Street corridor to the new High Tech station intensification node, pictured in Figure 1. Large office parks and big box clusters throughout Richmond Hill signify the importance once placed on separating land uses, something contemporary planners are now trying to remedy through transit improvements and densification.

Though geographically peripheral, Toronto's suburbs have always been politically powerful, and conservative. The suburbs' fast-growing population and right-leaning voting preferences helped install the conservative provincial government of the 1990s whose 'common sense revolution' of deep cuts and austerity have had lasting negative impacts on the availability of affordable social housing.[12] Like its 1990s predecessor, the current conservative provincial government–in power from 2018 to the time of writing in summer 2024—champions expressways and housing subdivisions but now also promotes a transit-oriented development agenda. Public investment in transit and advocating for higher residential densities are not the hallmarks of suburban conservatism. This begs an important question: what factors underpin this push for a 'post-suburban'[13] landscape in Richmond Hill?

Onwards and... Upwards

Development in Richmond Hill has reached the municipal boundaries. The days of predominantly outward horizontal expansion are over, and a new period of vertical expansion through infill and redevelopment is underway. Densification provides a 'spatial fix' for growth and tax revenue generation.[14] The High Tech TOC lands are not undeveloped suburban greenfields; there are big box and strip plaza retail sites, a government office (Figure 4), a bus station, and associated large parking lots. One of the anchor tenants is a movie theatre, a sector that has yet to fully recover since COVID-19 (Figure 3).[15] Vacancies in the area signal a stalling of capital circuits through this overinvested built form. Suburban retail landscapes are widely critiqued as sprawling, car-centric, ugly 'geographies of nowhere'[16] which represent the demise of traditional downtown urbanity. Big box shopping precincts struggle to cultivate aesthetic affection in terms of architecture and landscape design, thus offering fertile ground for a spatial fix that would replace the unloved form and derided symbols of suburban sprawl.

Province as Regulator and Developer

In the High Tech TOC, the province of Ontario is not only the planning and environmental regulator, but it is also a development partner. As the planning regulator, the Province has exempted development from the legislated planning processes that would otherwise be typical, such as amending the Official Plan, rezoning each site, and reviewing site plan details with municipal planners. The province has used its power to issue an Enhanced Ministerial Zoning Order (EMZO) to override local-level planning regulations. Furthermore, special legal agreements will be established and development projects will be expedited to the construction permitting stage. Put simply, these various actions are about cutting through so-called 'red tape' and removing 'bottlenecks' from any planning 'standing in the way of housing supply'.[17] Although this area has long been planned as an urban growth node or peripheral centrality, the latest development permissions amplify the scale and speed of change. Aligned with the provincial government's fast growth ideology,[18] the zoning order accelerates the gradual 'transformation from suburban to urban' envisioned in the Richmond Hill Official Plan.[19]

Despite its stated role as a developer in the High Tech TOC, it is unclear where exactly the province's involvement and investment begin and end. The project website shows the provincial government's logo alongside two for-profit landowner-developers: Metrus and Condor Properties. Notably, both of these companies are tied to the same parent company, Con-Drain, which is owned by one of Canada's wealthiest families (who are also major donors to the Progressive Conservative Party).[20] The community engagement report states that 'the site will be developed by the Province'.[21] This suggests that the Province is doing more than its 'traditional' role of providing transit infrastructure. As a developer, then, this raises questions around the extent to which the province is using public money to facilitate the flows and accumulation of capital through the private housing market.

Densification: Public Good and Policy Panacea for a Crisis Narrowly Defined?

The crisis of housing supply and affordability in Toronto, Ontario, elsewhere in Canada—and internationally, for that matter—is the primary problem that enables densification to be positioned as a public good, even in the historically low-rise suburbs. As noted on the Province's website:

> This is not just a big-city crisis. The housing supply shortage affects all Ontarians: rural, urban and suburban, north and south, young and old. The problem is clear. There simply aren't enough homes being built. And the solution is equally clear. We need to get more homes built faster.[22]

The housing crisis is narrowly defined as a *supply* crisis, with a seemingly uncomplicated solution: facilitate the private market to build more homes at a faster rate. During the High Tech virtual open house, project proponents described an unprecedented crisis as one that is clearly and simply a problem of supply. Building high-density residential condominiums was framed as the clear and simple solution to this problem. For example, a representative from Infrastructure Ontario stated that '[t]he fundamental driver of housing affordability problems is supply… We have a brewing housing crisis—a housing supply crisis that we've not seen in our lifetime'.[23]

While affordable housing advocates in the region point to problems including limited rent control, displacement through renovation, and lack of commitment to building new affordable housing,[24] the provincial government asserts that the housing crisis is a market supply crisis. Despite the mention of a crisis, there are only a few nods to affordable housing in the High Tech TOC planning reports, and these are largely without details or specific commitments. Instead, the focus is on market-rate housing supply, described at the open house as the middle of the housing affordability bell curve.

This invocation of a crisis draws on a long lineage of characterising markets as broken or in disequilibrium to justify political economic restructuring.[25] Critical scholars like David Madden and Peter Marcuse identify the problem as a commodification of housing that reiterates one of capitalism's central contradictions: the crisis is the result of markets working as intended, not a result of markets breaking down.[26] In Ontario, the housing supply crisis is the justifying rationale for a suite of planning reforms, including zoning orders—like the one fast-tracking the High Tech TOC—a repealed regional growth plan, decreased time to review development applications, and a reduced scope for site-plan review.

From Crisis to Convincing Aesthetics

Out of this crisis, amid the fading embers of an unloved suburban commercial landscape, rises the image of the High Tech TOC. There are two dominant aesthetic styles used to represent and visualise the High Tech TOC: sketching and photoreal digital rendering. Both are used to translate the conceptual imaginary into the look and feel of the future node. In urban design, sketching is used to develop concepts and is a soft, approachable way to present ideas to the public that invites iteration in design, feedback, and change (Figure 2). Photoreal renderings, like Figure 1, are generally created and used for multiple objectives: to convince, to sell, and to win design competitions. Releasing both the sketches and the renderings (Figure 6) at the same time—in the package of development documents presented at the public open house—reinforces the fact that the EMZO is an expedited, condensed process.

The planning documents include a series of sketches which, in the urban design tradition of serial vision, show vignettes of urbanism and public life from an eye-level perspective as if the viewer is moving through the future space. The streetscapes are abuzz with

Figure 3. 'Fugly' existing big box movie theatre ripe for a spatial and symbolic fix. Source: Photo by Katherine Perrott, 2023

Figure 4. No civic square where a regional government office fronts onto the back loading dock and parking for the Beer Store. Source: Photo by Katherine Perrott, 2023

pedestrian movement, showing interaction with active, tree-lined retail frontages (Figure 5). The hand-drawn renderings soften density and communicate the notion of a work-in-progress, even though the zoning order enables skipping past the typical process for collaboration and negotiation on design.

Photorealistic renderings are as concrete an image as you can get of an unbuilt space before the actual concrete is poured. They give life and light through a hyperreal photo finish applied to flat computer-generated models. Renderings present a crisp, more cemented vision of the future than sketches; however, they too include strategic softening through fade-outs, transparencies, and improbable reflections of greenery that appear far up the towers. The images are bright and optimistic, with only enough shadow to communicate three dimensions. While glassy, shiny and new, the rendered model accentuates the scale, height, visual repetition, and concrete underpinnings of the infrastructure, echoing an older generation of government-supported suburban housing blocks that Paul Maginn and Nicholas Phelps call 'brutopianscapes'.[27] The sketches must work then to counteract a sense of the inhumane or 'brutal' hardscape with a softened, more fluid and humanely scaled place image.

Rendering software is becoming more technologically accessible to the average computer user, though much of this work over the decades was outsourced to specialist architectural visualisation companies in China.[28] The High Tech TOC renderings were produced by a company called Frontop, based in Guangzhou, China. They boast a 'render farm' of 300 linked computers used to generate significant computing power and produce impressive visualisations.[29] These visualisation artists may have only been given a basic massing model and the location to create this vision from overseas. The rendering process highlights the productive tension between the forces of centralisation and extended urbanisation in the globalised production of place image. The spatial imaginary of the High Tech TOC, a new centre on Toronto's periphery, is relationally linked to Guangzhou through extended global circuits of capital and labour. This illustrates the mobility of the global spatial imaginary of the 'urban', which is consolidated through the movement of images and ideas transferred over digital cloud space.

Figure 5. The High Tech Transit-Oriented Community eye-level sketch of urbanity. Source: Lead architect: BPD Quadrangle; sketch by IBI Group

Figure 6. A sketched bird's-eye view of the subway station and adjacent greenspace, with the photoreal rendering showing the same view with an unlikely reflection of greenery. Source: Lead architect: BPD Quadrangle; sketch by IBI Group; rendering by Frontop

Conclusion: A Suburb Rises, but to What Challenge?

Density on this massive scale in the suburbs has the potential to generate negative public reactions related to neighbourhood impacts (like wind and shadow) or be dismissed by the public as developer avarice. So, how does high density become publicly palatable and even desirable in the suburbs? This examination of the future centralised periphery of High Tech TOC demonstrates the intertwining of economic logics and affective aesthetics to present land-value optimisation as a cause for public optimism. By mobilising the rhetoric of housing supply crisis, its proponents aim to justify the dramatic change in the built form as simple common sense and a *good* thing, which will be worth the public investment and truncation of the planning process. Facilitated by public funds, the development will include various physical public 'goods'—as in the constructed transit infrastructure—while densification itself is positioned as 'a public good' with positive impacts on the collective social problem of housing supply.

Although the housing crisis is multifaceted, requiring a range of interventions including direct investment in affordable non-market housing by the provincial government, the dramatic densification of Richmond Hill is presented as a one-size-fits-all solution to the oversimplified challenge of a market *supply* crisis. High Tech TOC represents a suburb rising in height and density, and it may yet rise to the challenge of supplying market-rate housing. However, the need for affordable housing will likely remain unmet through the current plans. The rising suburb carries costs for the planning process and public budget, which is why this image production matters early in the process. The images replace a derided suburban sprawl with a vertical urbanity that can be seen as intervening in a housing crisis, and as these images circulate, civil society is being called on to embrace density as a public good.

Endnotes:

1 The extension of Toronto's Subway Line 1, which currently runs up Yonge Street north to Finch, will be the second line extension of the subway system outside of Toronto.
2 Currently High Tech is projected to have 21,000 housing units, generating 9,500 jobs in office space, and various retail and entertainment uses. Parkland will be clustered around the subway station. Less than 500 metres south, another station area (called Bridge TOC) is planned. It will be of a similar magnitude, separated from High Tech by a major expressway and a municipal border. Between Bridge and High Tech TOC's, some 42.2 hectares (over one hundred acres) of land are greenlighted for densification.
3 Lehrer, U. 'If you lived here...': Lifestyle, marketing, and the development of condominiums in Toronto, *Scapegoat, 3*, 2012, p. 23.
4 Engage High Tech project website and video stream link to recorded public open house on December 9, 2021; https://www.engagehightech.ca/.
5 Charmes, E. and Keil, R. The Politics of Post-Suburban Densification in Canada and France: Debates & Developments, *International Journal of Urban and Regional Research, 39* (3), 2015, pp. 581–602.
6 Xing, L. They're called 'transit-oriented communities'. But to some GTA residents, they're a 'condo wasteland', *CBC News*, January 23, 2022; https://www.cbc.ca/news/canada/toronto/richmond-hill-markham-transit-oriented-community-development-doug-ford-1.6320951.
7 Goonewardena, K. The urban sensorium: Space, ideology and the aestheticization of politics, *Antipode, 37* (1), 2005, pp. 46–71.
8 Philo, C. and Kearns, G. Culture, history, capital: A critical introduction to the selling of places, in: G. Kearns and C. Philo (eds.) *Selling Places: the city as cultural capital, past and present.* Pergamon Press, 1993, pp. 1–32, quote from p. 3.
9 Angelo, H. *How Green Became Good: Urbanized Nature and the Making of Cities and Citizens.* The University of Chicago Press, 2021.
10 Canada Mortgage and Housing Corporation, Housing Market Information Portal; https://www03.cmhc-schl.gc.ca/hmip-pimh/en#TableMapChart/3519038/4/Richmond%20Hill%20(T) (accessed on October 12, 2022).
11 Latchford, T. Tallest building in Richmond Hill's history, 29 storeys, approved by OMB, *YorkRegion.com*, September 13, 2017; Wang, S. Richmond Hill's high-rise boom spurred by pro-development council, profitmaking developers: experts, *YorkRegion.com*, March 18, 2021.
12 Boudreau, J., Keil, R., and Young, D. *Changing Toronto: Governing urban neoliberalism.* University of Toronto Press, 2009; Walks, R. A. Suburbanization, the Vote, and Changes in Federal and Provincial Political Representation and Influence Between Inner Cities and Suburbs in Large Canadian Urban Regions, 1945–1999, *Urban Affairs Review 39* (4), 2004, pp. 411–40.
13 Phelps, N. *Sequel to suburbia: glimpses of America's post-suburban future.* MIT Press, 2015.
14 Harvey, D. *The Limits to Capital.* Verso, 2006 [1982]; Nethercote, M. Melbourne's Vertical Expansion and the Political Economies of High-Rise Residential Development, *Urban Studies, 56* (16), 2019, pp. 3394–3414.
15 Drost, P. Movie-goers are returning, but theatres are still waiting for a blockbuster year, *CBC*, February 23, 2023; https://www.cbc.ca/radio/costofliving/movie-cinemas-pandemic-recovery-2022-1.6732574.
16 Kunstler, J. H. *The geography of nowhere.* Touchstone, 1994.

17 Minister of Municipal Affairs and Housing Steve Clark quoted in Gray, J. Ontario to cut fees for affordable housing, rental construction, *The Globe and Mail*, October 25, 2022; https://www.theglobeandmail.com/canada/article-ontario-2022-housing-plan/.

18 Perrott, K. and Grant, J. L. From smart growth to fast growth, *Plan Canada, 63* (fall), 2023.

19 City of Richmond Hill Official Plan, January 2023 consolidation; https://www.richmondhill.ca/.

20 Project website: www.engagehightech.ca; on DeGasperis family see: Canada's richest people: The DeGasperis family, *Canadian Business*, December 24, 2015; https://archive.canadianbusiness.com/lists-and-rankings/richest-people/rich-100-degasperis-family/; on suburban landholdings and donations see: Jones, R. P. Wealthy Ontario developer close to winning long battle to build homes on protected Greenbelt, *CBC News*, November 22, 2022; https://www.cbc.ca/news/canada/toronto/developer-greenbelt-pickering-1.6658896.

21 AECOM. *Engage High Tech Final Report*, February 2022; https://www.engagehightech.ca.

22 Ministry of Municipal Affairs and Housing. *Minister's Message*, published October 25, 2022, updated: April 3, 2023; https://www.ontario.ca/page/more-homes-built-faster.

23 Engage High Tech project website and video stream, December 9, 2021; *op. cit.*

24 Doucet, B. Ontario's 'affordable housing' task force report does not address the real problems, *The Conversation*, February 10, 2022; https://theconversation.com/ontarios-affordable-housing-task-force-report-does-not-address-the-real-problems-176869.

25 Klein, N. *The shock doctrine: The rise of disaster capitalism.* Picador, 2008.

26 Madden, D. J. and Marcuse, P. *In Defense of Housing: the Politics of Crisis.* Verso, 2016.

27 Maginn, P. J. and Phelps, N. A. Making Sense of Twenty-First Century (Sub)Urban Landscapes: Blandscapes, Blendscapes, Brutalscapes and Brutopianscapes, *Built Environment, 49* (1), 2023, pp. 5–22.

28 Mayer, A. N. Urban fantasies in China: Architectural visualization, *CLOG:RENDERING*, 2012; https://www.chinaurbandevelopment.com/urban-fantasies-in-china-architectural-visualization/ (accessed September 25, 2024).

29 Frontop business profile: https://www.linkedin.com/company/frontop-digital-technology-company/about/.

Tales from the Road: An Experience of Critical Visual Narration along a Suburban Motorway

Martina Loi

Introduction: Understanding Peripheral Centralities through a Situated Perspective

When dealing with the topic of peripheral centralities, it is difficult to ignore urban infrastructures, the 'enablers'[1] that actually make these centralities possible. Infrastructure is in fact the foundation of suburbanisation, as well as urbanisation broadly speaking. Since the very early work of the infrastructural turn, it has been clearly established that its enabling status makes infrastructure a key element of urbanisation—in its planetary connectivity, it represents one of 'the most basic elements of collective consumption (and collective disposal) organising social, economic, and environmental lives.'[2] Infrastructures also embed an intricate set of material and mediating elements between different systems, constituting the largest and most sophisticated human artefact, one that provides the environment and conditions for daily life.

With the role of infrastructure in the contemporary urban(ised) world now squarely acknowledged, working on infrastructure raises several other epistemological issues and, consequently, analytical-methodological ones. The first one is a matter of defining infrastructure. Infrastructures constitute a complex relational ensemble, fully immersed in the socio-political context that produces and manages them. Ash Amin describes them as 'sociotechnical assemblages',[3] intended as a set of technological processes, material components, cultural and discursive practices, and political relations, and for this reason 'social in every respect'.[4] Therefore, it is almost impossible to find a one-size-fits-all definition. However, it can certainly be emphasised that infrastructure's ontological specificity lies in the relational character of things and relations between things, or spaces that produce and connect other spaces.[5] One might think of it as a 'plural ensemble': an oxymoron that conveys the need to find different and more situated reading lenses without adopting a single, universal definition. Therefore, a situated knowledge of infrastructure must combine a focus on the processes shaping the infrastructure system—and their spatial and social effects—with a reading of infrastructures as materialities and spaces in their own right. This attitude requires reflecting as much on the characteristics related to the role of infrastructures as on the urban life that unravels in infrastructural spaces beyond the strict functionality of infrastructure.

Moving beyond a hypothetical 'infrastructural ideal' that considers infrastructure supply solely as an aspirational apolitical asset—managed and distributed as a public and collective good—a reading of local infrastructure's heterogeneous configurations[6] can help make sense of the actual possibilities and opportunities infrastructure could offer to those navigating its socio-materiality, beyond its technicalities and constraining power relationships. Infrastructures emerge here as proper urban spaces, not just as relational and connecting urban elements. Infrastructural peripheries can be urban life spaces as much as their more represented counterparts, producing configurations that do not necessarily respond to predetermined paradigms, can sometimes be crossed by marginalised subjectivities, or generate alternative spaces of freedom and experimentation.[7]

Adding to the issue of definition, a further epistemological and methodological question emerges: without wanting to reiterate detached and telescopic views on infrastructure, how can we interact with and know infrastructural peripheries?

One viable way is offered through feminist epistemologies, which can be mobilised to build a strongly situated viewpoint about urban infrastructures as living spaces that give rise to specific peripheralities. In particular, it is possible to follow Cindi Katz's invitation to work on the 'empty spots'[8] often disregarded by infrastructural studies, e.g. interstices and interstitial practices around infrastructure. For decades now, feminists have been pushing to assume a truly 'peripheral' stance, meant as a perspective from which the agency and subjectivities that produce space daily can be acknowledged. The periphery is thus symbolically no longer a residual and less valid element of urban processes—the suburban as somehow less-than-urban—but a critical standpoint, a new centrality for reading urban life from an off-centred (and thus potentially renewed) perspective.

Methodologically, one possible way to work along these lines is to embody the research, crossing spaces with the body, and producing situated (but no less objective)[9] narratives of the spaces that emerge from the body–space interaction. It is in other words a matter of staying in these marginal spaces, from which we can even look at the centres using a rich *urban–peripheral vantage point*.

Tales from the Road: Encounters with a City in the Making

The spaces of an urban motorway are a favourable context for experimenting with this attitude, especially when situated in a non-central location, as in the case of Sardinia and the road called 'SS 554'. The road is one of the local expressions of the modernist planning paradigm of the 1950s and 1960s, centred on fast, modern infrastructure as triggers for urban development. It was built in a not-yet urbanised context, as part of the big post-war investment plan aimed at regional industrial development (the so-called 'Rebirth Plan'). The city, however, did not develop as planned, probably because the road in its design tried to reproduce an external model of modernisation that didn't completely align with the characteristics of a medium-sized southern European town.[10] Over the decades the city has grown within this symbolic boundary. When reaching and crossing the road border, however, it has not followed definite development patterns, instead giving rise to a multi-layered patchwork[11] the administration is still struggling to interpret or intervene in. This patchwork combines a great mixture of functions with a lack of conventional planning regulations, merging a certain degree of informality with the strong permanence of historic agricultural land patterns. Viewed from another perspective, it has led to spatial configurations that more closely approximate the actual needs of the inhabitants, following the paths of 'anticipatory urbanism'[12] that administrations should acknowledge and integrate into planning processes.

Extensive and immersive fieldwork has been carried out, using visual methods to develop a situated representation of these hard-to-read infrastructural peripheries. Walking and cycling were tools employed to stress the infrastructural dimension and the constraints it poses to body movements, enabling participants to encounter this city in the making. Some excerpts from the fieldnotes help us to make sense of this space.[13]

> I'm not sure how to deal with the spaces on the edge of the urban motorway I'm studying, so I decide to take my bicycle, cross and let the space cross me, in the company of my camera, a tape recorder, and a notebook.
>
> The general idea that this infrastructural periphery gives is that of being in a part of the city that is coming into being, where construction companies are in the midst of their building activity. But the houses, the finishes, the first signs of time, say something else. It is a strange contrast, and it makes me wonder what led these families to live (and build, I would say) in this rural area. Matters of affordability or the inheritance of family land, the search for open space, the dream of country life without renouncing the possibilities offered by the city.
>
> It really strikes me how the landscape can change with such rapidity. It is clearly an expansion area that is growing without any real awareness. But I'm also fascinated by that because of the gap between the idea of the city as a theoretical entity, the market logic, and the construction drive that gives rise to these strange clusters of houses that land here from who knows where.
>
> At one point, the asphalt gives way to a bumpy dirt road and then starts up again just beyond, with no apparent reason.
>
> It is a strange urbanisation that will perhaps arrive, though perhaps not.... A little bit spotty, a little bit autonomous, even a little anarchic. There is a small hill that I had never noticed. The hill, however, clearly looks lived in. Beer cans, pizza boxes, handkerchiefs. It is indeed a good place to hang out. Or to hide.

> From the hill I can see these big structures (the railroad, the road, etc.) that come into being. And that's it. But around it is nothingness. This part of town continues its life of fields, artisanal businesses, and little more, and doesn't seem to notice the city that wants to grow. The same happens with the scattered houses.
>
> It is a speckled landscape. Like the coat of a Dalmatian dog. Little spots in the indistinct magma of the slow peri-urban countryside.
>
> And this is a piece of wild city. The streets are just dirt, and yet people live here. And maybe even well. The houses take all kinds of forms, from quasi-shacks made of concrete blocks and sheet metal fencing to cottages with fine finishes.
>
> The city is born before the city thinks of it. And it is good that way.
>
> I can't tell what is more alien: the city trying to take the countryside or the wasteland that is not being settled. Is it an unfinished city or is it a countryside where some families have homes?
>
> The question I constantly ask myself is what drives people to build and live here.
>
> I don't think it's only economic issues, it's obvious that some of these families are wealthy enough to build houses paying all the fees.
>
> But maybe that's the interesting part, the choice to consciously live outside the norms, in a liminal situation, not the necessity or expulsion from the city.

What emerges as the main characteristic of this periphery is precisely its illegibility, the fact of it being at once unplanned and still in formation. It conveys a certain inertia, not attracting investment or redevelopment and thus remaining a margin within the margins,

Figure 1. A view of the SS 554 from an overpass. Source: Photo by Martina Loi, 2022

Figure 2. Around the SS 554: a growing city in a speckled landscape.
Source: Photo by Martina Loi, 2022

Figure 3. Around the SS 554: the 'Emanuela Loi' bridge, an infrastructure for the city to come.
Source: Photo by Martina Loi, 2022

Figure 4. Around the SS 554: an unfinished city or a countryside where some families have homes? Source: Photo by Martina Loi, 2022

Figure 5. Around the SS 554: taking care of the public space with a self-built garden-square. Source: Photo by Martina Loi, 2022

in a southern region of the Global North. It is a condition shared with many southern European cities, which tend to exist outside of the great flows of capital and yet produce suburban forms worth interrogating.

Amid the self-built houses and agricultural remains of these hard-to-read suburbs, a familiar spatial form emerges, somehow a reassuring epiphany. Here, in the middle of the brushwood, someone is spontaneously taking care of a corner of public space. They are creating a small garden, or, to use the urban lexicon, a sort of square. Specifically, the square was created through the placement of ornamental potted plants, adopting an idea of 'positive' nature as a means of legitimacy[14] in contrast to the wild and uncultivated nature that characterises these areas and contributes to associated images of degradation and squatting. This small and simple spontaneous green architecture puts together plants that were certainly already there (especially the fig tree), potted plants, and newly planted fruit trees waiting to grow, along with typical urban furniture such as benches and small decorations. It is a space made perhaps to trigger some kind of community bonding in a neighbourhood where the private dimension prevails, houses are extremely introverted, and there is no public meeting space.

The care of public space through the creation of such a space can then be interpreted as a claim for citizenship status not yet fully recognised by the municipality, which here manifests itself in the appropriation of a small area and the daily production of a known (therefore recognisable, and also legitimising) urban form. At the same time, it is a form of anticipatory urbanism. Although the neighbourhood came into being informally, it has been regularised over time. The municipality has not yet provided the services that typically accompany urbanisation, and the neighbourhood maintains its indefinite status, slightly abandoned and degraded. The small and daily gestures of care that led to the small square being established thus suggest the realisation of a new centrality—one that anticipates the (possible) formation of a city to come, self-produced through daily practices. The absence of an administration leaves this space in an interstitial position, whereby the appropriation of the space by its inhabitants—through non-conflictual, purposeful modes of caring—can highlight their agency and their self-representation.

The square thus frees itself from the not-yet implemented urban plan, emerging as a sign of relationality and belonging between the inhabitants of the self-built houses and the residual, evolving public space. A new centrality is produced, without the intervention of any structured planning processes. The administration has not yet found (or sought) the appropriate tools to intervene in the area. Instead, it should now learn how to integrate the performance of citizenship that the small square's maintenance represents, and the implied forms of care this act entails.

Conclusion: A Peripheral Standpoint for (Re)Figuring the City to Come

These reflections were made possible by immersion in the space, which allowed me to stumble across this micro-episode of spontaneous urbanisation. Moreover, situating oneself within and observing from the margins with a peripheral standpoint is a strong way to build an understanding of local processes of peripheralisation, revealing the radical possibilities[15] that margins enable. Together with these explorations, narrating everyday practices and interstitial scenarios that do not conform to planning paradigms makes it possible to challenge dominant narratives and telescopic views. This approach will eventually allow for the emergence of radical, diverse standpoints on contemporary global peripheries and peripheral centralities.

This small tale of the self-produced square has increased its visibility and, with it, its representational force. By performatively producing an account oriented towards the unravelling of interstitial practices and spatial alternatives, one contributes to strengthening the actual spatial possibilities observed. If language can be considered an actor, the narrative of the spaces of SS 554 contributes to 'productive ontological interventions.'[16] Just as equipping a small corner of public space with plants and furniture constitutes a meaningful form of spatial production that gives rise to a new peripheral centrality, narration is a vital contributing factor in (re)imagining and (re)figuring the city to come.

Endnotes:

1 Filion, P. and Keil, R. Contested Infrastructures: Tension, Inequity and Innovation in the Global Suburb, *Urban Policy and Research, 35* (1), 2017, pp. 7–19.
2 Tonkiss, F. Afterword: Economies of Infrastructure, *City, 19* (2–3), 2015, p. 384.
3 Amin, A. Lively Infrastructure, *Theory, Culture & Society, 31* (7–8), 2014, p. 138.
4 Amin, 2014, *op. cit.*
5 Larkin, B. The Politics and Poetics of Infrastructure, *Annual Review of Anthropology, 42* (1), 2013, pp. 327–343.
6 Lawhon, M. et al. Thinking through Heterogeneous Infrastructure Configurations, *Urban Studies, 55* (4), 2018, pp. 720–732.
7 Loi, M. Urban motorways as spaces of possibility: Urban interstices and everyday practices around a motorway in Sardinia, *Urban Studies, 61* (13), 2024, pp. 2548–2564.
8 Katz, K. Splanetary Urbanization, *International Journal of Urban and Regional Research, 45* (4), 2021, pp. 597–611.
9 Haraway, D. Situated Knowledges: The Science Question in Feminism and the Privilege of Partial Perspective, *Feminist Studies, 14* (3), 1988, pp. 575–599.
10 Leontidou, L. Alternatives to Modernism in (Southern) Urban Theory: Exploring In-Between Spaces, *International Journal of Urban and Regional Research, 20* (2), 1996, pp. 178–195.
11 Schmid, C. et al. Towards a New Vocabulary of Urbanisation Processes: A Comparative Approach, *Urban Studies, 55* (1), 2018, pp. 19–52.
12 Phelps, N., Keil, R., and Maginn, P. J. Introduction: The Periphery at the Centre, in this volume, pp. 11–24.
13 The notes were in Italian, and the translation provided tries to remain as close as possible to the original sense, with the inevitable gaps involved in the translation process.
14 Angelo, H. *How Green Became Good: Urbanized Nature and the Making of Cities and Citizens.* University of Chicago Press, 2021.
15 hooks, b. *Feminist Theory. From Margin to Center.* Second edition. Pluto Press, 2000.
16 Gibson-Graham, J. K. Diverse Economies: Performative Practices for 'Other Worlds,' *Progress in Human Geography, 32* (5), 2008, p. 614.

Iconic Architecture in the Periphery: Building the Ideal City of the Future

Amparo Tarazona-Vento

Introduction

The conceptualisation of model cities has long been one of the preferred ways for architects and planners to put forward their ideas on how to solve existing urban challenges and envisage what an ideal urban future should look like. Some of these conceptualisations have been widely influential as planning models, either in the form of theoretical ideas or actual developments that materialise those ideas. From Renaissance model towns to more recent concepts—such as Howard's Garden City, Wright's Broadacre City, Le Corbusier's Radiant City, or even phantasmagoria like Google's Sidewalk Labs' Quayside in Toronto and Saudi Arabia's NEOM project—these ideas continue to shape the built environment worldwide.

Valencia's Sociopolis was born as one such planning concept that aimed to prefigure the city of the future, a model neighbourhood that—although rooted in the past—intended to be innovative in how it tackled the challenges of twenty-first century urbanisation. The concept was later developed into a real neighbourhood, thus providing an excellent way into exploring the processes involved in translating ideas around 'the ideal city' into practice. The neighbourhood is located near the river, to the south of the city of Valencia, and is integrated into the farmlands as a way of preserving the city's cultural identity (see Figure 1). It includes eighteen buildings designed by internationally well-known architects. Master-planned by Vicente Guallart and María Díaz, Sociopolis was marketed as a socially sustainable urban quarter where social interaction would be encouraged by the well-designed urban environment.

The Theoretical Centrality of a Model Neighbourhood

The Sociopolis project was the initiative of a group of architects called Metapolis. The group was formed in 1998 and was led by a Valencian architect based in Barcelona, Vicente Guallart. This group of architects was also involved in the creation of the Institute for Advanced Architecture of Catalonia (IAAC) in 2001, an education and research centre funded mainly by the Catalan regional government, which was created, according to one of the members, with the intention of 'getting commissions from the public administrations through the institute, to do things that we thought had to be done'.[1]

In this context, Sociopolis was born in 2001 as a theoretical project in which a group of architects proposed their idea of how a city should be organised. Here, it was not the client—in this case the Valencian regional government—who contacted the architect, but the other way round. Guallart was friends with Rafael Blasco—who was at the time the regional minister of social welfare—and Consuelo Císcar, the director of the Valencia Biennial of Arts. Guallart recounts that, in a conversation with them, he proposed to 'look at that idea of doing an exhibition at the Biennial of Arts, invite some architects and draw up a project for designing a neighborhood, and then it can be developed'.[2]

As a result of this conversation, the first theoretical project—known as Sociopolis—was commissioned by the regional Ministry of Welfare. Guallart gathered a group of high-profile architects—including Ábalos & Herreros, Duncan Lewis, Alejandro Zaera Polo, Greg Lynn, Torres Nadal, Gausa, Vinymas, Eduardo Arroyo, François Roche, and Toyo Ito—who elaborated a project for an ideal neighbourhood that proposed new types of housing for young people who live alone or share flats, older people in homes, immigrants, and single-parent families.

Sociopolis was presented at the 2003 Valencia Biennial of Arts, whose topic was 'the ideal city', and in an international landscape conference in Valencia organised for that specific purpose. The model exhibited in the Biennale can be seen in Figure 2. The project also received the approval of the international architectural professional and cultural worlds. In 2004, it was exhibited at the prestigious centre for architecture, the Architekturzentrum of Vienna. Dietmar Steiner, director of the centre, commented that 'for the first time in the new millennium, the Sociopolis project is designing a really

Figure 1. Photomontage of Sociopolis. Source: Guallart Architects

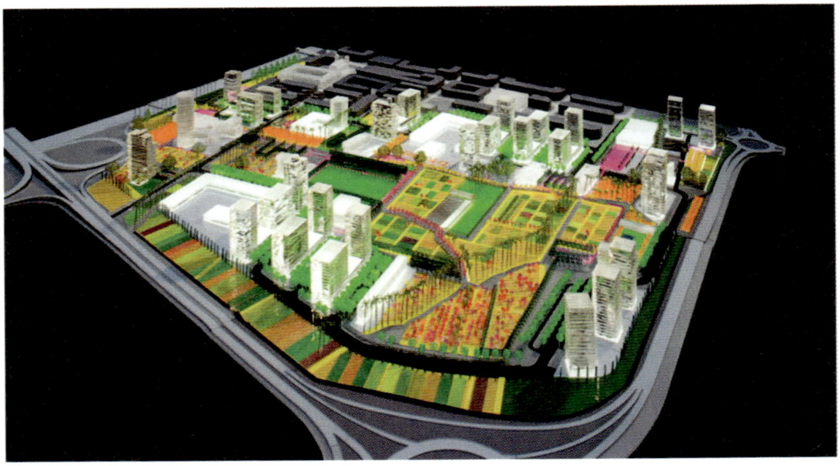

Figure 2. Model of the initial Sociopolis project. Source: Guallart Architects

integrative and hybrid vision for the new European city of the future'.[3] Later on, Sociopolis was one of the projects represented in the exhibition about contemporary Spanish architecture, *Onsite: New Architecture in Spain*, held at MoMA, New York, in 2005.

The opportunity for Sociopolis to become a real development project arrived when Blasco was appointed Regional Minister for Housing, Territory, Urbanism, and the Environment in 2003, and the Valencian Institute of Housing (IVVSA) was made responsible for its development. Sociopolis retained its primary aim of being a pioneering project from an architectural and urban design perspective, with the building commissions offered to prestigious architects. The project's other *raison d'être*, according to the Regional Director General of Housing, was to provide a sizeable proportion of the subsidised affordable housing needed in the Valencian region. This objective was interpreted as a way of satisfying the regional president's election pledge of building 100,000 subsidised affordable dwellings in a highly visible way.

Iconic Architecture in the Periphery

The IVVSA signed an agreement with Valencia City Council for the development of Sociopolis and, together, they selected a suitable site for the project. As shown in Figure 3, the site is located at the periphery of the city, on historical croplands in a dependent village within the Valencia city territory called La Torre. The plan was called La Torre Special Plan and included approximately 3,000 dwellings. The decision to build on protected croplands was very controversial but was justified by the author of the environmental impact study, on the grounds that this location would have the least detrimental effects (given that, in Valencia, any urban growth has to be made at the expense of the croplands or nature reserve land). However, the fact that the council offered up rural land as a location, arguing that there was no available land within the urban core of the municipality, was perceived by Guallart as an opportunity to look into the creation of a new rural–urban development typology—one which would integrate the croplands into urban life. Therefore, in addition to investigating new modes of dwelling, creating a laboratory of social housing, and proposing typologically and formally singular architecture, the project aimed to be innovative and experimental by exploring an urban design typology that would combine a rural environment with an urban one.

Since the General Urban Plan of Valencia did not allow building on the site selected for Sociopolis, the council reclassified thirty-five hectares of previously protected cropland, and ceded land previously earmarked for amenities for the development of social housing instead. The planning figure used was a 'special plan', which, as explained by an architect involved in the planning of the project, 'is called special because it has a very important public interest, which, in this case was the substantial quantity of subsidised housing to be built there'.[4] Therefore, making 80% of the project subsidised affordable dwellings was considered a way of justifying the occupation of protected croplands since it appealed to the project's strong public interest.

The official rhetoric of Sociopolis—namely, that it intended to create a sustainable neighbourhood with social aims—provided the project with popular support. However, urbanists, ecologists, intellectuals, citizens' groups, and the local socialist party opposed the project on the grounds that it would destroy Valencia's valuable rural environment. According to them, Sociopolis would *de facto* be a car-dependent neighbourhood, owing to its segregation from the urban area and its deficient public transport links. Moreover, it would not offer an effective solution to the city's housing problem. Instead, it would concentrate subsidised affordable housing in peripheral, badly connected areas of the city, leaving more appealing, more central areas for 'profitable' uses, such as tertiary or non-subsidised housing. Thus, it would not meaningfully intervene in the housing market by lowering prices in the core of the city. As summarised by a local urbanist, 'Sociopolis, as a concept, is a common and vulgar new town'.[5]

From Theory to Implementation

The project's implementation encountered many obstacles along the way. According to Guallart, building a neighbourhood is more difficult than building an iconic building because many more agents are involved in the former—landscape architects, botanists, ecologists, architects, engineers, and so on. Therefore, in the process, 'many hands intervene and, this, well, means that easily 20% to 25% of the quality is lost on the way, for various and even justified reasons, we

Figure 3. View of the Sociopolis site. Source: Guallart Architects

Figure 4. General view of Sociopolis. Source: Photo by Amparo Tarazona-Vento

could say'.[6] For instance, given the peripheral location, the connection to urban utilities was difficult, and the investment in infrastructures was therefore considerable. An agreement to retain one of the main historical water supplies for agriculture—namely, the irrigation canal of Favara, which was functional and still in use—was signed by the community of users and the Valencian Institute of Housing. However, although the original intention was to leave the layout of the irrigation canals and cropland paths as unchanged as possible, this feature of the project was ultimately lost, and the urbanisation of the landscape became more standardised (see a general view of Sociopolis in Figure 4).

Moreover, coordinating a group of 'starchitects' who are scattered around the world—and who have little knowledge of or interest in local building regulations and planning systems—proved difficult, especially given that each of them was involved in designing a small housing project with a limited budget rather than an iconic megaproject.

Utopia versus Profit

When the project changed from being a theoretical to a 'real' project, it also became less of an artistic and intellectual endeavour and became more closely linked to the urban development sphere. Guallart had selected all the participant architects for the theoretical project. In his words, they were 'friends of mine, let's say... We didn't contact anyone we didn't know but rather only people that we had worked with on past projects, in conferences, etc. in past years'.[7] When the Valencian Institute of Housing commissioned the architect for the master plan for the La Torre Special Plan, each of the architects in the initial group was assigned a plot of land on which to develop a housing project and given a new brief. In addition, other plots were assigned by public competition to teams formed by an architect and a developer.

The size of the site for the Special Plan grew sevenfold in comparison to the theoretical one, and the initial master plan elaborated by Guallart was modified in collaboration with architects from the Valencian Housing Institute so as to arrive at a more feasible final design. In Figure 5, a virtual model of the modified Sociopolis project

(La Torre Special Plan), including high-rise residential buildings in the middle of the croplands, can be seen.

Indeed, Sociopolis provides a clear illustration of the conflicts between producing architecture that stands out, making money, and managing to deliver an urban plan. Given that the project intended to create 'remarkable architecture', the construction costs of the new dwellings meant they were too expensive to qualify as affordable housing. To make the plan economically viable, a higher floor-area ratio than that established by the General Urban Plan was allowed. In addition, 20% of the dwellings would be sold at market prices instead of being affordable subsidised dwellings, as was initially planned. Moreover, because of the quality and singularity of the dwellings, most of those that were subsidised were at the higher price end for subsidised housing.

Despite all these changes, which were intended to improve the feasibility of the plan, the callout inviting construction bids for the projects was met with little response from the developers. This was owing in part to the level of technical and structural difficulty involved in building star architect projects, whose spec is generally far higher than is typical for social housing. Moreover, the fallout from the 2007 economic recession and the bursting of the real estate bubble affected the project since there was a lack of buyers for the dwellings and a lack of financing for the developers. By 2012, construction work had come to a halt and Sociopolis remained partially unoccupied. It was not until 2021 that a new plan to revitalise the neighbourhood—the Integral Plan of La Torre—was presented.

Conclusion

Sociopolis began its life as a model for what the city of the future should look like, placing architectural experimentation and intellectual exploration at its heart. Its final materialisation, however, is closer to a standard peripheral new development. Sociopolis's trajectory—from theoretical speculation to *in situ* development—raises a series of questions regarding the collective understanding of the urban, and our urban future.

First, it raises questions around the extent to which theory is independent from practice. Since Sociopolis was born as a result of a commission by the Regional Ministry of Welfare, the first theoretical

Figure 5. Virtual model of La Torre Special Plan (Sociopolis). Source: IVVSA

iteration of the project was focused on ideating new typologies of social housing. Later on, given the peripheral location of the site available for development, much of the conceptual emphasis turned towards exploring 'rurban' living. Thus, the theorisation of what an 'ideal city' should look like was influenced by the reality of the actually-existing city.

Second, it suggests that both architectural ideas and the practices involved in materialising them are heavily involved in the conceptualisation of the urban. In the case of Sociopolis, once the intellectual speculation became a real project, the need to make the project feasible outpaced the aim of creating a model for future living, and the reality of the implementation modified the vision still further. The density of the development was increased, the layout of farming gardens and irrigation canals profoundly modified, and the design of residential buildings adapted.

Third, the case of Sociopolis brings to light the dichotomy between utopia and profit, thus questioning to what extent it is possible to create a different urban future while the existing economic interests, processes, and actors are embedded in its development. Despite starting life as a utopian project, Sociopolis's objectives ultimately seemed more closely aligned with the interests of the construction and real estate sectors. The theoretical and political centrality of this project meant that developers could colonise formerly protected agricultural land, in this way providing an excuse for further development and real estate accumulation.

Finally, through the controversies surrounding its peripheral location and its continued theoretical and political centrality, Sociopolis highlights the importance of what it means to be urban in relation to location, accessibility, and connectivity. In other words, adding to questions regarding what the city of the future *should* look like and who will build it, Sociopolis asks a further question: namely, where should the city of the future be and just how much centrality can the periphery claim?

Endnotes:

1 Interview with Director of Sogo Architects, September 17, 2009.

2 Interview with Vicente Guallart, architect, author, and promoter of Sociopolis, December 14, 2009.

3 Alemany, L. La huerta valenciana 'invade' la ciudad con Sociopolis, *El Mundo*, May 2, 2006, p. 48.

4 Interview with author of the plot distribution project of La Torre, June 25, 2009.

5 Interview with former Head of the Mayor's Office, June 30, 2009.

6 Interview with Vicente Guallart, 2009.

7 Interview with Vicente Guallart, 2009.

The Role of Starchitects in 'Solving' the Peripheral *Problematique*

Lucia Cerrada Morato

Introduction

The role and responsibility of starchitects in the speculative urban regeneration that took place across Spanish cities between the late 1990s and before the 2008 financial crisis has already been generously documented. In the main, these urban renewal actions consisted of large public money investments that, at best, yielded low social returns.[1] This article opens with one of these megaprojects: namely The City of Culture designed by the American starchitect Peter Eisenman in the periphery of Santiago de Compostela, a medium-sized city in the northwest of Spain. Eisenman won the competition in 1999 and began work on the site in 2001. However, despite its budget tripling, it remains unfinished today.

While the above was happening, another starchitect–Britain's David Chipperfield–had moved his summer residency to a small village in the same region. In his own words below, he expands on the connection between him and Eisenman.

> He [Alberto Núñez Feijóo, President of the Region of Galicia] called me, knowing I was an honorary Galician and an architect, could I come and advise him what to do [with the City of Culture]? I really didn't have any suggestions [on how to complete or resolve the project] that are repeatable. Instead, I said what I would be more willing to do is give your administration advice on planning ... This part of Europe was not doing itself any good by a lot of developments ... It is a very identified condition called 'Galician ugliness' which is what they [Galicians] do. The President, aware of this problem, said 'it would be great if you can help us because we need to

> control the quality of our architecture [in the urbanised periphery]'.[2]

In this chapter I delve into what has unfolded since this conversation, in order to challenge the mainstream political and architectural discourse of how starchitects can 'solve' the urbanised periphery *problematique*. I argue instead that they are being instrumentalised to depoliticise the process, as a further mechanism of neoliberal planning ideology.

Context

There is a robust critical scholarship analysing the urbanised periphery, which demands that we recognise its existence, and its distinctive socio-spatial and environmental nature, but also that we develop a propositional agenda for its transformation.[3] This contrasts with the apparent paralysis of international, national, and regional institutions responsible for planning the urbanised periphery. The paralysis is twofold; on the one hand, there exists a lack of identification of the characteristics that differentiate these territories from bounded and dense urban areas; on the other, a lack of vision for their socio-spatial, economic, and environmental future.

Filling this gap in academic debate and policy practice, a series of starchitects in Europe have for some time now shown an interest in going beyond architecture and urban design in urban areas, investigating the urbanised periphery as a new object of study. Some examples include Rem Koolhaas's investigation on how peripheries are being transformed 'beyond recognition' in the Netherlands;[4] Herzog and de Meuron's and ETH Studio Basel's research into the impacts of processes of peripheral urbanisation on Switzerland's rural landscapes;[5] or Renzo Piano's call in his final years of practice to reflect on the physical and social transformations needed across suburbs and peripheries.[6] Overall, these initiatives have contributed towards efforts to recognise a different set of urbanisation processes and to reimagine these processes for the future.

As already stated, the role of starchitects in the contemporary urbanisation process has already been explored. Megaprojects, such as the Guggenheim in Bilbao, The City of Culture in Santiago de Compostela or the City of Science in Valencia—designed by starchitects during the 1990s and 2000s—marked the emergence of neoliberal policy, which favoured private investment and the deregulation of property markets, leading to social exclusion and the formation of new urban elites.[7] Furthermore, the materialisation of these urban megaprojects transformed governance at the local, regional, and national level, ultimately leading to the consolidation of less democratic forms of urban decision-making and governance. It has been argued that the preferred organisational model for the delivery of megaprojects was largely based on public–private partnership, authoritarianism and a lack of democratic accountability.[8] Following this early scholarship, other authors reflected on how lesser material aspects contributed to the implementation of such projects, including faith in the expertise of starchitects and the immaterial imaginaries that permitted this policy mobility.[9]

Twenty years on from some of these iconic urban regeneration interventions, the case of Chipperfield in Galicia raises questions around whether the intervention of starchitects will help unlock critical issues of the urbanised periphery, and whether the role of starchitects in querying and transforming the urbanised periphery represents a more participatory, bottom-up process or whether it simply replicates the democratic deficiencies of past megaprojects. To explore and unpack these questions, I conducted ten interviews with key actors in the planning ecosystem of the region—from local to regional governments through to academic institutions and professional bodies.

Chipperfield and Foundation RIA in Galicia

Galicia, in the northwest of the Iberian Peninsula, is one of twelve Autonomous Regions in Spain. A third of its 2,700,000 inhabitants live across seven cities and the rest inhabit the urbanised periphery, under differing spatial forms: from traditional rural settlements and their extensions to low-density dispersed growth or urbanised corridors. Historically, Galicia has been a region with a low level of industrialisation and high dependency on the primary sector, fundamentally for supplying its own consumption. Since the end of Franco's dictatorship in 1975, strong transformation processes have taken place both in terms of economic and infrastructural growth, but also from a political perspective—through the adoption of the Statute of

Figure 1. The City of Culture. Source: Photo by Lucía Cerrada Morato, 2023

Autonomy in 1981 and the subsequent creation of the regional government. Since then, the Regional Government of Galicia has been primarily governed by the right-wing party Partido Popular, with more progressive governments operating at the local level across the seven cities.

The Barbanza, where Chipperfield moved his summer residency, is a region of 244 square kilometres running in parallel to the Ría de Arousa. The area is located adjacent to the Atlantic Axis, an urbanised corridor that runs north to south from A Coruña to Oporto in Portugal, structuring the region of Galicia and its urban growth over the last forty years.

According to interviews and media reports, Chipperfield started to spend his summer holidays in Galicia in the 1990s. In the early 2000s, he built a house in Corrubedo, one of the rural settlements in the Barbanza region. Until 2016, his only economic and professional activity in the area consisted of a café in the village run by his family. In 2016, encouraged by the President of the region—as Chipperfield discloses in his lecture at the American Academy in Berlin—he decided to organise a workshop, run and coordinated by staff from his office, which allowed students from the University of Coruna and Barcelona to visit and analyse the territory in the Barbanza. The findings were presented in an exhibition organised in a public building in Ribeira. Numerous organisations attended, and an analysis of media documents shows that local and regional politicians also took part in the discussion sessions. This first phase was an exploratory exercise that provided an opportunity not only to investigate the urban, economic, and environmental issues in this peripheral area, but to assess the reception and demand of an external actor in the planning debate. Members of Chipperfield's team reported a warm welcome from a local municipal and regional government perspective, as well as from third sector organisations.

The second phase began with the creation of a non-profit foundation, Fundación RIA. As its by-laws establish, the foundation's purpose is the:

> ... analysis, debate, development and promotion of ideas to support the development and protection of the local economy, as well as the architectural, urban, natural and cultural values of the Atlantic estuaries of Galicia in north-west Spain. The Foundation seeks to reconcile

Figure 2. Peripheral urbanisation in Galicia. Source: Photo by Juan Luis Dalda, Manuel G. Docampo, and Javier G. Harguindey, 2006

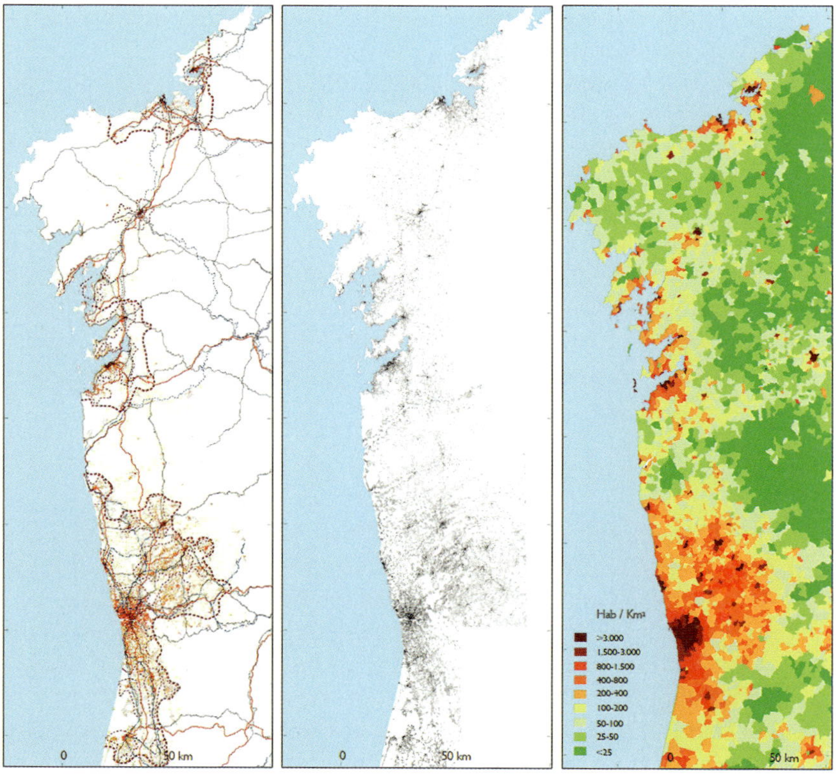

Figure 3. The Atlantic Axis. Source: Juan Luis Dalda, Manuel G. Docampo, and Javier G. Harguindey, 2006

The Role of Starchitects in 'Solving' the Peripheral Problematique

> and strengthen the efforts of individuals and public or private institutions related to these areas, and, where appropriate, operate as an instrument for coordination of these institutions.[10]

In this new role, the Foundation began to explore and develop studies around issues that affect Barbanza's extended urbanisation, such as urbanisation along roads, the issue of rural settlements, as well as more dispersed forms of urbanisation linked to land consolidation processes. Some of these initial projects, such as the AC-305 road study, were pitched to the regional government and to local authorities, and an agreement was signed for the Foundation to develop a more detailed analysis. In this second phase, we see numerous organisations—such as the Spanish National Research Council or the local authority of Pontevedra—approaching the institution for its support in developing a competition brief or seeking advice on urban and architectural issues.

The last stage of Chipperfield's role in Galicia marked a significant shift, both in terms of the Foundation's physical and symbolic location within the region, and in the scope of the works it has embarked on. On the one hand, Santiago's municipal government temporarily loaned the Foundation a public building to house their headquarters in the city. On the other, the Foundation launched a process to develop the territorial agenda for the region. In doing so, it signed a collaboration agreement with the regional government and the Professional Association of Architects of Galicia, through which all parties allocate funding.

Operating in a Peripheral Void

All interviewees pointed towards the 'critical vacuum' in which the figure of David Chipperfield and his Foundation—as an external actor to Galicia's governance landscape—was formed and continues to operate. This 'critical vacuum' was generally described as an absence of actors and initiatives that addressed the *problematique* of the urbanised periphery. Moreover, there are two fundamental controversial aspects that emerge from an analysis of the interviews. Firstly, why does this 'critical vacuum' exist in the urbanised periphery? And secondly, what is the actual *problematique* of these territories?

Figure 4. Corrubedo. Source: Photo by Cristina García Fontán, 2023

Figure 5. Typical detached single-family house in the Barbanza region.
Source: Photo by Lucía Cerrada Morato, 2022

The reasons why this gap exists are contested. Some interviewees point towards the shared responsibility of private and public actors—including governmental institutions and professional bodies—as well as the wider society. This discourse places equal responsibility on individuals for their actions (such as building a house in a particular manner) and institutions, which are framed as too weak or inept to control and guide this form of growth. However, other interviewees point towards the central and enabling role of regional government, not only due to its weak planning regulations, but its long-standing role in the provision of infrastructures that have supported and shaped this form of urbanisation over the last forty years. In fact, according to most interviewees, the urbanisation of the periphery was a deliberate strategy to allow individuals to capitalise on their land, through the construction of private homes. This approach, in a region with a *minifundia* land structure and highly dispersed landownership, was considered electorally advantageous.

To facilitate this institution-led process of peripheral urbanisation, a 'critical vacuum' was formed to eliminate antagonistic and disapproving voices. According to the planning and architectural consultants interviewed, the creation of this vacuum was operationalised by the regional government through a highly biased procurement approach which favoured (through very high capital requirements) large engineering companies to the detriment of smaller 'critical urbanism' practices. Consequently, projects and interventions have been addressed through 'hard' solutions that prioritise the efficiency and economic viability of these infrastructures, as opposed to good-quality placemaking interventions. This procurement approach eventually led to the disappearance of small and medium 'critical urban' practices working on the peripheral question.

The second issue is the actual nature of the problem itself. Local media and the regional government have framed the peripheral *problematique* as an aesthetic matter of poor-quality architecture. Bolstering this narrative, local media developed the concept of 'ugliness', which describes the deterioration and destruction of the traditional landscape through the abandonment of rural areas and/or actions that have little respect for tradition.[11] By doing so, they have focused the responsibility on individuals and their lack of 'taste' and culture, as opposed to developing a structural, institutional critique targeting issues of poor planning and a lack of political vision for what the economic future of citizens living in these territories should be. The ultimate outcome has been the reduction of the socioeconomic, environmental, and political complexities of the urbanised periphery to the status of aesthetic problem. The identification of a starchitect, one with a worldwide reputation, as the actor best placed to tackle the peripheral question thus only reinforces the regional government's aesthetic argument. In fact, as argued by one interviewee:

> Chipperfield has the prestige and a wonderful portfolio of first-class projects ... And he is also an apolitical and independent expert, and that's why actors of different kinds are approaching him to get studies done or get technical advice.[12]

This argument further contributes to the depoliticisation of the peripheral question, by reducing the issues to a purely technocratic question. However, an analysis of the work of the Fundación RIA, as well as Chipperfield's lectures and presentations, suggests that their diagnosis of what needs to be addressed in this context goes beyond aesthetic matters, requiring environmental and socioeconomic lenses that make the question of the peripheral a deeply political one.

The Planning Governance of a Peripheral Region

The shifting role of Chipperfield and his Foundation over the last five years is clear. From an independent, external actor—exploring a small area in Galicia through his private means—to a participatory actor embedded within the institutional landscape, undertaking studies—financially and politically supported by public funding bodies—that examine the region as a whole. Some interviewees justify the Foundation's current role, and its wide portfolio of projects, as a response to the demands made by numerous institutions seeking to address the peripheral *problematique*:

> ... as the Foundation is independent—it is not linked to the public sector, nor to the private sector—and in fact represents the society as a third actor, other institutions and individuals trust its members to unlock the problems of the territory.[13]

However, most interviewees point, firstly, to the fact that, although the Foundation has facilitated participatory processes, it cannot be considered representative of society since it has primarily engaged with 'a limited group of professionals and members of the elite such as international architects, planners, and business leaders'.[14] They emphasise, secondly, that, although non-profit, the Foundation is receiving public funding to develop studies and projects that have in the past generally been commissioned to private companies through competitive processes. Thirdly, the Foundation has selected *itself* as the leading actor for the development of a territorial agenda, a planning exercise that should ultimately be led and overseen by regional government, as captured in its by-laws. All these issues raise concerns around, firstly, the neglect of duties by regional government and the lack of democratic legitimacy of a non-profit entity establishing and moderating the governance of actors; secondly, the absence of transparency on how exactly funding for studies is allocated and negotiated; and, finally, deficiencies in the accountability process for a non-public organisation when considering project outcomes. According to this study it can be argued that the Fundación RIA goes beyond the public–private partnership model widely used across urban regeneration megaprojects during the 1990s,[15] effectively replacing public functions whose execution is now guided by a non-public, non-democratically elected entity.

Conclusion

In conclusion, this case has highlighted the limitations of traditional planning actors and tools in addressing the complex socio-political issues surrounding the urbanised periphery and, further, in articulating an agenda for its future transformation. However, it has also pointed towards the deficiencies of certain governance and partnership arrangements in chaperoning its transformation, which instead of advancing a progressive agenda of empowerment and democratisation, serve to reinforce weak democratic processes. In fact, the case of the starchitect Chipperfield in Galicia represents a paradigmatic example of a new wave of starchitects focusing on the urbanised periphery. Effectively, Chipperfield has moved beyond the purely analytical function of delivering according to a defined brief set by a governmental institution. Rather than a consultant, Chipperfield is now an embedded actor within the institutional landscape, one that has become central in leading and framing the planning of these territories. Indeed, Fundación RIA's replacement of the public sector represents yet another expression of neoliberal privatisation of governance and territorial planning that bears further scholarly inquiry.

Endnotes:

1 Medina, X. S. Governance, urban competitiveness and crisis in Spain, *Journal of Urban and Regional Analysis, 8* (1), 2016, p. 47.

2 Chipperfield, D. *Beyond Architecture: Identity and Sustainability – Fundación RIA in Galicia*, Marina Kellen French Lecture at the American Academy in Berlin, March 21, 2019; https://vimeo.com/325983770.

3 Sieverts, T. and Larup, L. (2012). Public Debate. New Dialogues 1, *Lacunas. The Middle Landscape.* Podium Discussion, January 23, 2012; https://vimeo.com/42182708.

4 Koolhaas, R. *Countryside: a report.* Taschen, 2020.

5 Herzog, J. and de Meuron, P. *Achtung: die Landschaft I, II & III*, ETH Studio Basel; https://archive.arch.ethz.ch/studio-basel/projects/achtung-die-landschaft/index.html.

6 Piano, R. The future of Europe's Cities is in the Suburbs, interview by Sylvia Poggioli, *WEMU. org*, March 10, 2015; available at https://www.wemu.org/2015-03-10/architect-renzo-piano-the-future-of-europes-cities-is-in-the-suburbs.

7 Swyngedouw, E., Moulaert, F., and Rodriguez, A. The world in a grain of sand: Large-scale urban development projects and the dynamics of 'glocal' transformations, in: F. Moulaert, A. Rodriguez, and E. Swyngedouw (eds.) *The Globalized City: Economic Restructuring and Social Polarization in European Cities.* Oxford University Press, 2005, pp. 9–28.

8 Keil, R. 'Common-sense' neoliberalism: Progressive conservative urbanism in Toronto, Canada, in: N. Brenner and N. Theodore (eds.) *Spaces of Neoliberalism: Urban Restructuring in North America and Western Europe.* Blackwell, 2002, pp. 230–253.

9 Tarazona Vento, A. Mega-project meltdown: Post-politics, neoliberal urban regeneration and Valencia's fiscal crisis, *Urban Studies, 54* (1), 2017, pp. 68–84.

10 Fundación RIA, *Vision*, 2017; https://fundacionria.org/fundacion/.

11 Santos, X. M. and Piñeiro-Antelo, M. A. Landscape and power: the debate around ugliness in Galicia (Spain), *Landscape Research, 45* (7), 2020, pp. 841–853.

12 Interview with local politician in a local authority in the region on December 8, 2022.

13 Interview with member of the Fundación RIA on January 11, 2023.

14 Interview with planner and academic in private practice and in an academic institution in the region on November 24, 2022.

15 Moulaert, F., Rodriguez, A. and Swyngedouw, E. (eds.) *The Globalized City: Economic Restructuring and Social Polarization in European Cities.* Oxford University Press, 2003, pp. 9–28.

Culture-led Peripheral Centrality: The Story of Songzhuang, the World's Largest Arts District

Linhao Chen, Oleg Golubchikov, and Justin Spinney

Introduction

Influenced by ideas concerning creative class and creative cities,[1] creative spaces and arts districts have gained much prominence in local policy, as one of the engines of postmodernist urban regeneration. There is now an extensive literature on the nexus of urban policy and cultural districts. However, most of these studies focus on central urban areas,[2] while very few explore the role of arts districts in shaping broader metropolitan morphology. Such a perspective is particularly relevant in China, which is currently undergoing a rapid expansion of its metropolitan areas.

In this chapter, we examine the case of Songzhuang in Beijing's Tongzhou District, which has experienced a remarkable transformation–from a farmland into what has become the world's largest arts district. What distinguishes it from the more 'traditional' arts districts is its location in the outer periphery of the city. This peripherality also means that Songzhuang is overshadowed by more 'famous' arts districts, such as the 798 Art Zone.

The formation and evolution of Songzhuang's Art District also represents an outlier in Beijing's wider urbanisation. Emerging organically and very much in opposition to the centrally prescribed regime, it remained a bottom-up, unplanned initiative for some time. More recently, Songzhuang Art District has been subsumed into the city's formal planning and development, as part of Beijing's 'sub-centre' in the Tongzhou District, which is a new mega-development seeking to decongest the inner city. The sub-centre also includes the Universal Theme Park and Zhangjiawan. The former is a world-famous amusement park and currently the only one in China. The latter is a national-level design industry town that is being built under the joint coordination of the municipal and district governments. Together with Universal Theme Park and Zhangjiawan, Songzhuang now forms a so-called 'cultural axis' of Beijing. This makes Songzhuang an unexpected point of spatial rupture in the morphology of Beijing. Nevertheless, due to its spontaneous origin, it remains very much an 'illegitimate child' in the eyes of the city government.

From Agricultural Periphery to a Cultural Centre

Songzhuang Art District originated in Xiaopu Village in the northern part of Tongzhou District, some 25 kilometres away from the centre of Beijing (Figure 1). At the time of writing, Xiaopu has become the central area of Songzhuang Town, adjacent to Beijing's new subcentre (Figure 2).

The town of Xiaopu had an incredibly modest start. Before the policy of opening-up China came into effect in 1978, Beijing's main industries and population were concentrated in the central city. Xiaopu was extremely poorly connected with Beijing and was still a small, backward village. Although farming was the primary source of income for locals, Xiaopu had poor land conditions, with more than 133 hectares of its agricultural land classed as sandy wasteland. In the 1980s, a chicken farm and a foundry were established in the village, but the everyday reality of poverty remained omnipresent. In the 1990s, when the country embarked on a boom of township enterprises, Xiaopu raised funds to build a village-level industrial park on abandoned land; thirteen enterprises moved in. Coupled with the opening-up of transport links, this development improved living standards for the locals. However, the biggest change came with the arrival of a community of artists displaced from another area in Beijing.

During the same time period, the contemporary Chinese art movement emerged across the country. This was partly an unintended consequence of artists losing their jobs or struggling to secure work in formal state institutions. In Beijing, these artists began to congregate spatially around Yuanmingyuan—located at that time in the urban periphery—forming the famous Yuanmingyuan Painters Village. The fragmented administrative control of this urban–rural area provided space and freedom for artists' survival and creativity.

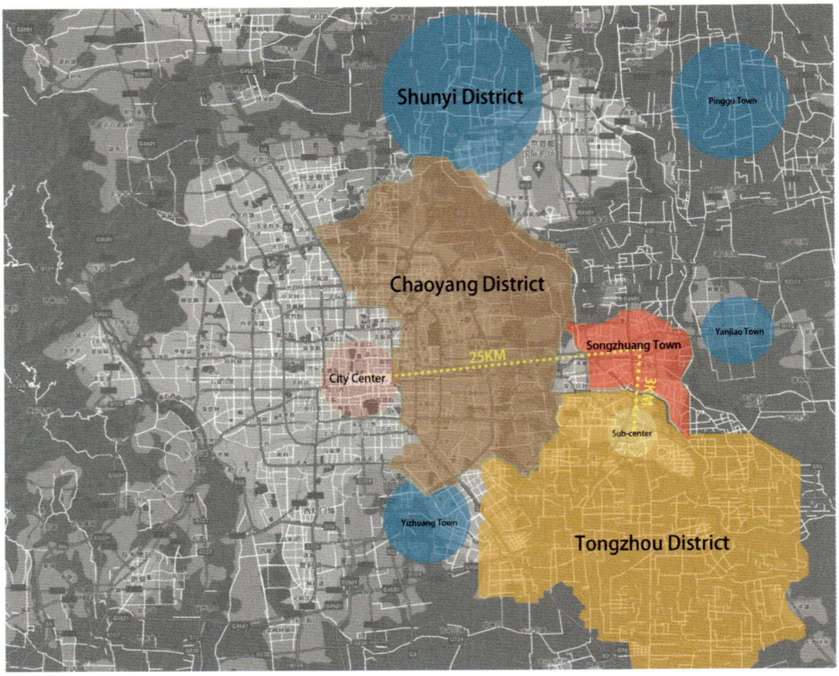

Figure 1. The location of Songzhuang and its links to the rest of Beijing City. Source: Google Maps, drawn by the authors

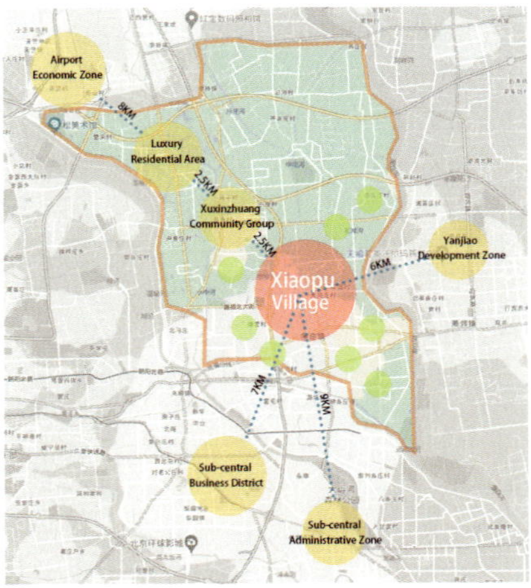

Figure 2. The location of Xiaopu Village and its links to surrounding communities. Source: Google Maps, drawn by the authors

As the area grew in influence, more than 300 artists moved in. However, the Yuanmingyuan Painters Village was seen by the local government as a destabilising factor and was disbanded in 1994. The emergence of Songzhuang was largely due to the relocation of artists from Yuanmingyuan.[3] In 1995, Fang Lijun, Yue Minjun, Liu Wei, Wang Qiang and other renowned artists of their era left Yuanmingyuan and, on the recommendation of a student, settled in Xiaopu Village. As more artists began to move in, both from Beijing and increasingly from other cities, a unique cultural atmosphere emerged in Xiaopu.[4] The villagers benefitted from this spontaneous process since they were able to rent their unused houses to artists to earn additional income. The emerging art colony also created demand for services to support artists and associated tourist activities.[5]

In 2000, the central government introduced the concept of a cultural industry which marked another watershed moment for Songzhuang. Arts districts were now seen as important carriers of the cultural industry, so that instead of alienating them, planning and other bureaucratic institutions began to support such developments. Beijing introduced its cultural and creative industries plan in 2005 and included Songzhuang in the first batch of officially 'certified' cultural and creative clusters, marking the beginning of more active government intervention in Songzhuang.

At the same time, Beijing's successful Olympic bid led to a forced relocation of low-end manufacturing-based township enterprises, which migrated still further into the outskirts of the city in an effort to accommodate urban expansion into once-peripheral areas.[6] This produced a large number of unused factory premises in Songzhuang, which further enabled cultural industry to be consolidated as a new pillar for the area. The 2005 Songzhuang Cultural Town Strategy Implementation Plan celebrated this new function and even introduced a district logo (see Figure 3).[7] In addition, the Songzhuang Township made 2,700 hectares of land available for investment in the cultural industry. In turn, this launched an era of commercial real estate that brought considerable income to the town.[8]

Figure 3. The entrance to Songzhuang Art District, with the 'Songzhuang, China' logo. Source: Photo by Linhao Chen, 2022

Figure 4. The Songzhuang Art Museum. Source: Photo by Linhao Chen, 2022

The Formation of an Arts-centred Ecosystem

The Songzhuang Art District developed rapidly, with the remaining factory premises converted into artist studios and exhibition halls. Songzhuang's preferential land policies attracted numerous art institutions. In 2006, the Songzhuang Art Museum was built (see Figure 4). Several official organisations were also established to coordinate relationships between the artist community and the government, with the additional aim of attracting investment into the art district space (see Figure 5). Among these were the Songzhuang Creative Industries Cluster Development Company and Songzhuang Investment and Development Company, which were set up with the sole purpose of profiting from real estate development.

These companies are commercial entities, with government officials occupying key positions, and are typical of the Chinese union of power and capital.[9] They provide government functions, such as approval applications for specific projects, while they also have a monopoly over land acquisition and leasing.

Another important player here is the village committee, which represents the interests of the farmers. Since rural land is collectively owned by the villagers, government land planning requires committee approval. The Xiaopu Village committee set up its own collective enterprise, headed by the village chief, to ensure that the original residents who hold land use rights benefit from land development. As shareholders, villagers receive dividends from land lease. Xiaopu is the only village in the vicinity that has established its own joint-stock company and distributed real estate profit to its residents. Other villages—typically those with fewer resources and weak bargaining power—tend to hand over their land use rights to more powerful government or real estate forces in the planning process.

This rapid spatial transformation of the village reached its peak in 2012. The village had thirty-five art exhibition halls, 113 galleries, more than 4,500 studios, and a total exhibition area of over 10,000,000 square metres.[10] With the completion of various art zones and museums, art institutions, painting and framing shops, and private galleries, Songzhuang has formed a fully-fledged art ecosystem. By this point, it was a comprehensive and self-sustaining arts community underpinned by art sales, art processing, art training and other related industrial chains (see Figure 6 and Figure 7).

Figure 5. Office buildings hosting official organisations in Songzhuang.
Source: Photo by Linhao Chen, 2022

Figure 6. Private galleries and art-related shops in Songzhuang. Source: Photo by Oleg Golubchikov, 2022

Figure 7. Locally organised auction sales in Songzhuang. Source: Photo by Oleg Golubchikov, 2014

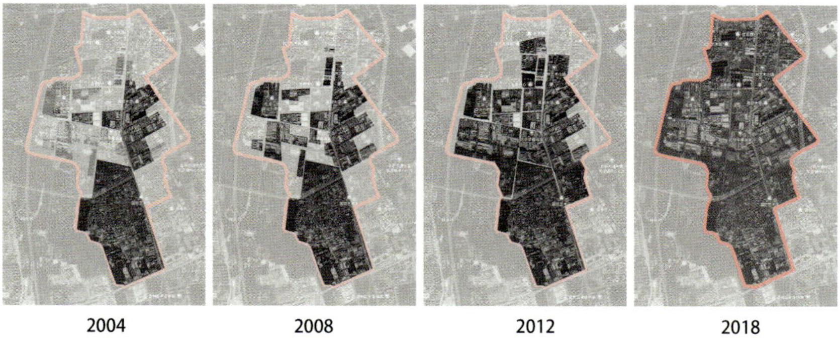

Figure 8. The evolution of land use in Xiaopu Village. Source: Baidu maps, drawn by the authors

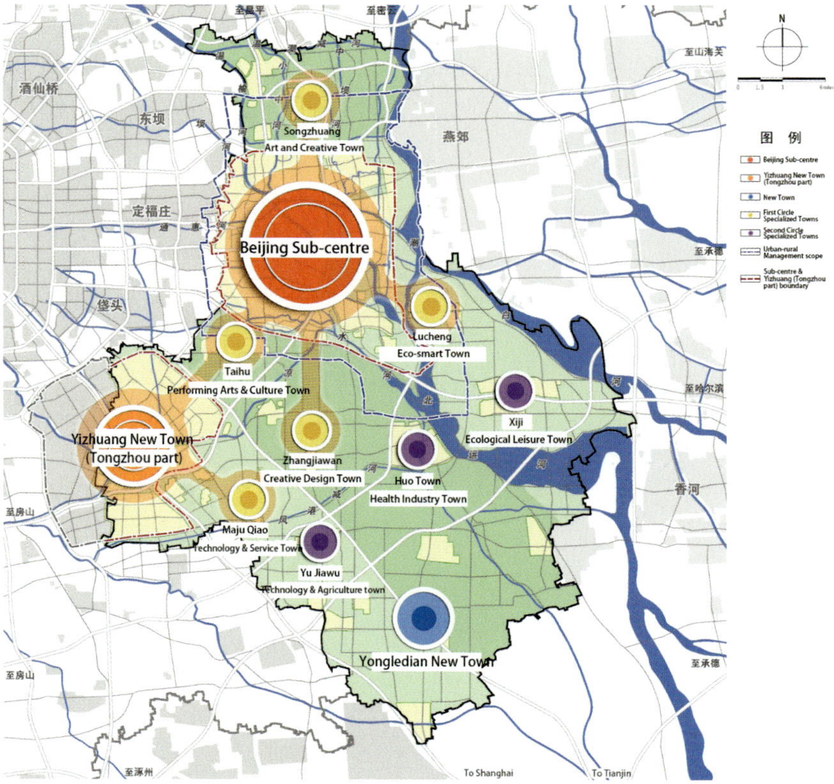

Figure 9. Sub-centre planning details. Source: Detailed Plan for Beijing's Urban Sub-centre

Figure 10. Sub-centre planning details. Source: Detailed Plan for Beijing's Urban Sub-centre

Figure 11. Ex-factory buildings hosting artists' studios are demolished.
Source: Photo by Linhao Chen, 2022

The construction activity continued northwards in line with the expansion of the art district and, after a series of transformations including the retreat of industrial plants, Songzhuang Art District took its current shape (Figure 8). The spatial pattern consisted of the original village in the south, a converted industrial area in the middle, and newly built independent artist studios in the north. More than twenty villages in the surrounding area[11] have also followed in Xiaopu's footsteps, witnessing a similar renewal based around the influx of the art community.

As people continued to flood to the region from all over the country, by 2011 the resident population of Xiaopu and its surrounding villages had exceeded the local registered population by nearly ten times (Table 1).

	1998	1993	1995	1998	2000	2002	2005	2007	2011
Householders	396	530	501	482	499	501	503	503	503
Domiciled population	1189	1553	1455	1351	1398	1404	1362	1367	1367
Resident population	1300	2300	2400	3300	4860	5600	6087	8010	10000+

Table 1. Demographic changes in Xiaopu Village. Data source: Xiaopu Village Committee

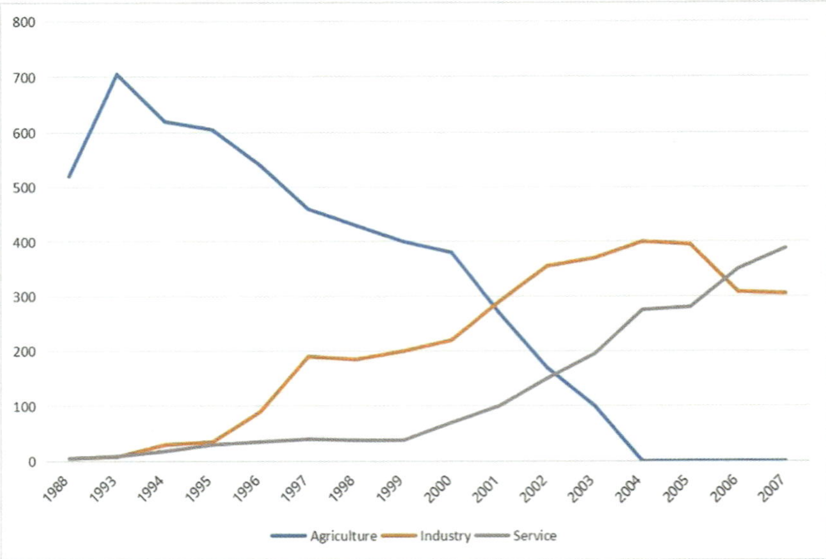

Table 2. Changes in the structure of the working population in Xiaopu. Data source: Xiaopu Village Committee

This new demographic includes art practitioners, business-people and migrant workers alongside a variety of other occupations, all revolving around the art industry. The number of villagers engaged in agricultural labour has plummeted, while the labour force in the secondary and tertiary sectors has continued to rise (Table 2).

The Beijing Sub-centre Plan and a 'Cultural Axis'

Beijing has long been looking for a means of de-concentrating its economic hub and alleviating population congestion in the central city. A major new mechanism in addressing this has been the 'sub-centre' strategy. The Beijing sub-centre is envisaged as an 'overspill' development which supplements the city centre by absorbing additional population, employment and public functions while at the same time boosting the economic development of surrounding areas. The Beijing Master Plan 2016–2035 identified Tongzhou District as the site most suited for establishing a major sub-centre. Tongzhou—located in the strategic belt between Beijing and Tianjin, on the borders of Hebei Province—now boasts excellent transport links to the surrounding areas. In addition to its function as a new centre, Tongzhou is also required to form its own polyfunctional relationships with its environs. Nine specialised towns will thus be established around the core sub-centre (Figure 9).

It is worth noting here that Songzhuang has been appointed as one of those secondary centres. Indeed, the district has developed over the past thirty years to a scale that cannot be ignored by urban planning—the plan for the sub-centre currently situates it as part of the first peripheral circle of the sub-centre and as an 'art and creative town'. Songzhuang Town will develop a spatial pattern of 'two zones' and 'two belts' (Figure 10). This involves strengthening the links between the Songzhuang Art District and the central area of Songzhuang Town, as well as building the Wenyu River International Exchange Zone and the Chaobai River Ecological Recreation Zone (along the Tongzhou Grand Canal). Songzhuang Art District will unite with the Universal Theme Park site to the south to form a complete cultural vision for the sub-centre; in local terms, Songzhuang Art District will act as a hub between the northern area clusters and administrative areas.

The future master plan for Songzhuang has been transferred from the town to the national level and incorporated into the sub-centre planning strategy. In terms of specific policies for the internal makeup of the Art District, the new plan will largely take the form of demolition and retention. The main buildings of the block will be renovated or their façades refurbished; however, a large number of artists' studios in former factory buildings that currently occupy the middle of the village will be demolished (Figure 11), with the area being rezoned as a 'reserve site'. Additionally, the foundation stone for China's largest China Artwork Trading Centre was laid in Songzhuang.

Songzhuang has thus completed its transformation from the world's largest spontaneously led artist colony to a government-operated 'art and creative town'. While this transformation has brought new opportunities to Songzhuang, it has also brought new conflicts. For instance, of the more than 2,000 artists affected by the demolition of the middle factory area, only a handful were adequately resettled, with most being forced to leave.

Although Songzhuang has accrued sustained artistic appeal over the past twenty years due to its extensive and well-known community of artists, and has thus maintained a degree of uniqueness in its development, it has not received more prominent support from the government. From the perspective of central government, the Songzhuang artist community has not lived up to its initial economic expectations. After nearly thirty years of development, Songzhuang is still reliant on profits from land rent and the circulation of artists' works (Figure 7). This is seen as a low value-added mode of growth. Although Songzhuang has had a decisive agglomeration effect in terms of attracting artists to the district and its surrounding area, it has not formed a complete industrial chain. Besides, many artists—including art institutions—are considered to be 'net consumers' locally. While they may produce their art there, they tend to rely on inner-city venues such as 798 for showcases and exhibitions, thus generating economic value outside of Songzhuang.

Even so, Songzhuang retains its unique status. It is the only specialised cluster of this kind to have formed spontaneously and to have survived until the present day. Although its prominence has declined, the nuanced structure of negotiation between officials and artist groups, developed over time, has not completely disappeared. With the inclusion of new stakeholders, it nonetheless continues to shape the spatial patterns of Songzhuang. The Art District's influence on the surrounding community has enabled it to remain as a subregional centre and (even if somewhat reluctantly) to be integrated into the government's own plans, as part of the cultural axis in Beijing's sub-centre strategy. Even though the artist community is highly mobile due to multiple changes in policy, shrinking its presence in the region, an official government source demonstrates its continued significance:

> There are nearly 5,000 artists living and creating in this art district, which remains the largest in scale and the most densely populated by artists and art venues in China—perhaps even in the world. About 7,000 people are employed in related industries derived from art creation [our translation from Chinese].[12]

Conclusion

Xiaopu Village, which used to be a deep periphery on the outskirts of Beijing, has transformed itself into one of the largest arts centres in the world. Not only has this changed its demographic structure and economic activity, but its influence has also spread to over twenty surrounding villages. Although its 'self-sufficient centrality' declined once it was subsumed into the city-wide planning regime, Songzhuang still maintains a greater number of active artists—more than any other art district in China.

This process is unique and important because it shows how a spontaneous, unplanned site in China has acquired its own gravitational pull from the fringes of government planning, gradually growing into a self-sufficient subregional centre. Ultimately, owing to the sheer scale of the area's growth, it can no longer be ignored and must now be incorporated into the government's own top-down strategies.

The story of Songzhuang also reveals the role culture plays in shaping alternative centralities within urban peripheries, beyond the purview of typical suburbanisation and 'anaesthetic' planning regimes. This is particularly enlightening in the Chinese context, since it gives another example of how allegedly omnipotent and omnipresent government planning is circumscribed in practice by local contexts as well as bottom-up dynamics.[13]

Endnotes:

1 Florida, R. *Cities and the creative class.* Routledge, 2005.

2 Hutton, T. A. *The new economy of the inner city: Restructuring, regeneration and dislocation in the 21st century metropolis.* Routledge, 2009.

3 Ren, X. and Sun, M. Artistic urbanization: creative industries and creative control in Beijing, *International Journal of Urban and Regional Research, 36* (3), 2012, pp. 504–521.

4 Huang, A. L. Leaving the city: Artist villages in Beijing, *M/C Journal, 14* (4), 2011.

5 Zhang, J. The geographic political economy of art district formation in China: the case of Songzhuang, *Geoforum, 106*, 2019, pp. 340–348.

6 Ren and Sun, 2012, *op. cit.*

7 Keane, M. and Wen, W. Managing Creativity on the Margins: A Comparative Study of Beijing's Songzhuang Art District and Hangzhou's White Horse Lake Creative Eco-City, *International Journal of Cultural and Creative Industries, 1* (1), 2013, pp. 16–29.

8 Ren and Sun, 2012, *op. cit.*

9 Zhang, 2019, *op. cit.*

10 Yao, Y., Si, X., and Ye, W. The spatial transformation mechanism of Beijing Songzhuang Cultural and Creative Industry Zone: a perspective of production of space, in: *2016 International Conference on Logistics, Informatics and Service Sciences (LISS)*, IEEE, 2016, pp. 1–4; https://doi.org/10.1109/LISS.2016.7854476.

11 Zhang, 2019, *op. cit.*

12 Tongzhou District People's Government of Beijing Municipality, Song Zhuang Art and Creative Town launches hand-drawn coffee map, *Beijing Urban Sub-centre News*, 2023; https://www.bjtzh.gov.cn/bjtz/fzx/202311/1682699.shtml (accessed July 11, 2024).

13 Wang, N., Golubchikov, O., Chen, W., and Liu, Z. The hybrid spatialities of post-industrial Beijing: communism, neoliberalism, and brownfield redevelopment, *Sustainability, 12* (12), 2020, p. 5029.

Conclusion

Towards an Epistemology of the Urban Periphery?

Nicholas A. Phelps, Roger Keil, and Paul J. Maginn

Introduction

The preceding chapters in this volume were organised to offer a thematic extension of an initial overview of various peripheral centralities—envisaged, planned, and built—seen through a historical lens.[1] Viewed through this lens, some peripheral centralities never made it off the drawing page, but remained a grand figment of the political-planning-entrepreneurial imagination, lost to the passage of time. For those peripheral centralities that were built, some were only half the vision of what was originally intended, while others 'lost' their peripheral centrality status as a result of being subsumed within an ever-expanding metropolitan frontier. Here, the emphasis has been on contemporaneous examples of peripheral centrality across the globe that offer a more textured exploration of three core defining elements—pervasiveness, agency, and social relations—that we previously identified and a 'new' element—namely technologies—in order to illustrate the centrality of the periphery in theorising and analysing city regions.

It is arguably the case that theories and methodologies applied to the analyses of the suburbs or suburbanisms, and processes of suburbanisation, peri-urbanisation, or extended urbanisation, have been the bridesmaid to theory- and method-development from a city-centric vantage point. In terms of empirical analysis, the suburbs and the urban periphery have been rendered somewhat invisible, a distant afterthought in mainstream urban studies, across critical theory-informed disciplines such as geography, environmental studies, planning, and sociology. Even in policy, socio-cultural, and popular cultural terms, the periphery tends to be overlooked or viewed with derision.

A major consequence of all this is that it remains unclear to what extent (and in what ways) the epistemologies typically employed to examine the city are applicable in any examination of the city's peripheries. In other words, is there a need or opportunity for the development of new epistemologies as a result of remaking urban theory 'from the outside in' and moving beyond 'methodological cityism'?[2] Important epistemological questions may accompany the theoretical inversion of seeing urbanisation from the periphery rather than established city centres. Developments in this regard have taken the form of reshaping existing theories from an urban-peripheral vantage point, seeking to ground extended urbanisation in new or additional repertoires of spatial planning concepts. Indeed, the linking of urban theory to methods of analysis and visualisation can bring urban theory closer to economic geographies of value chains.[3]

We do not elaborate here on these extant lines of work, which offer moves beyond methodological cityism. Instead, we sketch out some initial thoughts regarding the additional epistemological implications of the so-called 'invisibility' of urban peripheries relative to the urban cores they surround. More crucially, we explore the codependencies between centre and periphery that are required for each of these spatialities to exist and evolve.

Conspicuous Centralities: Learning from Las Vegas and Los Angeles

Learning from Las Vegas and Los Angeles: the Architecture of Four Ecologies drew attention to how the car and its associated road and parking structures offered a complete way of seeing at speed and living in increasingly extensive metropolitan areas.[4] These are themes that have since been elaborated as part of the systemic production of 'automobility', and the associated experiences of automobility and its distinct extended landscapes.[5]

This perspective is highly valuable in appreciating some of the unfolding elements of centrality in urban peripheral landscapes. Martina Loi's chapter in this volume depicts the centrality of the urban periphery in the form of a visual narrative, generated along a particular highway. The enormous physicality of transportation, logistics facilities, and other infrastructures that exist in basically all urban peripheries today are precisely the sorts of centrality that Julie Cidell focuses on in her contribution to this volume. These infrastructures project a certain sense of anonymity due to their austere architecture and design (*blandscapes*), and lack of signage or branding to signal their function or purpose. Yet, they loom large on the urban peripheral horizon on account of their scale (*brutalscapes*) and, as such, remain quite visible regardless of the mode of transport one might view them from when travelling through the urban periphery. These types of peripheral centrality have become fundamental in servicing capital accumulation and the conspicuous consumption needs, wants, and habits of industrialists, investors, and individuals. Ultimately, they provoke questions and curiosity about their function and purpose as well as our relationship to them.

Other buildings and mega-infrastructures constructed in peripheral centralities are self-consciously designed to draw the attention of observers–by virtue of their height, mass, or iconography. These can be individual signature buildings, such as the corporate head offices discussed by Steven Logan in this volume, or ensembles of offices forming edge cities, sprawling office parks, or transit-oriented developments. These can and have been considered 'artificial' downtowns grafted onto otherwise amorphous, centreless residential developments. However, as we have emphasised here and elsewhere, they have often been more intentionally orchestrated or constructed as centres in the urban periphery than this interpretation would suggest.

Regardless of the intentions and secreted functions underpinning some of these massive expressions of peripheral centrality out there in the urban hinterlands, they can still be clearly seen, even when moving at speed. There are also instances of peripheral centrality that lend themselves to representation, analysis, and interpretation with recourse to visual methods closely associated with architecture, landscape architecture, and urban design. As massive objects and spaces/places of interest, the building and physical infrastructure of centralities located on the urban periphery enable the extension of these methods. Indeed, scholars working in the context of a nascent 'geographies of architecture' literature can readily shift their focus away from city-centred objects onto urban peripheral objects.[6]

Observing peripheral centralities at speed and from afar is only one means of analysing and strengthening our theoretical and empirical understanding of these massive objects of anticipatory urbanism. However, analysing peripheral centralities up close and personal—not to mention at a slower pace—offers the potential for alternative and additional insights, thus leading to deeper, richer evidence for theory-building.

Stealthy Centralities

If some of the largest infrastructures necessary for contemporary living exist in the very visible forms suggested above, other vital infrastructures exist 'by stealth' in the urban periphery. There is a variety of less visible physical infrastructures here and, in some respects, their lineage dates to the corporate suburban office and research campuses of the 1930s, through which there was a mass relocation of employment land uses to residential suburbs.[7]

The likes of key storage facilities, security operations, fulfilment centres, and data centres do not typically draw attention to themselves. Again, in terms of architectural design they are often bland in an effort to try and blend into their local environments—a far cry from the remarkable signature 'flexspace' architectures Lehrer observed (often located next to bland 'sheds') along transportation routes in Switzerland over a generation ago, which she viewed as a telltale sign of the arrival of 'flexible' accumulation landscapes and post-Fordist economic space.[8] Assemblages of pallid coloured mega-warehouses that are often indistinguishable from one another are the physical manifestation of economic *blandscapes*. Notably, however, despite such aesthetic blandness, they conceal a range of uses—some of which may be the largest of their kind in their respective metropolitan or even national settings—and are an instrumental facet in the global flows of capital, consumption, and city-building. Figures 1 and 2 provide an indication of the blandness and scale of what can be termed *stealth peripheral centralities*.

In other instances, these markers of centrality in urban peripheries have been deliberately obscured from view. This can include military and other sensitive facilities that are not only highly securitised but may also have large curtilages and landscaping buffers to prevent even remote viewing. Others may exist in plain sight but are cunningly disguised in natural landscapes or as part of townscapes; as has been the case with some large data centres in China.

Figure 1. Warehouses in Brantford, Canada. Source: Photo by Roger Keil, 2021

Figure 2. Amazon Fulfilment Centre, Jandakot Airport Industrial Precinct, Perth, Western Australia. Source: Nearmap / Paul J. Maginn

Though less conspicuous than the consciously-extroverted architecture of individual buildings and deliberately designed new town centres, the majority share of these corporate and data control centres (despite their centrality to national urban systems) have been located in the suburbs for some time.[9]

Urbanity Unseen

Outcast London drew long overdue attention to the history of that particular city 'from below'.[10] There is now a corresponding need to unveil something of the outcast status of urban peripheries. This requires a focus not on massive objects, such as individual signature buildings or physical infrastructures, but instead on the people who animate and inject life into the urban periphery. After all, as Francois Maspero observed of gentrifying Paris in *Roissy Express*, it is real people who move to the outskirts and they do so for all manner of reasons. There is a distinctly human aspect to the centrality of the urban periphery, one that again raises questions of how best to investigate suburbanism as a way of life. Of course, the analytical gaze needs to move beyond the middle-class residential suburb made up of single-family detached houses, which now seems like a quaint and overly powerful trope in this extended moment of suburbanisation. Indeed suburbanism increasingly takes on forms of precarity, marginality, informality, and illegality that are not easily ascertained using desk-assembled secondary data or without recourse to extended original research on the ground.

The urban periphery may be central in an altogether more fundamental way, in the sense of being home to a diverse collection of those who are unwanted and unseen by mainstream urban society. This is the human face of inhuman attitudes towards urban peripheries. Here, contemporary urban peripheries once again take on something of the earliest roots of suburbia—as locations for people and land uses considered 'undesirable' within the walled city. The urban periphery, then, emerges as a potential locus for the informal urban economies that everywhere shadow the formal economy of cities. To say that they shadow the economy 'proper' in this way again does them a disservice. The scale of informal urban economies is not known with any precision, however there is some analysis to suggest that it may constitute as much as 80% of employment in Global South contexts.[11]

This shadow economy is only partially glimpsed in the storage spaces and scrap yards of urban peripheries, not to mention other 'grey' land uses that are found in green belts and other planning designations in metropolitan areas—such as those described by Astrid Safina in her analysis of Athens's outskirts in this volume.

These aspects of centrality in urban peripheries are not readily understood using visualisation tools such as Google Earth or even from the seat of a passing car or train. Their significance, vibrancy, and implication for formal urban economies may only be appreciated up close on foot or travelling by bicycle, by way of delicately negotiated access to informants as part of ethnographic and qualitative methodological data collection approaches. A focus on the informal—plus the need to use qualitative methods to get up-close and personal with those that live, work, and shape the identity and character of peripheral centralities—would be enough to exercise many, if not most, university research ethics committees.

Conclusion

In conclusion, each of these less-travelled research paths offer fruitful (and as yet largely unexplored) avenues in urban studies. Not least because while they have previously been deployed to analyse the aesthetic qualities, morphologies, geographies, and sociologies of historic city cores, or the political economy of contemporary downtown redevelopment, they have not been effectively used in considering the centrality of urban peripheries to the contemporary processes and experiences of urbanisation.

However, in the latter two guises of 'stealthy' or unseen peripheral centralities, these methodologies tend to privilege different starting points for considering centrality in contemporary times. The banality of urban peripheries makes them rather harder to read and interpret than 'traditional' urban cores and often demands the use of methods that are closer to the ground (and, accordingly, slower in the assembly of data). A landscape of 'ordinary' cities is paralleled by the significant, more geographically-extensive 'ordinariness' of the suburbs and populous urban peripheries—as sources of constant human inventiveness.[12]

Figure 3. Data Centre Badlands, Perth, WA. Source: Photo by Paul J. Maginn, 2021

The kaleidoscope of responses presented in this book generously respond to our editorial demand to venture into the peripheral centralities of our urban world, paving the way forward into a vibrant reality that awaits us all. From the containers of an Athens port to the peripheries of Jakarta and the greenbelt of Toronto, everywhere we look today we uncover the contours of a new (sub)urban world in which the conventional coordinates of up/down, central/ peripheral, and in/out are upended and recalibrated. Ultimately, in an era of globalisation and planetary (sub)urbanisation, our urban epistemologies need to adapt accordingly.

Endnotes:

1 Phelps, N. A., Maginn, P. J., and Keil, R. Centring the periphery in urban studies: Notes towards a research agenda on peripheral centralities, *Urban Studies, 60* (6), 2023, pp. 1158–1176.

2 Brenner, N. and Schmid, C. The 'urban age' in question, *International journal of urban and regional research, 38* (3), 2014, pp. 731–755; Keil, R. Constructing Global Suburbia, One Critical Theory at a Time, in: J. Harrison and M. Hoyler (eds.) *Doing Global Urban Research.* Sage, 2014, pp. 169–181.

3 Arboleda, M. *Planetary mine: Territories of extraction under late capitalism.* Verso Books, 2020; Phelps, N. A. Which city? Grounding contemporary urban theory, *Journal of Planning Literature, 36* (3), 2021, pp. 345–357. Phelps, N. A. and Wood, A. M. The new post-suburban politics?, *Urban Studies, 48* (12), 2011, pp. 2591–2610.

4 Banham, R. *Los Angeles: The Architecture of Four Ecologies.* University of California Press, 1971; Venturi, R., Brown, D. S., and Izenour, S. *Learning from Las Vegas, revised edition: the forgotten symbolism of architectural form.* MIT Press, 1977.

5 Sheller, M. and Urry, J. The city and the car, *International journal of urban and regional research, 24* (4), 2000, pp. 737–757; Edensor, T. Defamiliarizing the mundane roadscape, *Space and culture, 6* (2), 2003, pp. 151–168.

6 Jacobs, J. M. A geography of big things, *Cultural geographies, 13* (1), 2006, pp. 1–27.

7 Mozingo, L. A. *Pastoral capitalism: A history of suburban corporate landscapes.* MIT Press, 2011; O'Mara, M. P. *Cities of Knowledge: Cold War Science and the Search for the Next Silicon Valley.* Princeton University Press, 2005.

8 Lehrer, U. A. Images of the Periphery: The Architecture of Flex Space in Switzerland, *Environment and Planning D: Society and Space, 12* (2), 1994, pp. 187–205; https://doi.org/10.1068/d120187.

9 Gottdiener, M. *Planned sprawl: private and public interests in suburbia.* Sage, 1977; Muller, P. O. The suburban transformation of the globalizing American city, *The Annals of the American Academy of Political and Social Science, 551* (1), 1997, pp. 44–58.

10 Jones, G. S. *Outcast London: a study in the relationship between classes in Victorian society.* Penguin, 1971.

11 Charmes, J. The informal economy: definitions, size, contributions and main characteristics, in: E. Kraemer-Mbula and S. Wunsch-Vincent (eds.) *The Informal Economy in Developing Nations: Hidden Engine of Innovation?* Cambridge University Press, 1971, pp. 13–52.

12 Robinson, J. *Ordinary cities: Between modernity and development.* Routledge, 2013.

Julien Aldhuy is associate professor of Urban and Regional Planning and Studies at the Paris School of Planning, Université Paris Est Créteil, and a member of the Lab'URBA research unit. He researches discourses, policies, and practices of economic development in urban and regional planning and action. His publications include *Aménagement économique des territoires* (CNER, 2020, with Vincent Gollain and Fabien Nadou). Julien is vice-rector in charge of real estate, campuses, and sustainable development at his university.

Lucia Cerrada Morato is a research associate at King's College London. Her research focuses on the governance and planning of metropolitan areas, the relational geographies of urban and suburban development in them, and policy innovations in the context of a post-growth agenda. Lucia is the AESOP YA Ambassador for Southern Europe.

Cara Chellew is a PhD candidate in Urban Planning, Policy & Design at McGill University in Montréal. Her research interests include urban governance and the politics of public space. She is a member of the Urban Politics and Governance Research Group (UPGo) at McGill.

Linhao Chen is a PhD researcher at the School of Geography and Planning, Cardiff University. He is finishing his PhD thesis on the impact of arts districts on urbanisation in China. His broader research interests include urban public space and geographical political economy.

Julie Cidell is a professor and department head in the Department of Geography and Geographic Information Science at the University of Illinois Urbana-Champaign. She studies how local governments and individual actors matter in struggles over large-scale infrastructure and the corresponding urban environments that are produced, including airports, railroads, logistics hubs, and interstate highways.

Zachary Dark is a PhD candidate in Environmental Studies at York University. His dissertation research examines the role of state-owned hydroelectricity utilities in Canada's energy transition. His research is supported by a Social Sciences and Humanities Research Council (SSHRC) Canada Doctoral Scholarship.

Sharifah R. S. Dawood is associate professor at HUM, Universiti Sains Malaysia. She researches peripheral urbanisation, regional economic innovation, and sustainable transportation. Her publications include *Cluster Development in Selected Asian Countries* (USM, 2016, with Ghazali & Samat), and a book chapter in *Making 21st Century Knowledge Complexes* (Routledge, 2015, with Phelps).

Sophie Didier is professor of Planning and Urban Studies at the Paris School of Planning, Université Gustave Eiffel, and a member of the Lab'URBA research unit. Her research spans Southern California and South African cities, examining metropolitan growth coalitions, the variegation of neoliberalism and, more broadly, questions of spatial justice and the capacity of urban actors to effect change. Her publications include *Politics and community-based research: perspectives from Yeoville Studio, Johannesburg*, co-edited with Claire Bénit-Gbaffou, Sarah Charlton, and Kirsten Dörmann (Wits Press, 2019).

Erica Dorn is assistant professor of Design and Innovation at Oregon State University and founder of Suburb Futures. She researches relational design practices towards depolarisation and belonging in an age of plurality and extremes. Her recent book is titled *Relational Design for Transitions within U.S. Suburbs* (Carnegie Mellon University, 2024).

Brian Doucet is an associate professor in the School of Planning at the University of Waterloo. Originally from Toronto, he obtained his PhD from Utrecht University (2010) in the Netherlands. He is the co-editor of the four-volume series *Global Reflections on COVID-19 and Urban Inequalities* (Bristol University Press, 2021, with Van Melik and Filion) and the co-author of *Streetcars and the Shifting Geographies of Toronto* (University of Toronto Press, 2022, with Michael Doucet). His feature-length documentary *Thinking Beyond the Market: a film about genuinely affordable housing*, is released in 2025.

Federica Duca is a senior researcher at the Public Affairs Research Institute (PARI), University of Johannesburg. She researches spatial inequality and urban governance, with a particular emphasis on the role of elites in shaping and governing cities. Her latest publication on golf includes 'Golf, gates and the good life' (2022) for *The Sociological Review*.

Robert Freestone is a professor of Planning in the School of Built Environment at the University of New South Wales. He researches planning history, metropolitan development, and airport urbanism. His authored and edited books include *Australian Urban Policy* (2024), *Community Green* (2024), *Campus* (2023), *Iconic Planned Communities and the Challenges of Change* (2019), *Designing the Global City* (2019), *Place and Placelessness Revisited* (2016), and *Urban Nation* (2010).

Oleg Golubchikov is professor of Human Geography at Cardiff University. His research and publications focus on a spatial justice critique of urban, energy, and digital transitions. He is actively engaged in informing policy and has been the lead author of over ten substantive United Nations publications on urban and housing development and sustainable cities.

Philip Graus is a planner, urban designer, and architect. He is currently a PhD candidate at the City Futures Research Centre at the University of NSW, where he explores the role of urban design in metropolitan planning. He was a director of Cox Architecture before joining the Greater Sydney Commission, embedded in the planning and urban design of the Western Sydney Aerotropolis. Philip is an adjunct professor at the University of Technology Sydney.

Clarence Hatton-Proulx is postdoctoral researcher based at Université Paris 1 Panthéon-Sorbonne, Laboratoire Géographie-Cités. He studies the past and present of energy transitions, infrastructure, and environments in urban contexts. His work has been published in *Enterprise and Society, Journal of Urban History, Journal of Energy History, Flux*, and *Revue d'histoire de l'Amérique française*.

Sean Hertel is a registered professional planner (RPP), principal of Hertel Planning, and a lecturer in the planning programmes at Toronto Metropolitan University, University of Waterloo, and York University.

Sophia Ilyniak is a PhD candidate in the Faculty of Environmental and Urban Change, York University. She studies uneven geographical development, sub/urbanisation, neoliberal governance, and collective action. Her work focuses on the role of the third sector in the production of sub/urban space.

Frédéric Mercure Jolette is a professor at Cégep de Saint-Laurent. His research focuses on political representations, experts' claims to authority, and the history of urban planning in Montréal. His work has been published in *Planning Perspectives, La Revue d'histoire urbaine* [Urban History Review], and *Journal of Urban History*.

Roger Keil is distinguished research professor at EUC, York University. He researches global suburbanisation, urban political ecology, cities and infectious disease, infrastructure, and regional governance. Among his publications are *Suburban Planet* (Polity, 2018) and *Pandemic Urbanism* (Polity, 2023, with Ali and Connolly). Keil is a fellow of CIFAR's Humanity's Urban Future programme.

Hannes Langguth, an interdisciplinary urban scholar and architect, is a member of the DFG-funded research training group 'Urban Future-Making' at HafenCity University Hamburg. He works at the intersection of critical urban theory, urban ethnography, and urban-regional planning and governance. His current research explores the (trans)local urban effects of China's global expansion in the context of Europe's green transition.

Steven Logan is an adjunct faculty member at the University of Toronto. His research and teaching focuses on media infrastructures, histories of the media home, media theory, and consumer culture. His publications include *In the Suburbs of History* (University of Toronto Press, 2021) along with articles for *Spacing Magazine, Urban Geography*, and *The Conversation*.

Martina Loi is a postdoctoral researcher at the University of Cagliari, interested in the relation between urban infrastructures and (planetary) urbanisation processes, from a local perspective. Her PhD explored suburban motorways, focusing on the intersection between everyday practices, urban political ecology, and urban politics in the interstitial infrastructural space. Her latest article, 'Urban motorways as spaces of possibility', has been published in *Urban Studies*.

Sara Macdonald has a PhD in Human Geography and Spatial Planning from Utrecht University in the Netherlands. Her research interests include greenbelts, regional governance, land-use planning, and suburbanisation. She is the former coordinator of the City Institute at York University (CITY) and the 'Global Suburbanisms' research project.

Paul J. Maginn is the director of the UWA Public Policy Institute and an associate professor of Urban and Regional Planning at the University of Western Australia. He is the co-editor of ten books including: *Navigating Contemporary Sex Work: Gender, Justice and Policy in the 21st Century* (Palgrave, 2024); *Suburbia in the 21st Century: From Dreamscape to Nightmare?* (Routledge, 2022); *Disruptive Urbanism: Implications of the 'Sharing Economy' for Cities, Regions and Urban Policy* (Routledge, 2020); *(Sub)Urban Sexscapes: Geographies and Regulation of the Sex Industry* (Routledge, 2015); and *Planning Australia: An Overview of Urban and Regional Planning* (CUP, 2012).

Emma McDougall is a PhD candidate at the School of Planning, University of Waterloo. She researches transit equity, gentrification, displacement, and the value of lived experience data in informing urban change.

Katherine Perrott is an assistant professor and the associate director of professional practice in the School of Planning at the University of Waterloo. She is an experienced professional planner. Her research examines the urban design, visual representations, and policy drivers of densification.

Nicholas A. Phelps is chair of Urban Planning and associate dean international in the Faculty of Architecture and Planning at the University of Melbourne. He is author of *An Anatomy of Sprawl* (Routledge), *Sequel to Suburbia* (MIT Press), *Interplaces* (Oxford University Press), and *The Urban Planning Imagination* (Polity), in addition to being editor of *International Perspectives on Suburbanization* (Palgrave-MacMillan) and *Old Europe, New Suburbanization* (University of Toronto Press).

Simon Pinnegar is professor of City Planning and associate director of the City Futures Research Centre in the Faculty of Arts, Design and Architecture at the University of New South Wales, Sydney. He served as director for the UNSW City Planning programme between 2013–2017 and 2021–2023. Simon has researched and published widely on matters related to metropolitan planning, housing market dynamics, incremental forms of urban renewal, and suburban densification.

Dinar Ramadhani is an independent researcher based in Jakarta, Indonesia. Her research interests cover topics such as sustainable urbanism, public places, and suburbanisation. Some of her publications are featured in the *International Development Planning Review* (2021) and *Springer* (2021). Currently, she is a stay-at-home mum who writes about cities and short stories for children.

Astrid Safina is an urban geographer and postdoctoral researcher at Sapienza University (Rome). Previously, she has been a postdoc at Politecnico di Torino (2020–2023), visiting scholar at South China University of Technology (2017–2018), and junior researcher at Universidad Central Venezuela (2012). She researches urbanisation processes, global infrastructures, urban-rural relations, and global urbanism.

Tilman Schwarze is lecturer in the School of Social and Political Sciences, University of Glasgow. His research focuses on spatial theory, territorial stigmatisation, urban redevelopment in the U.S. Rustbelt, and racial economies. He is the author of *Space, Urban Politics, and Everyday Life: Henri Lefebvre and the U.S. City* (Palgrave, 2023).

Justin Spinney is professor of Transport and Mobility Studies at the University of the West of England. He is a human geographer and economic sociologist with particular specialisms in cycling and the political economy of transport. Among his publications are *Understand Urban Cycling* (Routledge, 2020) and the co-edited volumes, *Mobilising Design* (Routledge, 2017) and *Handbook of Travel Behaviour* (EE, 2024).

Amparo Tarazona-Vento is a lecturer at the Department of Urban Studies and Planning, University of Sheffield. Her research investigates the contested politics of urban regeneration, placing special focus on analysing the political mobilisation of iconic architecture and the contribution of grassroots politics to placemaking.

Loïc Vadelorge is professor of Contemporary History at Université Gustave Eiffel and a member of the research unit Analyse Comparée des Pouvoirs (EA 3350). His research focuses on the urban and environmental history of twentieth-century France. His publications include *Retour sur les villes nouvelles. Une histoire urbaine du XXe siècle* (Créaphis, 2014).

Sophie L. Van Neste is associate professor at INRS and holder of the Canada Research Chair in Urban Climate Action. Her research focuses on social mobilisations and changes in urban governance for climate action, considering the exacerbation of inequalities and politics of place. Her work has been published in *Environment and Planning C, Lien social et Politiques, Territory, Politics and Governance, Urban Geography*, and *Journal of Urban Affairs*.

June Williamson is professor at the Spitzer School of Architecture, The City College of New York. A registered architect, she documents transformations of obsolete suburban built form. Her books include *Retrofitting Suburbia* (Wiley, 2008, updated 2011), the sequel *Case Studies in Retrofitting Suburbia* (Wiley, 2021)—both with Ellen Dunham-Jones—and *Designing Suburban Futures: New Models from Build a Better Burb* (Island, 2013).

David Wilson is professor of Geography, Urban Planning, and the Unit for Criticism and Interpretive Theory at the University of Illinois Urbana-Champaign. His research focuses on the socio-physical restructuring of cities, the governance of land, property, and racialised-classed populations in cities, as well as the dynamics of urban racial economies. His latest book, *Toward a Dracula Urbanism: City Transformation in the Twenty-First Century* (with Elvin Wyly), is scheduled to appear in spring, 2025 (Routledge).

Imprint

Cover image: Marcus Glahn, 2024

Project coordination jovis: Franziska Schüffler
Copy editing and proofreading: Cecilia Tricker-Walsh
Cover and design concept: jovis Verlag
Layout and typesetting: Daniel Wittner, Stoffers Grafik-Design
Lithography: Stefan Rolle, Stoffers Grafik-Design
Printed in the European Union.

For questions regarding the General Safety Product Regulation,
please contact productsafety@degruyterbrill.com.

Bibliographic information published by the Deutsche Nationalbibliothek
The Deutsche Nationalbibliothek lists this publication in the Deutsche Nationalbibliografie; detailed bibliographic data are available on the Internet at http://dnb.d-nb.de

jovis Verlag
Genthiner Straße 13
10785 Berlin

www.jovis.de

jovis books are available worldwide in select bookstores. Please contact your nearest bookseller or visit www.jovis.de for information concerning your local distribution.

ISBN 978-3-98612-144-0 (softcover)
ISBN 978-3-98612-152-5 (e-book)